CORONARY

A True Story of Medicine Gone Awry

STEPHEN KLAIDMAN

SCRIBNER

NEW YORK LONDON TORONTO SYDNEY

SCRIBNER
1230 Avenue of the Americas
New York, NY 10020

SCRIBNER and design are trademarks of
Macmillan Library Reference USA, Inc., used under license
by Simon & Schuster, the publisher of this work.

For information about special discounts for bulk purchases,
please contact Simon & Schuster Special Sales at
1-800-456-6798 or business@simonandschuster.com

Designed by Kyoko Watanabe
Text set in Sabon

Manufactured in the United States of America

3   5   7   9   10   8   6   4

Library of Congress Cataloging-in-Publication Data

Coronary : a true story of medicine gone awry / Stephen Klaidman.
p. cm.
Includes bibliographical references.
1. Cardiologists—Malpractice—California—Redding. 2. Realyvasquez, Fidel.
3. Moon, Chae Hyun. 4. Cardiology—Redding. I. Title.

RC669.K52 2007
362.196'120092279424—dc22
2006050621

ISBN-13: 978-0-7432-6754-0
ISBN-10: 0-7432-6754-0

For Liam, Itai, Bella, and Shayna

CONTENTS

CORONARY

"You show them you have in you something that is really profitable, and then there will be no limits to the recognition of your ability. . . . Of course you must take care of the motives—right motives—always."

—JOSEPH CONRAD, *Heart of Darkness*

An Ill Omen

Felix Elizalde's mother died when he was six years old, which left him little choice but to follow his migrant-worker father each day into the fields and orchards of the American West. After several years on the trail his father found a job as a construction worker in Stockton, California. Settling down meant that Felix was finally able to attend school regularly. Although he was bright, at first no one noticed. He was treated, in the vernacular of that time and place, like any other "dumb Mexican." But because in fact he was smart and persistent he was able to overcome this stereotype. After finishing high school he worked his way through San Jose State University on the graveyard shift at a mental institution, earned a master's degree in broadcasting from San Francisco State University, and achieved professional success as a journalist, government official, and academic administrator.

In July of 1992 Elizalde was sixty-one years old. He was neither rich nor famous, but he was nonetheless living a version of the American Dream. That month he and his wife, Margaret, set out to see several Shakespeare plays at the world-class theater in Ashland, Oregon. To break the six-hour drive from their home in Castro Valley, near San Francisco, they stopped overnight in Redding, a small city in northern California. After checking into a motel they went out to eat at a Mexican restaurant. Later that evening, Elizalde experienced nausea and stomach pain. It seemed like indigestion to him and he wasn't especially worried, but Margaret was concerned and talked him into going to Redding Medical Center, one of two relatively large and modern hospitals in town.

He was met in the emergency room by a stocky, tightly wound, chain-smoking South Korean cardiologist named Chae Hyun Moon, who was several inches shorter than the five-foot five-inch Elizalde. Moon asked him curtly about his symptoms and within minutes, with no cardiac workup, hustled him off to the catheterization laboratory for an angiogram, an invasive test that, in the absence of acute symptoms, is normally preceded by an electrocardiogram and a stress test. Less than half an hour later Moon told Elizalde that he had bad blockages in his coronary arteries, one of which was known in the trade as a "widow-maker," and that he needed immediate triple bypass surgery. Elizalde, surprised and upset, but still able to make a rational judgment, said he would prefer to return to the Bay Area and get a second opinion. But Moon, who was imperious and did not much care for niceties such as respecting patients' wishes and informed consent, told him bluntly that he would not survive the trip.

A few moments later Moon introduced Elizalde to Fidel Realy-vasquez, the chief of cardiac surgery at RMC. Like Elizalde, Realyvasquez was a Mexican-American from a working-class background. He said he would perform the surgery. A nursing supervisor standing nearby tried to soften the blow by assuring Elizalde that the cardiac care at RMC was the best in northern California, an opinion widely held in and around Redding. In fact, National Medical Enterprises, Redding Medical Center's owner, was on the verge of becoming the second-biggest for-profit hospital chain in the United States and RMC was on track to be its most successful hospital.

The nursing supervisor said Elizalde shouldn't worry about a thing and that the hospital would arrange for a comfortable place for Margaret to stay. But Elizalde, who recently had undergone a treadmill stress test that was negative, was more than a little skeptical. Things were moving too fast for his taste. And he was put off by Realyvasquez, whom he found condescending, especially when he spoke to him in Spanish. Although it was the weekend, he succeeded in reaching his cardiologist, David Anderson, and asked his advice. After speaking to both Elizalde and Moon, Anderson had the feeling that what he was hearing didn't sound quite right. Nevertheless, he told Elizalde that he could not second-guess Moon over the phone. He said Elizalde would have to decide for himself whether to have the surgery.

Despite Anderson's hesitancy, Elizalde took away a different message. He thought Anderson's tone suggested that he probably should have the operation. But after talking it over with Margaret, Elizalde decided against it. Although bypass surgery was done almost half a million times a year in the United States and was considered routine, the operation carried with it the prospect of a long and painful recovery, the possibility of depression, a small chance of a stroke, and perhaps some lingering mental deficit. If at all possible, Elizalde wanted to avoid these potential consequences.

The next morning Elizalde was flown on a gurney to Summit Hospital in Oakland. Anderson met him there, reviewed his records from Redding, and did some additional tests. He was shocked to find that in his judgment Moon's diagnosis and treatment recommendation were baseless. Anderson called Moon and angrily told him that what he had done to Elizalde was thoroughly unethical. Moon replied, "You had to be there" to make the diagnosis, a comment Anderson found incomprehensible because he saw absolutely nothing on Elizalde's angiogram that indicated a need for heart surgery. A week or two after coming home to Castro Valley Elizalde's symptoms returned and he threw up blood. Soon thereafter he was diagnosed with an inflamed gall bladder, which almost certainly was the cause of his nausea and stomach pain in Redding.

Both Anderson and Elizalde wrote to the California Medical Board about the incident. The board sent Elizalde a form letter saying the matter was under review. Four and a half months later the board notified him by mail that it had closed the case without taking any action because the staff could find no violation of the law. In the 1992–93 fiscal year the board reported to the state legislature that it had received 6,749 complaints and took 149 disciplinary actions. To anyone familiar with the inadequacy of oversight of medical practice around the country these statistics would come as no surprise. California's medical board, like most others, was underfunded and understaffed. Elizalde's experience and the board's failure to act went virtually unnoticed in Redding, but Anderson recalls worrying that the case might be "a harbinger." He was concerned that RMC's relatively new but fast-growing heart program was operating without sufficient oversight.

At the time of Felix Elizalde's long night in Redding, Moon, Realyvasquez, and RMC already had well-established reputations throughout northern California. Moon was considered to be a magician with a catheter and was widely known for doing an unusually high number of angiograms for the time, which was a source of pride for the hospital and the community. The same was true for the number of cardiac operations being done at RMC—mostly by Realyvasquez—which was higher than expected given the small population the hospital served. This statistic also conveyed bragging rights in Shasta and the even more rural counties surrounding it. A few physicians in town considered Moon's and Realyvasquez's practice patterns overly aggressive. But no one was suggesting that either was guilty of malpractice. Indeed the more common view was that they were practicing medicine on the cutting edge.

Besides, RMC was just about the only game in town when it came to treating heart disease. Mercy, the other big hospital in Redding was just starting an open-heart program, but no one expected it to seriously challenge the primacy of the California Heart Institute, as RMC's cardiac program was formally known. At the time it was an article of faith among the residents of the 40,000-square-mile area surrounding Redding that RMC's heart program was not only the best in northern California, but that it was fast becoming one of the best in the country. And Moon and Realyvasquez were considered by almost everyone to be exceptionally talented physicians. The citizens of Redding and the scattered populace of the rural counties had all seen the big billboards that said so. They'd seen the newspaper ads, watched the television commercials, and heard the radio spots, all driving home the same message—RMC's California Heart Institute was one of the nation's leading programs.

By 2002, a great many people in Redding and the surrounding counties had heard that HealthGrades, a nationwide online rating service, consistently ranked RMC's heart program among the best in the United States. RMC's mortality rate for bypass surgery was around 2 percent, about as good as it gets. And by 2002, the hospital was approaching a thousand bypasses a year. Volume is generally considered one of the most reliable indicators of quality for surgery. But what probably carried the most weight in Redding and the surrounding towns was that almost everyone knew someone—a friend, a relative, a colleague—whose life had been saved by Moon, RV (as Realyvasquez was widely known) or, most frequently, by both doctors. Unsurprisingly, in a small, traditional community like Redding, word of mouth from grateful patients and families was more resonant than slick, high-powered advertising. The thousands of Redding area residents who had undergone heart surgery at RMC had heard the good news over and over again, from nurses and technicians, and, if they were his patients, as most were, from Dr. Moon himself. They knew they were incredibly fortunate because they were being treated by two of the best doctors at one of the best hospitals any-where. And they were the living proof. When Moon came to see patients after surgery, just in case they didn't already know how lucky they were, he would tell them. And who were they to doubt it?

1

A Historical Precedent

Felix Elizalde's experience in Redding, as unpleasant as it evidently was for him and for his wife, Margaret, did not necessarily have wider implications. It could easily have been a simple case of medical error or just a difference in clinical judgment between two cardiologists. Medical errors occur with much greater frequency than most people are aware or would like to think, even at the best academic medical centers, and variations in clinical judgment are only natural. Cardiology in particular has many gray areas, and good clinicians frequently differ about the most appropriate treatment. The California State Medical Board, like most of its counterparts around the country, requires a pattern of questionable practice to investigate a physician, not just a single complaint, which makes sense. Doctors should not be held to a standard of perfection nor should they be expected to make identical cookbook diagnoses. Malpractice, of course, was not out of the question in Elizalde's case, but neither was it a certainty. And the possibility of fraud had not entered anyone's mind. In retrospect Elizalde had no definitive reason to be suspicious of Redding Medical Center, its owner, National Medical Enterprises, Dr. Realyvasquez, or, to be completely fair, even Dr. Moon.

Yet at the same time there was something potentially relevant to the situation that Elizalde knew nothing about—a lengthy episode involving National Medical Enterprises that was deeply troubling. In the late 1980s and early 1990s a number of NME-owned psychiatric hospitals had engaged in a cold-blooded scheme that was ongoing at the time of Elizalde's Redding experience and destined to end in criminal convictions. Had Elizalde known about these activities he might have been even more skeptical about his own treatment.

About fifteen months before Moon diagnosed Felix Elizalde with
triple-vessel coronary artery disease, late in the afternoon of April 12,
1991, a repainted police car pulled up to Sid and Marianne Harrell's
modest ranch house in Live Oak, Texas, a middle-class suburb of San
Antonio. The light blue Dodge had a flashing red light on top and the
words Sector One painted on the trunk. There was a prisoner cage in
the back seat. Marianne and her fourteen-year-old grandson Jeramy
watched two bulky, uniformed men get out. One of them told her
curtly, "We're Sector One, Mobile Crisis Unit, and we're here to pick
up the boy." Marianne thought they meant Jeramy's twelve-year-old
brother, Jason, who was undergoing an evaluation at Colonial Hills, a
psychiatric hospital in San Antonio owned by a company called Psychiatric Institutes of America. She said, "He isn't here. What did he do?"
But one of the men, who introduced himself as "Lieutenant" Joe Saenz,
said, "That boy," pointing at Jeramy. She asked again what he'd done,
but they wouldn't tell her.

Marianne, Jeramy, Saenz and the other man, whose name was Ulysses
Jones, went inside where Sid Harrell, a retired army staff sergeant, was
sitting at the kitchen table. Saenz and Jones told the Harrells they were
operating under orders from a Dr. Bowlan at Colonial Hills and that if
Jeramy didn't go with them they would get a warrant under which he
could be held for twenty-eight days. They also indicated that if this happened he would have a police record.

Marianne was both frightened and angry. She called Colonial Hills
and was told that the officers were authorized to bring Jeramy to the
hospital. When she asked the reason, she was told for substance abuse,
truancy, and because he was a victim of child abuse. Sid then called the
local police to try to establish whether Saenz and Jones had the authority to take Jeramy. By the time a police officer showed up Jeramy was
handcuffed and in the cage in the back of the Sector One car. The officer reviewed the papers the men showed her, which did not include a
warrant authorizing Jeramy's detention. Nevertheless, she told the Harrells that Saenz and Jones were licensed security officers and could
indeed get a warrant to hold Jeramy for twenty-eight days. If the Harrells let their grandson go with the security officers, she said, they could
probably have him released within twenty-four hours. At this point the
distraught grandparents gave up and let the two uniformed men take
Jeramy away.[1]

Dr. Mark Bowlan's "diagnosis" of drug abuse and the allegation that Jeramy was an abused child had been based solely on Bowlan's interview with Jeramy's twelve-year-old brother Jason. Bowlan, a psychiatrist who at the time had a temporary, limited medical license, which he would lose that summer for falsifying letters of recommendation, waited four days before seeing Jeramy, even though he had asserted that the boy was so dangerous that he had to be brought in by a pair of professional bounty hunters and admitted to Colonial Hills on an emergency basis. After six days, during which time his grandparents, who were his legal guardians, were not allowed to see him, Jeramy was released on a writ of habeas corpus obtained by state senator Frank Tejada. The senator went to the hospital himself and threatened to kick the door down if they didn't let the fourteen-year-old go. A bill for $11,000 followed. Jeramy's younger brother Jason was kept in the hospital for two weeks. His bill was $15,000. Both bills were paid by CHAMPUS (Civilian Health and Medical Program of the Uniformed Services), the U.S. government's health insurance program for members of the military.

Jeramy Harrell's experience of being forcibly taken from his home and being incarcerated in a mental hospital was not unique in the annals of the Psychiatric Institutes of America, a subsidiary of National Medical Enterprises. And, as bad as the Harrell case was, it was far from the most egregious in the company's history. Nor would it be the last. Something seemed to be awry in the corporate DNA.

At least as far back as 1984, some Texas psychiatrists knew what was going on at the Psychiatric Institutes of America hospitals, and some were benefiting from it handsomely. Dr. Charles S. Arnold, a San Antonio psychiatrist, tape-recorded a conversation on June 12 of that year with the administrator of Colonial Hills, the hospital to which Harrell would be taken. Arnold said he recorded the conversation "because of what I had already learned about the hospital." The administrator told him that if he went along with the program, the hospital would make him rich, as it had done for other psychiatrists who had cooperated. The administrator then cited a Houston physician as an example: "They called [name deleted] and said 'Look, you want to be rich? You let us set up this program the way we want to set it up. All you do is be the admitting psychiatrist and we'll make you rich.' We made him rich."[2]

The administrator who contacted Dr. Arnold was executing a key part of the company's business plan—to identify and admit patients with good insurance coverage. Harvey Friedman, the psychiatric unit's vice president for program services, said that Ron Bernstein, the chief operating officer, had issued a directive to "Fill the beds at any cost. Hire sleazeballs. These are his words. Anything it takes. That was his philosophy."[3] A year after NME's approach to Arnold, Norm Zober, president and CEO of its Specialty Hospital Group, which included the psychiatric facilities, scribbled the following hand-written note at a planning meeting: "Kinds of doctors we are looking for? Guys that will admit." At a similar meeting thirteen months later, Zober wrote that the "incentive" contracts that were being discussed were "Deals to sew up M.D.'s."[4]

The doctors were the linchpins of this scheme. And because what they were being asked to do—accept bribes for referrals among other things—was illegal, NME cooked up ways to disguise these bribes. The company relied on the doctors to do what was expected of them and in return rewarded them with titles that required no work and paid handsomely. At the psychiatric hospitals, cooperating doctors were usually given contracts as chiefs of treatment units. Peter Alexis, who was regional vice president of Psychiatric Institutes of America for Texas, explained that the doctors were paid salaries ostensibly for providing services expected of someone holding the title they had been given. Alexis also said the size of a doctor's salary was directly linked to the number of his referrals.[5]

Mark Bowlan, the psychiatrist who admitted Jeramy Harrell and eventually pled guilty to charges of making false claims, theft of public money, and forgery, said he received $250,000 from NME his first year under contract, $400,000 in his second year, and was offered $750,000 for a third year. He later told the *Houston Chronicle* that "Doctors became addicted to the money, whether in terms of lifestyle, financial obligations or recreation."[6] Dr. Arturo Torres of Laurelwood Hospital charged $125 for each patient visit. He averaged twenty-four patients in the hospital and billed for five visits a week per patient, from which he grossed $780,000 in one year. The visits, when they occurred at all, were cursory. Hi, how are you feeling today? Fine, that's good. Bye.

Each hospital's business was driven by extremely ambitious bottom-line requirements that effectively ruled out acceptable patient care. Marketing was everything. James Hutchison, an executive at Baywood Hospital, told an investigative committee of the Texas Senate and the

Select Committee on Children, Youth and Families of the U.S. House of Representatives that "every employee, from groundskeeper to program director, from office secretary to nurse, was obliged to conduct weekly marketing calls." Russell Durrett, controller of Psychiatric Institutes of America's Twin Lakes Hospital in Denton, Texas, from November 1988 to July 1989 told the House Select Committee in 1992 that at the Twin Lakes program those with the rank of director and above were given a weekly quota of contacts—his was five—and received prizes for referrals. He testified that, "We had an insurance remaining report that we completed on a weekly basis [and] the patient was discharged on that particular day when their insurance benefits ran out."

Jose Carranza, a physician at Laurelwood, said that 80 percent of the patients arrived at the hospital without a referring doctor[7] in response to advertising and hotlines. According to Texas Attorney General Dan Morales, one hotline received $155,000 a month from NME for "operating expenses."[8] Other paid referral sources were school counselors, social workers, and probation officers. The psychiatrists and psychologists with the best referral records were rewarded by being assigned patients for whom they could bill insurers $100 to $150 a day. The doctors would then pay back the administrators by making sure the patients stayed in the hospital until the last penny of their insurance was exhausted.

In mid-1991 Morales initiated an investigation of various abuses in the psychiatric hospital industry. By that time enough concern had been raised about NME's highly aggressive patient-recruitment strategies that the company hired the law firm of McDermott, Will & Emery to investigate its psychiatric hospitals. The firm delivered a 240-page report with three hundred appendices to NME, but it never saw the light of day. An NME executive told a Texas Senate committee that any wrongdoing was the work of one or two individuals who were no longer with the company and assured the House Select Committee that the investigation disclosed "no evidence of systemic practices that negatively affected the quality of patient care." The next day, NME's CEO, Richard Eamer, and its president, Leonard Cohen, sent the same message to shareholders. But four years later, after reading a summary of the McDermott report, Texas State District Judge Fred Edwards, in response to a motion by plaintiffs' lawyers to make it public, would rule that its findings "substantially differ" from NME's representations.

The precise consequences of NME's relentless, single-minded pursuit of profits are hard to calculate. How do you measure the human costs of deceiving parents into allowing their children to be imprisoned in mental institutions where at best they were warehoused and at worst they were subjected to alleged therapies that resembled torture more than treatment? What were the psychic costs for the young children and adolescents? How would they affect their ability to develop into stable confident adults? What did these experiences do to their capacity to trust their parents or critical institutions like the medical system? How much guilt did it instill in their parents? The answers to these questions are unquantifiable, but perhaps the best way to understand the human costs of this scandal is to hear what happened to Jeannie Warren, just one of the many young persons shanghaied into a Psychiatric Institutes facility.

A thirty-eight-year-old Fort Worth psychiatrist named Robert Hadley Gross was enamored of a now-discredited form of treatment at the time called "rage reduction" therapy. In theory it was intended to help children and adolescents who were unable to form normal emotional attachments with others. It was to be done only in the presence of and with the informed consent of a parent. It was supposed to involve four people holding the patient down while the therapist prodded or tickled him or her to produce anger, which it was hoped would be cathartic. Warren was Gross's patient at the Psychiatric Institute of Fort Worth. She told the *Houston Chronicle* that she was subjected to this "therapy" two dozen times for two to five hours at a time. She said she signed a consent form she wasn't given a chance to read. No parent was present. In preparation for one of her treatments she was taken to a snack room and held down on some gym mats by eight people.[9] Here's how she described what followed to the *Chronicle*'s Mark Smith:

> My whole body was covered with people touching me and holding me down. [Gross and another staff member] would make a fist and stick out their knuckles and bore and grind into my ribs. I was crying, hyperventilating. . . . They had their hands over my nose and mouth so I couldn't breathe. They were attempting to muffle my screams. I stopped breathing twice. When I started breathing again they would slam me back down on the mat. When finished, I had burst blood vessels on my face and chest.

A nurse at the hospital confirmed that Warren had swelling and pur-plish-red welts on her side after one session.[10] Years later Warren said, "I have dreams of my doctor standing over me screaming and coming after me. My nightmares won't go away." Willem Duard Bok, a psychi-atrist at PI–Fort Worth testified to the House Select Committee that rage-reduction therapy was at best worthless and sometimes caused physical harm. Bok said rage-reduction therapy often caused severe pain and bruising: "in some of the female preadolescent and adolescent patients there was tissue injury in the form of severe bruising incurred in the nip-ple and breast areas." In 1996 a Tarrant County judge ruled that War-ren had been the victim of assault and intentional infliction of emotional distress and ordered Gross to pay her $8.4 million.

On July 20, 1996, Gross was convicted of criminal contempt and was facing a possible six months in prison and a $5,000 fine on this count. Released on his own recognizance, he fled to England. On August 13, Gross was indicted on four counts of mail fraud and two counts of filing false insurance claims for services that were not provided. The fugitive psychiatrist was accused among other things of accepting kickbacks of $861,000 for patient admissions between 1988 and 1991. These were partly embedded in the $329,000 he was paid by NME during one two-year period. The rest were included in his billing of insurers at $150 per patient per day for the twenty to twenty-five patients a day on average he was assigned by hospital management. Using the smaller number of patients and five days a week, that works out to $780,000 a year. By the time Gross went into hiding he was facing twenty years in prison and more than $1 million in fines. He was finally returned to the United States where, in a plea bargain, he was sentenced to a year and a day in prison to be served concurrently with his six-month sentence for crimi-nal contempt of court.

In July 1993, with NME facing civil lawsuits by thirteen insurance companies and more than a hundred individual plaintiffs, two of the company's founders, Richard Eamer and Leonard Cohen, the vice chair-man and president, resigned. Jeffrey Barbakow, a board member with little hospital experience who was an investment banker and film exec-utive, took over as chairman. On August 26, 1993, six hundred federal agents led by the FBI raided NME/PIA hospitals in seventeen states, regional headquarters of NME, and the company's corporate headquar-ters in Santa Monica, California. The raid led to criminal and civil charges against the company and individual executives and physicians for battery; bribing doctors, school counselors, and others for patient referrals; coercing parents into committing their children; locking up patients until their insurance coverage was exhausted; providing unnecessary treatment, grossly inflating charges, and billing for treatment that was not provided. The allegations against the company, its hospitals, and the psychiatrists who worked in them were hard to believe at first. And many people wondered whether, if indeed such a thing could happen at all, it just involved greedy doctors acting on their own rather than an extensive conspiracy managed at the corporate level.

The answer came ten months after the FBI raid when Peter Alexis agreed to cooperate with the federal investigation. On June 29, 1994, National Medical Enterprises pled guilty to one criminal count of conspiracy and six criminal counts of paying kickbacks and bribes to induce doctors and other professionals to refer patients to their psychiatric hospitals. The company paid $379 million in fines, penalties, and civil damages. The $33 million criminal fine that was part of the agreement set a record at the time. Alexis, two hospital administrators, four psychiatrists apart from Gross, but including Bowlan, one psychiatrist's office manager, and one counselor were convicted criminally. The longest sentence—eight years—went to Bert Wayne Bolan, who ran a counseling service that channeled patients to NME hospitals. Mark Bowlan was sentenced to five months in prison and three years of supervised release.

No one in NME's top management was convicted of anything and neither were the dozens of others, including mid-level executives, hospital administrators, physicians, psychologists, therapists, and counselors, all of whom appeared to be deeply implicated. NME, however, was required to divest itself of all of its psychiatric hospitals and to enter into a corporate integrity agreement committing it to better patient care and compliance with federal healthcare regulations. The document was signed for NME by the associate general counsel, Christi Sulzbach. It was still in effect a decade later, by which time Sulzbach was general counsel and a senior vice president of Tenet Healthcare Corporation, the name NME took in 1995 in an attempt to shed its tainted reputation after the psychiatric hospitals debacle.

The federal fraud case was over, but for NME the problems were just beginning. By late 1994, a pack of ex-patients and personal-injury lawyers were on its tail led by Jim Moriarty, a motormouthed forty-eight-year-old former Marine door gunner in Vietnam. Moriarty's small but successful law firm occupies a large redbrick house on a quiet, tree-lined, mostly residential street in Houston's Museum District. Apart from the noncommercial appearance of the neighborhood, nothing about the setting seems out of the ordinary. But to cross the threshold is to know instantly that you're not in a typical law office and you are not about to meet white-shoe lawyers like the ones at Gibson, Dunn & Crutcher, the big Los Angeles firm that represents Tenet.

The office, just a bit weirdly, is a monument to hunting, flying, and taxidermy. The wood-paneled waiting room is furnished with a stuffed wild pig and a tiny desert deer, and a large zebra rug. There are books on hunting, fishing, and guns, and a great big coffee-table history of the Marine Corps. And a short trip down the hall to the restroom brings you face-to-face with a big-horn sheep. But the sheep's just a tease. The really unsettling presence sits placidly to your left, right next to the toilet, clutching a very big beer can. He is a massive, hairy, pot-bellied, glassy-eyed baboon. One flight up, in Moriarty's private quarters, the décor is even more eclectic and less likely than that in the waiting room. On the wide-board pine floor a saddle, boots, a lariat, and other western gear are carefully arranged. Elsewhere there are Indian rugs and canoe paddles and what at first glance might be mistaken for two car seats for giant children. In fact, one of these is from a Harrier, a vertical-takeoff Marine aircraft, and the other is from an A-4 Skyhawk fighter jet. Moriarty flies Skyhawks and helicopters at air shows.

As for the man himself, Moriarty is not necessarily someone you would like to have on your tail. When he focuses on something—it could be anything from a big, consolidated lawsuit to racing his hopped-up go-cart at 120 miles an hour—it is with the tenacity of a junkyard dog. He is a short, compact Irishman with wavy gray hair and squinty, faded blue eyes. The day I met him he looked like an unusually well-groomed wrangler in jeans, a checked shirt, and crocodile cowboy boots. He looks you directly in the eye with the somewhat pugnacious gaze of someone who wants to intimidate, and he has a gift for summing things up: "Tenet's big plan is remarkably simple," he said, presciently substituting the present tense for the past and the company's new name for its old one. "Bribe the docs." He added, by way of characterizing the company's message to parents in the psychiatric-hospital cases, "Bring us your troubled children and we'll teach 'em not to suck eggs." A loose translation from the Texas vernacular: If your kid has a behavior problem, give him to us and we'll beat it out of him.

A couple of months after NME's federal guilty plea in June 1994 a lawyer in Houston named Tommy Fibich asked Moriarty for his help. Fibich had three clients interested in suing, but he knew he needed more to take on a big company with deep pockets and he wasn't sure how to sign them up. Moriarty had been following the case in the press as he did with mass-tort cases generally, but he hadn't thought about pursuing this one. Fibich's call changed his mind. His dormant instinct for the big case was reawakened. This, combined with a sense of outrage about the abuse he was convinced had been inflicted on vulnerable children, made this one a natural. Moreover, what he viewed as dereliction of duty by many parents in giving up their children to mental hospitals left a bitter taste in his mouth. He and his associate Kevin Leyendecker teamed up with Fibich and brought on board several other lawyers. These included Steve Hackerman, a tall, deceptively easygoing man who took charge of developing the evidence in the case, and Richard Frankel, who was looking for a change and had the medical malpractice expertise Moriarty's team was lacking.

The media-savvy Moriarty, whose approach to cases can be as exotic as his dress or décor, came up with a seductive weeklong radio and newspaper advertising campaign that played off of NME's misleading ads. They were directed at the parents who had been deceived into handing their children over to NME psychiatric hospitals. The newspaper ads featured a photograph of a Moriarty employee staring into the middle distance looking depressed. The headline said: "Therapy or Abuse?" The rest of the copy asked specific questions like "Were you put in four-point restraints?" or "Were you billed for therapy sessions you never attended?" In a relatively short time the ads brought in hundreds of clients.

The lawyers built their case around the obvious premises that psychiatrists, administrators, and others had lured their clients under false pretenses into various NME hospitals and kept them there for the sole purpose of capturing their insurance benefits,[11] and that NME targeted minors. Four hundred and sixty-three of the plaintiffs were under the age of eighteen when the abuses occurred. The suit went well beyond the federal charges of kickbacks for referrals and billing fraud, alleging that patients were confined in psychiatric hospitals with no legitimate medical justification—that is to say, imprisoned—and that many of them were harmed mentally and physically.

On July 30, 1997, the eve of what would have been the actual start of a civil trial, a settlement was reached. Tenet and the doctor defendants agreed to pay $101 million to the plaintiffs represented by Moriarty and his team. Tenet had already settled the claims of more than a dozen insurance companies for $300 million. Together with the criminal fines, penalties, and civil damages paid to the federal government, and a subsequent $17 million settlement, the company had paid out more than three quarters of a billion dollars to settle the bulk of the claims arising from the NME psychiatric-hospital scandal.

Considering the widespread nature and the magnitude of the crimes and abuses committed by NME, very few people went to jail. At least part of the reason for this is the subjective nature of psychiatry. A considerable number of the victims had behavioral problems and there was little doubt that some—possibly many—of them might have benefited from appropriate therapy. Trying to get more criminal convictions against psychiatrists in these circumstances was a formidable—although not necessarily insurmountable—challenge for federal prosecutors. As a result they used their limited resources to go after NME for the money bilked from federal healthcare programs, letting executives like Eamer, Cohen, and Bernstein go scot-free.

Was this a wise strategy? With hindsight it looks like the fines in excess of three quarters of a billion dollars were seen by NME more as a cost of doing business than as a deterrent. By the time the criminal and civil cases had been completely resolved, the company had already moved on to greener pastures. As things turned out, though, not too far into the new millennium Tenet Healthcare, as the company would by then be known, would once again meet up with Moriarty et al. This time however there would be no high-level insider like Alexis to give away the game. Instead the company would find itself confronting an unusually determined and tough-minded FBI agent, some smart local lawyers, and a pair of unlikely outsiders who were not easily intimidated.

2

The City

The widely held geographical misconception that San Francisco is in northern California is easily corrected by a glance at a map. The city by the bay is in fact only about two-thirds of the way between the Mexican border and the Oregon state line. The real North State, as the local residents call it, begins at the top of the Sacramento Valley, in Redding, the small city where in 1992 Felix Elizalde narrowly avoided unnecessary bypass surgery. The drive to Redding from the Bay Area begins on heavily trafficked Route 80 near the coast. At Vacaville, where Genentech, the big biotechnology company, has a facility, it cuts east along Route 505 to Interstate 5. For the first sixty miles on I-5 there is nothing to break the monotony but a few small cattle herds, clusters of silos, rice fields, and an occasional farm hamlet. But just past the rice fields and still more than 120 miles away, a 14,000-foot volcanic monolith materializes on the horizon. This is Mount Shasta, the sacred mountain of the Modoc Indians. The gold miner and natural-born poet Joaquin Miller, who lived for a time among them, described the mountain a bit fulsomely, but not entirely without justification. "As lone as God, and white as a winter moon," he wrote, "Mount Shasta starts up sudden and solitary from the heart of the great black forests of Northern California. . . . A shining pyramid in mail of everlasting frosts and ice."[12] No less of a natural wonder, but hidden from the highway, is the fast-flowing Sacramento River, which carved the valley over millennia and was said once to have been so filled with salmon that you could walk across it on their backs.

The city of Redding, the Shasta County seat, straddles the Sacramento River, its setting a gift from God, a figure of speech that many who live there take literally. But the devil never being too far away, from

May to November nothing cools the valley. In midsummer, no one even starts talking about the heat until the thermometer registers 110 degrees. On the whole the scenery seems more salutary than the weather. Redding is the gateway to a 40,000-square-mile rock-rimmed wilderness of fast rivers and man-made lakes behind colossal dams, with likely more deer than human residents and surely more trout. Shasta County is 75 percent national forest and parkland. Mount Lassen, which spilled molten lava into the valley below as recently as 1914, rises forty miles to the east. And between Whiskeytown Lake, just to the west of Redding, and the Pacific Ocean, the wild and beautiful Trinity Alps shelter small herds of Hereford cattle and some of the biggest methamphetamine laboratories in the United States.

Trinity County was an ideal setting for illicit drug manufacturing because it was rural, heavily wooded and there was very little local law enforcement. Making the methamphetamine requires little space and equipment and is as simple as baking a cake. Before it was shut down by state drug agents, a fairly typical super lab had been situated on the Trinity-Shasta line on an isolated hilltop overlooking the road with clear sight lines so that anyone approaching could be seen from miles away. The drugs manufactured at the site were shipped to Los Angeles and two other large cities. But not all of the meth cooked in the Trinity Alps was being sent out of the area.

Methamphetamine had long been a big problem in Redding and its environs. A lot of ex-cocaine addicts had switched to meth because it was cheaper, produced a longer, better high, and didn't eat up your nose. They were blissfully unaware of meth's more ravaging effects. Former users who subsequently became informants told a California narcotics agent that if an orgasm was a 10, meth was 100. Anyone familiar with the telltale signs of methamphetamine addiction—twitchiness, an inability to focus for more than a couple of seconds, ruined gums and teeth, and a ravaged body and face—was likely to spot several users on the street in Redding on any given day. Less visible were the drug's effects on the cardiovascular system, which can result in sudden death.

Of course, most people who lived in Trinity and the other counties surrounding Redding did not earn their living making and selling methamphetamine. This craggy, densely forested land was also home to a small, socially and politically conservative, churchgoing scattering of folk. Many of them tended to be suspicious of government, especially of

the federal variety, but accepting of the traditional authority of preach-
ers and physicians. The area was also an outdoorsman's paradise. That
fact, like the existence of a nearby airport, also played a role in bringing
down powerful men in Redding and the institution with which they were
closely associated. Sportsmen came from all over to fish the Upper and
Lower Sacramento, the Pit, McCloud, and Fall rivers, and Hat Creek.

The people of rural northern California on the whole seemed content
with their isolated lives. Even in Redding itself, many residents, with a
certain amount of sophisticated irony and pride, called themselves red-
necks. There were those among them who still talked longingly—in jest
in some cases, but not all—of the State of Jefferson, the name a small
group of secessionists gave to the breathtakingly beautiful pine-forested
land comprising four counties in northern California and one in southern
Oregon in 1941.* Their proclamation of independence specified that the
new state would have no sales tax, no income tax, and no liquor tax. Services would be financed through a small royalty on mining and timber
development. Although this grand project ended abruptly on December
7 when the Japanese launched a sneak attack on Pearl Harbor and the
United States entered World War II, the spirit survived. A man I met in the
tiny gold miners' hamlet of Old Shasta, which straddles Route 299
between Redding and the ghost town of French Gulch, got it just about
right when he said he was "happy living where the altitude [3,500 feet
measured at the lower end of town] was higher than the population
[3,630 in 2003]." And everyone seemed to put up easily with the long,
hot summers and the cool, but rainy winters.

Gold was Redding's first boom and signaled the end of dominion for
the Modoc, Wintu, and Yana Indians, tribes that had hunted in the great
northern forests for centuries. Not long after it was discovered at Sut-
ter's Mill on the American River east of Sacramento, Pierson Barton
Reading, who operated a ranch on a Mexican land grant in the area,
traveled to the mill to have a look. When he returned home, he noticed
that, like the foothills around the gold strike, his property was rich in red
clay and manzanita, which is still ubiquitous in the area. It wasn't much
of a hint, but it was enough to get Reading into nearby Clear Creek
where in three days he sifted $800 worth of gold. He then supplemented

---

*Del Norte, Siskiyou, Modoc, and Lassen in California, and Curry in Oregon.

his own labor with that of some local Indians who worked for him, went north to the Trinity River, and in six weeks recovered about $80,000 worth of gold. Shortly thereafter a group of Oregonians threatened to kill his Indian workers, and Reading, who was already very well off, decided to get out of the gold business. Soon prospectors were flooding into the area from all over. By 1872, gold had attracted a large enough population for the Central Pacific Railroad to build a branch line up the Sacramento Valley to serve new towns like Maryville, Chico, Tehama, and Red Bluff. But they needed a railhead, which was built thirty-five miles north of Red Bluff along the river and was named for Benjamin Bernard Redding, the general land agent for the railroad and Sacramento's first mayor.

The gold was about worked out, but the arrival of the railroad and construction of the town were followed by a copper boom that began in the 1890s and ended when the last of five smelters shut down in 1919. The mining and smelting stoked the local economy, but the smelters kept Redding under an almost permanent stinking and poisonous cloud for the better part of twenty-five years. The demise of the copper industry was the beginning of a boom-and-bust cycle that has continued to this day. Redding sank into a depression a decade before the stock market crash of 1929. The city began to emerge from it only in 1938 when the federal government sent a construction team from the newly completed Hoover Dam to begin building the Shasta Dam, whose floodgates were opened at the end of World War II. To this day many of the children and grandchildren of these construction workers still live in Redding and the surrounding area. For quite a while after the completion of the dam the great expanses of pine forest provided jobs in logging and mill work, but by 1990, largely because of concerns about preserving old-growth forests and protecting the northern spotted owl, several million acres of federal land were closed to logging and the industry withered.

By 2000, Redding had become largely a city of service workers toiling in retail and other low-paying jobs, although building and real estate were beginning to pick up because retirees from Sacramento, the Bay Area, and even from around Los Angeles were beginning to move there. These so-called equity refugees would sell houses where they lived and buy bigger ones in Redding for one-third the price. Physically the city had turned into something approximating a giant mall; a model of the new, cookie-cutter, minimum-wage economy. You could get just about anything you wanted in Redding, although little of anything was made there. Shoppers from Yreka and Dunsmuir, Weaverville and Etna, Red Bluff and Shingletown crowded Best Buy and Circuit City, Sears and Mervyn's, Costco and Wal-Mart, Bed, Bath & Beyond and the smallest Macy's in America, inside of which ran Redding's first and only escalator. The transition began in the 1960s, when a handful of local movers and shakers joined together to roof over three blocks of the old downtown to form a covered mall, a seemingly sensible strategy in a city that swelters in the summer and is raw and rainy in the winter. But before long more modern malls mushroomed across the river along Hilltop Drive and Dana Drive, leaving the downtown desolate and dying, its shops boarded up and its respectable old hotels reduced to SROs. For a long time, with two exceptions, almost the only thriving business left downtown was Jack's, an institution on California Street that from the outside looked totally derelict, but inside was warm, smoky, crowded, and noisy. Jack's served big, pan-fried steaks that were so good patrons regularly waited an hour outside in the heat or rain for a table. The other exceptions were the two big, modern hospitals. Redding Medical Center provided 1,200 mostly middle-class jobs to the local economy and about $800,000 a year in tax revenues. Mercy Medical Center provided a similar number of jobs, but because it was a nonprofit, no tax revenue.

Despite its ups and downs Redding, with a population of about 85,000, was the metropolis of the North State. Heading toward Oregon you had to drive more than 120 miles, past Yreka, where Dugan Barr, the city's best-known personal-injury lawyer grew up, and across the state line to get to the next town with a population over 5,000. In many ways Redding was typical of middle-class rural America, relaxed and friendly, at least on the surface. It was a place where people were generally polite and talked to strangers on the street and in the supermarkets. It was the kind of community in which a retired funeral director like Rudy Balma could get together with a group of friends, form a new bank, and make a go of it. The city's closely knit upper middle class—doctors, lawyers, bankers, and county, state, and federal officials mostly—met weekly at Rotary luncheons. The desire to participate in Rotary was so high that Redding supported five separate clubs. But a majority of the city's elite belonged to the biggest, oldest, and most prestigious club, known simply as the Rotary Club of Redding, which met every Thursday at noon over lunch at the Riverview Golf and Country Club on Bechelli Lane.

The meetings were informal but ritualistic affairs. After ten or fifteen minutes of friendly chitchat, members placed their hands over their hearts, pledged allegiance to the flag, and said grace. Then, while sharing jokes and gossip and eating meatloaf and mashed potatoes or the like, members dreamed up civic projects. After lunch there were committee reports and at each meeting a different member was called on to say a few words about what he or she had been up to lately and to pledge an unspecified sum of money—$100 wasn't unusual—to the general fund. The club also assigned all of its members to service teams with responsibilities for activities such as socials, blood drives, and charitable giving. Reflecting Redding's continuing love affair with the Old West, during 2002–3 these teams were given names like the Earps, the Jesse James Gang, and the Hole in the Wall Gang. The two teams headed by women were named for Belle Starr and Annie Oakley.

As might have been expected, these same men and a smaller but growing circle of women regularly golfed and dined together at Riverview, the social nexus of well-to-do Redding. The unimposing two-story frame clubhouse sat on a low bluff on the east bank of the Sacramento River ten minutes from downtown. Its glass-walled upstairs and downstairs dining rooms overlooked a manicured putting green and beyond that a wide stretch of the river and the eighteen-hole golf course, which was built along the east bank and was thick with scrub oaks that were old when the course was built in 1947. The property was still habitat for deer, red and gray fox, badgers, beaver, and an occasional mountain lion. Bald eagles and osprey regularly perched on the withered gray trunk of a dead oak that jutted out from the bank of the river at about a 20-degree angle. The clubhouse had been designed by a local architect named Bill Woodward, who in the 1950s had helped Frank Lloyd Wright build a small church in Redding. Like similar clubs everywhere, it was a place where acquaintances with common social and business interests were afforded an easy opportunity to become friends in a comfortable environment over drinks, dinner, or a round of golf. If and when business was actually transacted there, members tended to be discreet about it.

Riverview was significantly different from many other country clubs in that it had no initiation fee, at least in the traditional sense. To become a proprietary member—one with voting rights—one bought a share in the club, which could be sold at any time at market value. In 2005, a number of shares were available at the relatively modest price of about

$3,000. Proprietary members, limited to five hundred, paid monthly dues of $250, which included golf and tennis privileges. There were also less expensive nonproprietary memberships, which did not require any payment up front. Social memberships cost just $60 a month. These included everything except golf and tennis, which meant use of the swimming pool, the dining rooms, and club facilities for weddings and other events. Nonproprietary tennis memberships were also available. The low prices and a generally nondiscriminatory admissions policy made the club accessible to the city's growing middle class, including the equity refugees. And the process of becoming a member, like much else in Redding, seemed quite informal. If someone wanted to join he presented himself to either the club manager or the golf pro, both of whom were authorized to conduct an initial interview. According to Bill Woodward, a former president of the club, if the applicant were not a habitual criminal or sociopath, the manager or pro would find members to sponsor him. The final admissions decision was made by the board.

A quick perusal of the membership list suggests that most are in business, the professions, or retired. Their names and a couple of visits to the club also suggest a religious and ethnic mix roughly representative of Redding's business and professional community: overwhelmingly white and Protestant. The club appears to have its fair share of Catholics, Asians (most of whom are physicians), perhaps as many as a dozen Jews, and a Muslim or two. There is at least one black member, James Tate, a Jamaican-born physician who runs a boutique hospital in Redding. Chae Moon, without a doubt the most prominent physician in town, is also a member and a regular on the golf course. So is Riaz Malik, a surgeon at Redding Medical Center.

Of course, all this easygoing fellowship at Rotary and Riverview did not mean that the usual undercurrents did not run in Redding, the same as in any town, big or small. There was gossip, some of it just petty, some of it mean, sexual intrigue involving doctors and nurses and doctors and doctors, occasional dark rumors, some false, some with a grain of truth to them, and occasionally more than a grain, and the usual unspoken animosities. And, like small cities all over America, but especially in the Sun Belt, Redding was going through change, some of it wrenching.

Beginning in the 1990s, growth-related problems had put considerable strain on Redding's social fabric. By 2000, retirees from the big cities to the south were arriving in increasing numbers. Apart from the relatively low price of houses, these newcomers were attracted by the beautiful scenery, lower living costs, and medical care that was plentiful and generally believed to be unusually good. On the whole, these comfortable retirees seemed certain to be an asset to the community. Nevertheless, some perceptive locals worried that if they kept coming, before long they would drive up real estate prices, making it difficult for young families to buy starter houses. And there were those who worried that they would bring their city values with them, which, they believed, would erode the small-town character of the community. Still others, embarrassed by the redneck image that many of their neighbors embodied and a smaller number cultivated, saw in the recent arrivals potential supporters for their pro-development policies, both economic and cultural, and were more welcoming.

Despite these incipient communal tensions, there was still, among the men and women of Redding, a tangible sense of community not easy to find in bigger cities or, increasingly, in small towns either. Mike Warren, Redding's city manager since 1995, thought he knew why Redding had been able to preserve these evanescent qualities. He had worked in small towns in Oregon and California and he believed that people were kinder in Redding. They were more tolerant, he said, less political, and they contributed more to their community. "At first," he said, "I thought that it was something in the water supply [but] what I've come to realize is they're different . . . because everyone that works here lives here and everyone that lives here works here. As a consequence, you almost have to get along. It's your community. No one is driving longer than ten or fifteen minutes to work. It is the people's community. They feel very loyal to it and they feel very loyal to one another."

There might be something to Warren's assessment. People in Redding seem unusually civic-minded. In recent years, with substantial community support, the city has added a sports complex that includes three-quarter scale replicas of the baseball fields at Yankee Stadium, Wrigley Field, and Fenway Park, and a world-class aquatic center. The city government, with the help of local citizens, has beautifully restored an old art-deco movie theater and turned it into a performing arts center that draws talent ranging from Ricky Skaggs to the Emerson Quartet.

At the same time, it is undeniable that certain tensions were bubbling to the surface in May of 2000. Perhaps the most concrete expression of the divisions resulting from the changes underway was the controversy over the Sundial Bridge, which spans the Sacramento River, connecting the city's arboretum to the Turtle Bay Exploration Park and museum. The project was conceived in 1995, the year Warren arrived in Redding. Arguably, nothing better represented the growing disparity of interests between the relatively small professional and managerial class in Redding and the bulk of the population. Redding's doctors and lawyers, bankers and business owners, the Rotary and Riverview set, saw the bridge as part of a long-term plan to encourage economic growth and to bring cultural and other amenities to their city. What ultimately made the project possible was the McConnell Foundation, established locally on the Farmers Insurance fortune of Carl and Leah McConnell, which was estimated to have assets of half a billion dollars.

The foundation's approach was ambitious, audacious, and expensive. Its executive vice president, John Mancasola, happened to have seen a book depicting the work of the now-renowned Spanish architect Santiago Calatrava, who subsequently designed the main Olympic stadium in Athens and the transportation center at Ground Zero in New York. Mancasola picked up the phone one morning and called Calatrava at his office in Zurich. The architect answered the phone himself and quickly agreed to design and build the bridge. Had the project been brought in anywhere near its original cost estimate of $2.8 million there probably would have been little controversy over its construction. But the cost ballooned to $23.5 million, with the annual upkeep estimated at $200,000. Many Redding residents thought the money could have been put to much better use, even though in the end the foundation picked up $20.5 million of the cost. But when the bridge was inaugurated on July 4, 2004, almost everyone agreed that it was an engineering and esthetic triumph. Walking across it and stopping for coffee or lunch in the cafe at the Turtle Bay end became a favorite outing for Redding citizens, including many who had opposed its construction.

Meanwhile, as the city struggled with its economic and social transition, the two hospitals continued to thrive, especially Redding Medical Center. At the millennium the hospitals were the two biggest and most influential private enterprises in town. Redding was physically, and to some considerable extent economically, dominated by these modern concrete-and-glass medical facilities, each sited on high ground and easily visible from the hundred-foot-high red bluffs across the river. Together, they were a source of more than two thousand jobs, almost a million dollars annually in tax income for the city, and a great deal of civic pride, not to mention an unusually broad range of medical services for a city the size of Redding. Just about everyone in northern California, and some in nearby Oregon and Nevada, was proud of the first-rate medical care available at highly profitable RMC and at Mercy, the Catholic nonprofit hospital across town. But most of all they were proud of RMC's heart program, which, at a word from Dr. Moon, would send its helicopter aloft to ferry in heart patients from the hinterlands.

3

Old-West Medicine

Medicine in Redding wasn't always state of the art. When Jim Charles came to town to open a medical practice in the 1940s, doctoring had more in common with Dodge City and Tombstone in the 1840s than with contemporary Los Angeles and San Francisco. Redding was an isolated lumber and railroad town with a population of under 10,000. Even a decade later, around the time that angiography, which revolutionized coronary care, was invented in Cleveland, medical care in Redding was still reminiscent of the Old West.*

The only hospital in town when Charles arrived was St. Caroline's, built in 1907 at the corner of Pine and Sacramento streets. A man named Thomas Wyatt practiced there. According to Charles, Wyatt, who was short and weighed in at about 200 pounds, would come into the operating room shirtless, with his beer belly hanging out, and grab a surgical gown. Charles said Wyatt used to brag about his speed, but the surgeon's pace was a problem sometimes because "he had a few bleeders that he couldn't quite control." He said typically Wyatt would be playing cards in one of the bars on California Street and he would get a call that a patient needed an appendectomy. He would run over to the hospital, race through the surgery, and return posthaste to the card game. Wyatt also was reputed to have locked the operating room doors and done quite a

---

*By way of illustration, Rush Blodget, another retired Redding physician, tells a story about a patient who was brought to a Redding hospital one day from the hamlet of Hayfork in Trinity County after having been shot. He was supposed to have had three bullets in him, but the surgeon, a man named Bridgman, as best Blodget was able to remember, could find only two. Bridgman, presumably not wanting to have to explain the missing bullet, shot one of his own into a board in his backyard, dug it out, and turned it over to the sheriff with the two he took out of the patient. One can only hope that he was better at surgery than ballistics, however, because his bullet was of a different caliber from the ones he extracted from the victim.

few abortions at St. Caroline's, which was a Catholic hospital. It is Charles's recollection that Wyatt was asked to leave St. Caroline's because of the abortions, after which he founded Memorial Hospital in 1945. A dozen investors, including Charles, bought it from Wyatt seven years later and in 1972 sold it to National Medical Enterprises, the forerunner to Tenet. It was renamed Redding Medical Center in 1984.

In Charles's early days in Redding, the general practitioners did everything but thoracic surgery. Charles said that before the first neurosurgeon arrived "they even cracked a skull every once in a while. If someone came in with a depressed fracture they would open the skull and remove the debris and whatnot. We weren't afraid to do anything, lots of gall bladders." Charles eventually had to give up his practice in the late 1990s because he didn't have malpractice insurance. "I was one of the unusual ones," he said. "I had faith in my patients."

After NME bought Memorial, however, some things began to change. In 1977, the same year that Andreas Gruentzig, a charismatic German physician working in Zurich, first did coronary angioplasty, the new owners rebuilt the hospital from the ground up. St. Caroline's was also modernized and moved to a prime hilltop site overlooking the city and renamed Mercy Hospital. Little Redding was on its way to having two well-equipped, up-to-date medical facilities. Meanwhile, Shasta College's two-year program was turning out a steady supply of nurses for them, many of whom would never experience medical practice outside of Redding. The two hospitals, together with Redding's beautiful setting and very livable, inexpensive, small-town environment made it an attractive place for doctors, especially those with young families looking for a safe, homogeneous place to raise their children. It was also appealing to anyone who enjoyed the outdoors, like Harry Daniell, a Harvard-trained primary care doctor who hiked and rode his mountain bike and whose wife couldn't stand the cold. And it was a place where by and large the churchgoing, socially and politically conservative population was comfortable with the idea that doctors were trustworthy, autonomous professionals whose judgment should rarely if ever be questioned. Very few members of the community gave a thought to concerns like quality and cost controls in healthcare, and, like most of the physicians in town, they were hostile toward managed care. They were happy with things the way they were.

When asked why he thought Redding physicians were so opposed to managed care, Daryl Cardoza, COO of Hill Physicians, an HMO that did business in Redding between 1995 and 2000, but couldn't survive there, said: "They were against accountability." The "they" Cardoza was referring to were doctors who wanted to practice medicine without anyone checking to see how well they were doing it. Without managed care, and without effective peer review in the hospitals, which by all accounts was virtually nonexistent, doctors were free to do as they pleased and to charge pretty much what they wanted. "They charged more because they could," Cardoza said, adding that a lack of competition in Redding, particularly among specialists, enabled physicians to keep managed care out. George Anderson, a vice president of Health Net, which also tried to operate an HMO in Redding, but pulled out in 1999, told the *Sacramento Bee* that "What you have there is a community where physicians really have left urban areas to escape managed care. You have a fee-for-service payment structure. You end up with a lot of unnecessary procedures and higher-than-normal utilization of elective surgeries. We had no ability to cover the cost of care."

And it wasn't only the doctors who were raking in the big bucks in Redding, the hospitals were, too. Even by Tenet's exacting standards, RMC was a cash cow. The average revenue per patient day earned by Tenet nationwide in 2001 was $1,661. The average for Redding Medical Center was $3,181, nearly twice as much, with heart procedures setting the pace. Catholic Healthcare West, Mercy's owner, made $1,310 per patient day that year. Mercy Hospital earned $2,088. From the mid-1990s on, RMC was at or near the top of the charts for the rate of bypass operations done on Medicare patients. In 1996, the city of Redding was number one in the country and RMC was doing twice as many bypasses as Mercy. By 1999, the bypass rate in Redding for Medicare patients was twice as high as in Sacramento, 144 miles to the south on I-5, or Medford, Oregon, 124 miles to the north. Redding by all accounts was still a place where doctors could practice pretty much as they pleased, doctors and hospitals could charge what they wanted, and third-party payers, both public and private, picked up the bills and asked few questions.

The Doctors

The people of Redding and its six surrounding counties seemed happy with the hospitals and the care they provided. They especially admired the two relative newcomers, Chae Hyun Moon and Fidel Realyvasquez. Moon arrived in 1978, left for a practice in Orange County near Los Angeles for about a year, and then returned. Realyvasquez came to Redding at Moon's invitation, first as part of a rotating team of surgeons from Sacramento in 1987 and then full-time two years later. Just about everyone gave these physicians credit for the RMC heart program's high ratings and the economic benefits it provided to the community.

While their achievements were renowned in Redding, in some ways what was more interesting, though rarely discussed, was that the two men were held in such high esteem despite the fact that they were geographically and ethnically outsiders. When each arrived, Redding's population was well over 90 percent white, largely Protestant, and, except for a thin layer of professional cream, working class or lower middle class. That these local inhabitants wholeheartedly embraced a highly aggressive, razor-tongued Korean whose religious affiliation if any was generally unknown and a moody, introspective, Roman Catholic Mexican-American, seems to testify to Moon and Realyvasquez's accomplishments and to the community's open-mindedness.

In the decade before Moon came to Redding, major changes had taken place in American medicine that had set the stage for Moon and Realyvasquez's acceptance by the community. Perhaps the most important of these was the passage of Medicare and Medicaid legislation in 1965, which in its first two decades provided hospitals with a huge cash windfall. By the end of the 1970s, partly as a result of new technologies and procedures and partly because of free-flowing Medicare and Medicaid funds, cardiac medicine had become a major growth industry in the United States. Angiography, which identifies blockages in arteries, had been developed in the late 1950s and bypass surgery in the late 1960s, both at the Cleveland Clinic. The use of angioplasty, in which a balloon on a catheter is inflated to open blocked arteries, had begun in the late 1970s in Switzerland. Tenet's forerunner, NME, like hospital corporations all over the country, was looking to capitalize on this trio of new, high-revenue-producing procedures.

The company's hospital in Redding was situated in an area in which few cardiac services were available and therefore it represented a significant business opportunity. NME needed an ambitious, aggressive cardiologist who could build a program quickly. They found their man in Chae Moon. Moon had attended Yonhap Medical School in Seoul,

South Korea, where he grew up. He came to the United States in the mid-1970s to do a residency at Metropolitan Hospital in New York, after which he spent two years at the Cleveland Clinic training in cardiovascular medicine. He was recruited by NME and in 1978 set up a cardiology practice in Redding. Although he was not board certified in cardiology, he soon began doing interventional procedures such as angiograms and angioplasty at RMC. He also began actively and generously lobbying primary care doctors in Shasta and neighboring counties to send him their cardiac patients. He would, for example, arrange for NME to buy them treadmills for exercise stress tests that would both enhance their practices and increase the number of cardiac referrals they made. These tests, in which a patient walks on a treadmill, whose speed and elevation are steadily increased while an electrocardiogram tracing is generated, indicate whether the patient's heart muscle is getting enough oxygen. Treadmills are basic diagnostic tools for primary care physicians and their results frequently determine whether the doctor will recommend that the patient see a cardiologist for further evaluation.

There were only a few cardiologists in town in those days and Moon was a prodigious worker. He was much faster at doing procedures than his colleagues and made himself available at any hour of the night or day, which endeared him to the primary care doctors, whose patients he would sometimes see at the hospital in the middle of the night. Other cardiologists would often try to avoid getting out of bed and going to the hospital by asking the on-duty doctor, "Are you sure it's an MI [heart attack]?" Some, like Gary Crawford, were offended by Moon's frequent failure to alert them to the fact that he was about to perform an angiogram on one of their patients, but Crawford, too, was grateful not to be awakened in the middle of the night. When Moon did call, Crawford said, he would typically say, "Your patient had 99.9 percent stenosis," or blockage. "He loved the nines."

Moon built his practice rapidly and, for the time, did a high volume of procedures. By the mid-1980s, he was doing a fair number of angioplasties and he arranged for cardiac surgeons, including Realyvasquez, to rotate through Redding to provide backup. In those early days it wasn't unusual for the procedure to fail and for the patient to be rescued with a coronary bypass. By the time these rotations began Moon was on the verge of creating a full-scale open-heart program at RMC. The hospital had operated a shell program since 1976 with the grandiose name of the California Heart Institute. But now Redding Medical Center was going to build a new four-story tower for it and promote the institute heavily as a nationally ranked cardiac program. This effort turned out to be wildly successful; the California Heart Institute became a financial bonanza for NME and it made Moon, and to a lesser extent Realyvasquez, a living legend in Redding.

Moon was soon putting up numbers in the cath lab that in their own worlds Michael Jordan and Barry Bonds could hardly dream of. He was doing four and five times as many catheterizations as his peers elsewhere, even at major academic medical centers. This, of course, was good for Realyvasquez's business, too. In Moon's world, the world of RMC, and also Mercy Hospital where he maintained a small practice, there were a few skeptics among the physicians, but almost everyone else chalked up their skepticism to envy. On the whole Moon was revered as much by the doctors and nurses as he was by the public and was treated with deference and respect, as was Realyvasquez. Bill Browning, a perceptive retired army colonel who was the chief pharmacist at RMC for six years, observed that both Moon and Realyvasquez reveled in this treatment and speculated that it was "because they weren't from white American backgrounds." Although both men earned much more than any other Redding doctor, Browning believed the adulation was more important to them than the money.

For the most part, though, the reverence in which Moon was held was strictly professional. Even those who liked him could not help but notice that he was egotistical, short-tempered, and insulting to patients, nurses, and even other doctors. And he was not at all averse to throwing his weight around. At the same time he could be generous. He supported training programs for nurses with his own funds and bought rain jackets for the men who worked on the hospital grounds. He was a gregarious, assertive, self-promoting bundle of energy who, despite his ungrammatical and inarticulate English, would speak in public at the drop of a hat. He never hesitated to tell anyone who would listen that he was one of the ten best cardiologists in the country, and that he was way ahead of the technological curve in his practice. Moon behaved as if other cardiologists in town, like Bob Pick and Roy Ditchey at Mercy Hospital, were medical bumpkins even though both were board-certified interventional cardiologists and Ditchey had spent about fifteen years in academic medicine at the universities of Vermont and Colorado.

To get a better sense of Chae Hyun Moon, it helps to *hear his voice*. Thanks to a tape recording made at a "meet-the-doctor" session with Moon in 1996, it is possible to do so. Here is an excerpt from his colorful, freewheeling, foulmouthed, syntactically challenged discourse, which awkwardly entangles his thoughts on how his father practiced medicine in Korea and his own gifts as a physician with a spirited defense of his locally renowned failure to keep records.

When my dad was a family practitioner practicing in town, all we could afford during Japanese and China wars—and he didn't have any autos or nothing and he was doing house calls, down a river, horse and buggy or riding in a sleigh going to an emergency or an operation and thing like that. Where are the medical records, huh? When Dr. Schwartz [sic—did he mean Albert Schweitzer?] was in Africa, where was the goddamn medical records? Do you know what I'm saying? Last year in Redding Medical Center I did nineteen hundred procedures by myself. How many patients died? Zero. Huh! That's the quality of medicine. Not because I have a legible handwriting or, you know, this and that bullshit. I said why are you guys doing it? You look like Democrats. Too much paperwork! When are we going to have time to take care of patients?*

Like Moon, Realyvasquez could be intimidating. In 1987, just before moving his practice to Redding full-time, he met with Kevin Linkus, a member of his surgical group who was then the resident cardiac surgeon at RMC. Linkus was excited because he thought Realyvasquez was going to offer him a partnership. Instead Realyvasquez told him coldly over lunch in the cafeteria that he was fired and refused to explain why. The ostensible reason was that Linkus could not get along with Moon and the cardiologist wanted him gone. Linkus said he did not learn until the next day that Realyvasquez was his replacement. Realyvasquez sometimes berated nurses and technicians with foulmouthed tirades. At one point, operating-room nurses complained to

---

*Neither Moon's lawyers nor Realyvasquez's lawyers would permit their clients to be interviewed for this book. Just before completing it, however, I met Realyvasquez and spoke to him for almost an hour and a half. Later I spoke to him again by phone for about half an hour. This quotation from Moon is taken from the transcript of a tape recording made on February 6, 1996, by the daughter of one of Moon's patients.

the administration at RMC that he created a hostile work environment in the OR.

In January 1999, Steve Schmidt, Redding Medical Center's CEO, wrote a memo to Dennis Brown, Tenet's regional vice president, complaining that the surgeon's "verbal abuse, profanity and total disrespect for the staff had escalated to the point that they were all seeking new jobs." Schmidt also wrote that Realyvasquez refused to curtail his profanity because he said it was part of his personality. Like Moon, Realyvasquez was at times abusive to other physicians. In one case he threatened to sue a local cardiologist for defamation of character. The cardiologist backed off and after that kept his criticism to himself. Realyvasquez was subject to angry outbursts less frequently than Moon, but he held grudges longer, often not speaking to people for weeks after blowing up at them. Bill Browning and others said that both Realyvasquez and Moon refused to accept review of their work by other medical professionals and neither the medical staff nor the hospital administration could or would force either of them to do so.

But in other ways, Realyvasquez was a different type altogether, both physically and in temperament. He was about five feet ten inches tall, of medium build, with dark hair that had grown thin on top and soft brown eyes. He had the long, tapered fingers often associated with pianists and surgeons. While not especially imposing physically he had a presence, at times steely and commanding, at other times gentle and charming. He was neither ascetic nor self-effacing; rather he was reserved and private, and in some ways enigmatic. While he was articulate in direct conversation, he was a poor public speaker who often mumbled or stuttered as if he were nervous, although his command of English was that of a well-educated, native-born American. He was confident about his intellect and professional skills, and off the public platform, generally speaking, he had the quiet bearing of a man who did not suffer fools and did not need to bluster. He was, however, given to outbursts of anger when those around him didn't perform up to his standard.

Realyvasquez went to medical school at the University of California at Davis and completed his training at Stanford and the University of California at Irvine. Unlike Moon, he was interested in basic research, traveled frequently to professional meetings around the country, and published in surgical journals, although perhaps not as much as he would have liked. But he never published a landmark paper, and therefore never became well known among leading surgeons elsewhere in the country. Given his not inconsequential ego, this probably rankled. One thing he did have in common with Moon, however, and with a great many other physicians, was a lack of patience when it came to record keeping. Hours spent dictating charts are hours not spent caring for patients; neither are they billable hours. He also tended to let his physician's assistants handle most postsurgical patient visits.

Realyvasquez's Mexican-born father was an auto mechanic in South San Francisco. He and Moon were reared in radically different social and cultural surroundings, although economically the difference might not have been as great as the occupations of their fathers suggest. Moon's goal as a teenager was to follow in his father's footsteps professionally, but not economically, and certainly not as far as status was concerned. His father was sometimes rewarded for his skilled services with a live chicken, a form of payment that Moon found demeaning and that likely served as an early motivator for him to work toward a high-income practice in a prestigious specialty. Realyvasquez showed no interest in becoming an auto mechanic like his father. Nevertheless, as a teenager he was a James Dean–style tough guy in a motorcycle jacket who played high school football and at least early on was a mediocre student with no notable academic or career ambitions. At some point, however, a hard-working and academically successful cousin moved in with the family, stirred his competitive juices, and inspired him to study. Against the odds, this ultimately led him to medical school and a career as a cardiac surgeon.

As different as their childhoods were, the two doctors had much in common. They both were highly ambitious, self-promoting, driven workaholics. Moon in particular could be found at the hospital at all hours of the day or night. Professionally, both men were loners; each had only a single partner in his medical practice during his years in Redding and neither partnership lasted. Coincidentally, both of them came from large families in which all of the children were boys. Moon had five brothers. Realyvasquez had six, but one died while still a baby. Both men cared about art, Moon as both a collector and a practitioner. Some of his own canvases were very large blood-red abstractions. He once told a reporter for the *Record Searchlight,* Redding's Scripps Howard–owned daily newspaper, that he found painting therapeutic and that he made big paintings because his mind was big and he was not someone who saw life in small scale. Realyvasquez's involvement was principally as a collector of Western art, including works by Remington, although a close friend who had seen his doodles said he showed a talent for drawing. And both men were philanthropic. Realyvasquez donated a suite of seventy-five Ansel Adams photographs from the Museum Set, images Adams selected as his favorites, to the Turtle Bay Museum in Redding. And Moon supported Redding's municipal exhibition space in the old city hall and commissioned several abstract stone pieces by a Korean artist for a sculpture garden in front of the current city hall.

In the few waking hours when he was not out cathing patients, Moon liked to paint in the studio he had built at his sprawling Mediterranean-style house on Texas Springs Road, about a fifteen-minute drive from Redding Medical Center. He lived there with his wife, Sun, and three children. The large white house with red roof tiles was set on twenty rolling, tree-covered acres with a stunning view of Mount Lassen; it was surrounded by a fence topped with barbed wire. Somewhat incongruously, it had sliding Japanese-style screens instead of doors inside. It also had a swimming pool and tennis court. But Moon's game was golf, which he played as often as he could at the Riverview Country Club.

Realyvasquez, who said that one of the reasons he came to Redding was because "I like shit on my boots," spent leisure time riding a big lawn mower around La Baranca, his 1,000-acre Palo Cedro ranch just east of Redding. The property had spectacular views of both Mount Shasta and Mount Lassen. He lived there with a nurse named Theresa Ratterman, his longtime companion, and their two children. Unlike Moon, who seemed proud of his heritage and attributed his work ethic to having been brought up in a Korean family, Realyvasquez identified more with American cowboys than Mexicans. His 7,000-square-foot house, which he said blended Spanish, Mexican, and Pueblo elements, could easily have been mistaken for a Mexican hacienda. He likes to vacation in Santa Fe and he brought craftsmen from there to do the fine woodworking on the house. When he put the place up for sale in the spring of 2004, it was billed as "Santa Fe style," not Mexican. The asking price was $6.375 million.

One fact not widely known in Redding, except among a small segment of the elite, was that the two physicians did not like each other. Jim Grant, the genial president of Simpson College, a four-year institution in Redding with a strong Protestant religious orientation, said they wouldn't even speak to each other. Grant should know, because he was chairman of the board of the RMC Foundation and served on the hospital's governing board. He also said they would not appear together in public unless business interests demanded it. Grant told a story to support his assessment.

When Redding Medical Center was building its cardiac tower, there was a meeting in which Moon and Realyvasquez had to be together to approve the plans. After they both signed off on them, Moon left. Realyvasquez stayed, and asked the only other person there, "Do you understand what kind of meeting this is?" The response was "Well, yes, obviously it's an important meeting." Realyvasquez then supposedly said, "No, this is the first time I've been in the same room with this little son of a bitch." Realyvasquez said later on that his own memory of the meeting was somewhat vague, but the quote rang true. Nonetheless, the mutual benefits of their relationship must have outweighed the personal drawbacks because it continued year after year.

4

A Case of Abandonment

At the same February 1996 meet-the-doctor get-together in which Moon talked about his father and "Dr. Schwartz," the outspoken cardiologist soliloquized on his records-related problems once again, this time specifically at Mercy Hospital where he had admitting privileges, but saw few patients. His recorded remarks suggest a kind of messianic arrogance combined with a highly combustible personality. Added to the value he placed on speed in doing procedures and seeing the maximum number of patients these qualities would contribute to a tragic outcome for one of his patients later that year.

"What is the hospital gonna say?" Moon asked his audience rhetorically.

I don't know. No, I say to the hospital, I say that Mercy Hospital tried to kick me off the staff two years ago. This is true story, huh, this is true story. Well, doctor, you didn't do your medical records. I said the reason I didn't do medical records is because your hospital shut me out of your ER. You lied to my patients when they go to the Mercy Emergency Room, Dr. Moon doesn't come here anymore. Why? Because I'm a director at Redding Medical Center. . . . So finally I said fine, if you're going to treat me like that I'm not going to do medical records. I know they're going to try to kick me off the staff. I wanted it to become a legal issue. You understand what I'm saying? You cannot treat medical staff unlegally because one is the director of a program of another hospital, a competing hospital. You understand what I'm saying? So I hired a lawyer. It cost me $45,000 in two months. I went to the board and I said, Listen, at twelve years old—a kid—God told me to become a doctor. I'm a crazy man in a sense; I love medicine for the sake of medicines. My body might be old, my hair might be turning gray, I might have arthritis and all that, my lungs might have black tar and emphysema. I would still take care of my patients.

Mercy did not kick Chae Moon off its staff over his record keeping or anything else, then or ever, although an incident involving the cardiologist in 1996 led a few people in Redding to think the hospital should have. On July 17 of that year, a former patient of Moon's named Charles Kenneth Brown went to Mercy's emergency room. At the time all but a handful of people in Redding felt incredibly fortunate to have a "world-class" cardiologist like Moon practicing in their small city. Just about everyone knew he was often abrupt with patients, dismissive of their concerns, and arrogant. But most were willing to overlook his unpleasantness because of the quality of care he delivered. But Brown, a sixty-seven-year-old country-and-western singer who also worked in the wood molding business, and his wife, Geanetta, a vocational nurse and country guitarist, were exceptions. When Charles Brown's blood pressure spiked to 329 over 101 and he had mild chest pain, Mrs. Brown brought him to Mercy Hospital specifically to avoid having him cared for by Moon.

Brown had been seeing Moon for his hypertension and he and his wife were not happy with the care he was getting. Unlike Brown's doctor in Reno, where he lived before moving to Redding, Moon did not seem able to get his blood pressure under control. Moreover, Brown had experienced a previous bad episode with Moon. In November 1990, Moon had performed an angiogram on Brown, and Brown had reacted badly to the contrast dye. It had to be quickly flushed out of his body. Moon had been either unaware of or had paid no attention to the fact that sometime in the late 1980s, while living in Reno, Brown also had reacted badly to contrast dye, developing acute kidney failure and high blood pressure as a result.* After the 1990 angiogram Moon had referred Brown to Realyvasquez for triple-bypass surgery, which could not be performed until he recovered from his reaction to the dye.

---

*This was a potential problem Moon should have been fully aware of because he'd had a similar experience with one of the first patients on whom he had ever performed angioplasty. Contrast dye from the angiogram performed on that patient compromised her kidney function for the rest of her life.

Although Moon rarely did procedures at Mercy, he happened to be present the day in 1996 that Brown was brought in. When Norman Arai, Brown's primary care physician, told Moon that Brown was in the emergency room, Moon went to the ER and told Brown, who was sedated, that he was going to do an angiogram. The reason for performing this angiogram was not clear. Nothing in Brown's chart indicated that he needed it and Arai had told Mrs. Brown that tests he had run showed no heart damage. Later, while still partially sedated and groggy, Brown told his wife that Moon said he needed an angiogram and it was scheduled for nine the following morning. Mrs. Brown told him that she was going to stop the procedure, but by the time she arrived at the hospital the next morning her husband had already been taken away.

Kim Schlenker, one of the nurses, spoke to Brown just before he was taken into the holding room at 8:30 a.m. Her notes on the case that day said, "Patient alert, responsive, verbalizes understanding of pending procedure. Patient remains conscious and oriented." Moon arrived at the cath lab after Brown was prepped, draped, and ready and began the procedure at 9:45. Schlenker said that Moon, working at top speed as always, was operating with a right coronary catheter. The procedure is risky because the catheter can flick off material from arterial walls that can migrate to the brain, causing a stroke. But just a few minutes into the delicate procedure, Moon decided to inject contrast dye into Brown's left internal mammary artery. Schlenker said that normally one would change catheters, but Moon was impatient—he said he had many cases across town at RMC—and it was possible to do this by injecting the dye into the subclavian artery, from which it would flow through the vertebral artery into the left internal mammary artery. Done carefully, this is acceptable technique, but Moon was in a hurry and appeared to have caused an embolism in the patient's brain. Brown began to scream in pain and suffered a stroke.

Brown's systolic blood pressure spiked immediately from 170 to 230 and his speech became incomprehensible. Schlenker needed help. She had a nurse named Mary Roach paged to come to the cath lab to help her monitor the patient's neurological status. Moon announced that Brown was having a stroke and they had to infuse him with esmolol, a medication intended to get his blood pressure down. Then, instead of following through with additional orders or action, he took off his gloves and, sounding irritated, shouted that he had to go crosstown because he had seven cases waiting at RMC.

Roach was transporting a patient when she heard the overhead page. It sounded urgent. She dropped off the patient at the CCU and went straight to the cath lab. When she arrived minutes later Moon was already in the foyer area and unscrubbed. Kim Schlenker filled her in on what was going on while she and Bonny Purcell, the scrub nurse, continued hanging drugs for IV delivery. Roach glanced at the patient, noting immediately that he had a low level of consciousness, he was having a hard time speaking, and one side of his body was not moving. Moon was yelling at the nurses to get the patient's blood pressure down and Purcell and Schlenker were trying to find out what else he wanted them to do. They asked whether he wanted a CT scan. They also asked whether he wanted them to call him. But Moon left without giving any additional orders.

The nurses couldn't believe that he was abandoning a neurologically unstable patient and leaving them without a physician to help them resuscitate him and manage his care. It was about 10:10 a.m. when Moon headed out the door. Brown's wife was waiting, and he told her, "Your husband's heart is okay, but if you don't do something about his kidneys he's going to die." She told him, "We have an appointment with a very good kidney specialist in Nevada," to which Moon shot back, "Oh, so what do you want me to do, fly him to Nevada now?" She asked Moon, "What's going on, what's happened?" But he ignored her question, spun around, got on the elevator, and disappeared. Someone called Bill Jennings, the cath lab supervisor, to come and help stabilize Brown.

At 10:30 a.m. Moon telephoned the cath lab and a nurse named Patrick Green answered the phone and passed it to Schlenker, who asked Moon if he wanted her to get another doctor to take charge of the patient. She told him the esmolol was not working and asked if she should switch to Nipride, another medication. Moon, seeming rushed and speaking curtly, ignored her question about getting another doctor to take over, but approved the switch to Nipride, which did bring Brown's blood pressure down. He also ordered a CT scan. Schlenker went out to talk to Brown's family while Roach, Purcell, and Green worked to stabilize the puncture wound in his groin from the insertion of the catheter and to monitor his airway and neurological status. She told the three waiting family members that he had suffered a stroke and that he would not look the same when they next saw him. She also told them that they should get a new doctor. Brown's daughter, obviously very upset and angry, told Schlenker that Moon had told Geanetta Brown that her husband was going to die and that it was her fault for not bringing him to the hospital soon enough.

Not knowing what else to say or do, and needing to get the patient to radiology for the CT scan, Schlenker wheeled him out of the room. As he passed through the area where his wife, daughter, and grandson were sitting, he managed to say, "He hurt me, he hurt me bad." At the end of the day Schlenker prepared an occurrence report as required, documenting that a patient had suffered a stroke in the cath lab and that Dr. Moon had abandoned him in unstable condition. Over the next three weeks Brown underwent dialysis for kidney failure. He died twenty-three days after arriving in the Mercy emergency room. Moon's July 19 report on the angiogram, under the heading "Complications," says "None." According to the death certificate, which was signed by Dr. Arai, Brown died on August 9, 1996, of "cardiac arrest due to cardiac arrhythmia, due to renal failure, due to contrast dye." Mrs. Brown never heard from Moon again.

At noon on August 27, Dr. Nena Perry called to order a meeting of the Mercy Hospital Medical Staff Executive Committee of which she was chairman. Apart from Perry, six members were present and one was excused. George Govier, the CEO of the hospital, also attended the meeting as did Jim Campbell, Sr., the hospital's medical director. According to the minutes, the committee discussed Moon's behavior in the Brown case and considered a subcommittee recommendation that Moon's procedures in the cath lab be monitored. Another incident involving Moon was also discussed. A motion was passed asking Moon to respond within thirty days as provided for under the committee's rules. A second motion was passed approving the recommendation that Moon be monitored in the cath lab and assigning Dr. Perry and Dr. David Short to draft a letter conveying the committee's determinations to him. The letter, dated August 28, said the following:

> Dear Dr. Moon:
> Issues relating to patient care and employee safety have been brought to the attention of the Medical Division and the

Executive Committee. The Executive Committee requires your response to the following concerns about the management of Charles Brown.*

1. This patient suffered a stroke during cardiac catheterization. It is alleged that you left the hospital without clear instructions to the staff about how the complication was to be managed, made worse by the fact that the patient was unstable. Leaving the nurses to deal with the complication was inappropriate and a serious quality of care issue.
2. There is no evidence in the patient's chart of adequate pre-evaluation.
3. There was no dictated report on the patient's chart.

Your written response is required within 30 days of receipt of this letter.

In addition to patient care concerns, employee safety issues were discussed.

In one case a nurse [Kim Schlenker] suffered a needle stick during a case and you would not allow the time to inspect and clean the wound, nor was she given time to reglove.

Due to the seriousness of the above patient care concerns and issues of employee safety, the Executive Committee passed a motion on August 27, 1996, to require concurrent monitoring on all catheterization procedures, effective immediately. The monitoring will be carried out in the following fashion:

- *All procedures performed in the Cath Lab* will be monitored.
- The medical director of the Cath Lab (Dr. Tretheway) or his designee will be your monitor. It is *your responsibility* to contact him prior to the procedure.
- The case *will not proceed* without the monitor in attendance.

---

*This letter is reproduced from a redacted text. The patient's name has been edited out and the author has filled in Mr. Brown's name. In the first sentence of the next paragraph two words have been edited out. The author has filled in the words "stroke" and "catheterization" in that order.

- You *will not* jeopardize patient safety. Cases of extreme emergency will be closely reviewed for adequate documentation.
- Monitoring will continue until the Executive Committee is satisfied that patient and employee safety is no longer compromised.

If you have any questions, please contact one of us.

Sincerely,

Nena L. Perry, M.D., chairman,   David Short, M.D., chairman,
Medical Staff Executive Committee   Medical Division

As of September 27, Moon had not replied to the letter from the executive committee, which he had received on August 29. Perry wrote to him again advising him that his failure to respond within the one-month time limit would result in automatic suspension until the response was received. On September 30, Perry received a hand-delivered, six-page, single-spaced letter from Moon filled with grammatical errors and misspellings, including Perry's first name, which he rendered as Nina. In this letter he wrote that Brown was suffering from chronic renal failure and high blood pressure that was difficult to manage. The reason for the catheterization, Moon wrote, was that Brown had experienced "an episode of prolonged chest discomfort." He went on to say that the patient was intelligent and aware that he could suffer a second heart attack, a stroke, or kidney failure as a result of catheterization, therefore he left it to the patient to decide whether he should undergo the procedure.

Moon wrote that he saw that Brown was having a stroke immediately after completing the procedure. What happened next, however, is not clear from Moon's letter, which in the version available from court records is heavily redacted. But he appears to have written, in direct contradiction of the sworn testimony of Roach and Schlenker, that he ordered a CT scan before leaving the cath lab. He also wrote that "immediately afterwards," he called Dr. Norman Arai, Brown's primary care physician, discussed the case, and asked Arai to involve a neurologist, an intensive-care specialist, and Dr. William DeVlaming, a nephrologist. He said he then told Arai that he didn't think he needed to be involved in Brown's care any longer, but that he would be available as necessary. There is no indication of any of this in the patient's chart, including the alleged involvement of any of these other physicians.

Moon also complained in the letter that "the person who made the allegation" against him had had a run-in with him at RMC that the committee members knew about and disregarded in their deliberations. It seems likely that he was referring to Mary Roach. He did not appear to be aware of the occurrence report written by Kim Schlenker or that all of the other nurses present had also written letters expressing their concerns about his abandonment of Brown in a neurologically unstable condition.

Moon denied the charge that he did not let Kim Schlenker, the nurse involved, change her glove after the needle stick she received. He wrote, "I cannot imagine myself not allowing a scrub tech to change their gloves in the incidence of needle stick. A needle stick is a needle stick, once you have felt the needle how much can you examine yourself and worry about it, and it does not merit to stop the procedure."

After making a series of procedural objections, Moon requested a hearing by the executive committee or a review of the case by a body independent of the executive committee. He then wrote pointedly: "I do not want to make this a legal issue outside the hospital, but if your committee continues to pursue this in an illegal manor [sic] I do not have any course but to take legal action against the committee and the hospital." He followed this threat by writing, "The only way to analyze this situation at present that I am in with your committee is that this is a political vendetta that Mercy Hospital and the Medical Staff Executive Committee is executing. With single allegation by [sic] a nursing staff that after sixteen years of practicing in Redding to be requested to be put on monitoring status which also has nothing to do with the procedure itself is very questionable decision by your committee." Moon then questioned Perry's ability to be impartial because he had refused to help her husband in what he referred to as "a political fall out" at Redding Medical Center. Finally, he asked for a prompt reply from the committee "because I have to make the decision regarding taking the case to court. . . ."

On October 15, Perry wrote to Moon that monitoring should not be construed as disciplinary action but rather as an investigative activity designed to evaluate the quality of care he was providing. The committee subsequently invited Moon to make his case, which he did on November 27. He restated the defense he offered in his long letter to Drs. Perry and Short. The minutes of this meeting cite an unnamed committee member as saying: "You have answered our questions. The abandonment is probably a non-issue after hearing your description of events." The minutes also cited another member saying, "The patient's chart (re abandonment) does not note anything that he [Moon] stated happened. Communications with nursing isn't recorded as having taken place." The committee then revised its original ruling and restricted monitoring of Moon to two cases. It did not restrict the monitors to cardiologists, and permitted Moon to select the monitors. The minutes were too cryptic to discern the reason this action was taken and members were unwilling to discuss the matter. The committee also ordered a letter to be placed in Moon's file expressing the concerns of the cath lab personnel.

Geanetta Brown said years later that she wrote to Dr. Campbell on November 20, 1996, describing what had happened and complaining about Moon's behavior. She said Campbell responded in a phone call that a review of the case was underway, but that he would not be able to share the results with her. She then told Campbell that she was going to report Moon to the California State Medical Board and she said he told her, "That's a good thing to do." The board looked into it and eventually rejected the case. She also looked into the possibility of suing Moon for malpractice, but she was turned down by two lawyers. She said James Wyatt in Redding told her that Moon had harmed his mother. He and a lawyer named David Smith in Sacramento, to whom Wyatt referred her, both made it clear that taking on Moon in Redding was a losing proposition, even though Smith had Brown's records reviewed by two cardiologists who said the angiogram was not necessary. Finally, Mrs. Brown said, "I just got tired. It's not just fighting city hall, it's fighting all of Redding and the State of California and I just got tired."

Almost exactly a year later, Moon demanded redress, perhaps even revenge. He was angry, he acted as if he had been victimized, and he lashed out at the hospital, its management, and medical staff. First, on Sunday, February 2, 1997, he placed a four-column advertisement in the *Record Searchlight* informing his patients that from then on he was restricting his hospital practice to Redding Medical Center. Then he sued Mercy, its owner, Catholic Healthcare West, the medical staff, the chair of the medical staff executive committee, and the CEO of the hospital. He sued in Shasta County Court for unfair business practices and in federal district court for violation of federal antitrust statutes, violations of the Business and Professional Code, defamation, loss of business opportunity, interference with his right to pursue his profession, and interference with prospective economic advantages. The federal case was dismissed on September 16, 1999, and the case in Shasta County Court was dismissed on December 27, 1999.

Years later, Jim Campbell told Patrick Campbell, another Redding physician to whom he is not related, something he did not tell Geanetta Brown. Mercy Hospital never reported Moon to the State Medical Board after the Brown case came to light because they signed an agreement with Moon precluding them from doing so as a condition of the minimal sanctions imposed on him. The Brown case was covered by the *Record Searchlight* and talked about around town in the late summer of 1996, but in time it was largely forgotten. It did not seem to do any damage to Chae Moon's reputation or hurt his practice. Most people, unlike the Browns, reasoned that no one was perfect and continued to think Moon was the best and that they were lucky to have him in Redding. One thing that few of them knew, however, was that Charles Kenneth Brown was not the first patient Moon had been accused of abandoning in extremis. Another man, Cornealous "Tex" Morrison had died of an overdose of potassium while under Moon's care. A medical expert hired by the family to review the case, which was settled for $40,000, concluded that "Dr. Moon, the primary physician, was unavailable and unreachable for several hours while the patient was in a critical condition. This falls below the standard of care for an on-call physician."[13]

5

The Outsider

The quality of medical care available was not on Father John Corapi's mind in the spring of 2000 when he drove 160 miles north from Sacramento in search of a new home somewhere near Redding in sparsely populated Shasta County. At age fifty-three Corapi was vigorous and as far as he knew in excellent health. Redding's appeal was its proximity to fast rivers full of salmon and trout and woods full of game. Just over 160,000 souls were scattered throughout the county's 3,785 square miles, which suited Corapi's solitary nature. Along with the good fishing and hunting he liked the fact that housing was cheap and that Redding Airport was nearby, a necessity dictated by his unusual priestly duties. These were the reasons Corapi chose to settle near Redding, but he had no way of knowing then that his decision to do so would prove providential. He did not divine that he would be subjected to a physical and psychological ordeal that would burden him for years. And he had no way of knowing that because he was an outsider with no links to Redding's establishment his actions would radically change the fortunes of a great many people.

Very likely none of this would have happened had Corapi lived an ordinary life before becoming a priest. Nor would it have happened had he become an ordinary priest. Since his ordination by Pope John Paul II in 1991 he had never been assigned to a parish. He had served as an itinerant preacher in the tradition of St. Paul, who was converted on the road to Damascus and walked through Asia Minor bringing Christianity to the Gentiles. Like Paul, the born-again John Corapi, who was forty-four years old by the time he entered the priesthood, traveled far and wide delivering homilies. By today's standards his deeply conservative sermons were almost as radical as Paul's, except that Corapi's audiences were in no obvious need of conversion. But Corapi did not see it that way. He believed that most of the Roman Catholic "faithful" to whom he preached did not know their faith very well and therefore could not live it very well. The message he preached to them was to return fervently and fully to the One True Faith. This he delivered from the depths of his soul based largely on his own twenty years of precarious wandering on the frontiers of hell.

Corapi was the product of a traditional Italian Catholic upbringing in Hudson, New York. His father, Anthony, half Sicilian and half Calabrese, was a journalist and his mother, Veronica, who was half Milanese and half French Canadian, was a nurse. The problem was that Anthony Corapi, a good-looking, athletic man, chased women, drank too much, and gambled. And each time Veronica discovered a new liaison, there would be an eruption of yelling and screaming. Anthony never hit Veronica nor did he ever hit his son, John, or his daughters, Carol and Mary Ann, who was killed at age fourteen with four of her classmates in a car accident coming home from a football game. Instead, he cursed and belittled them, often in a menacing drunken rage. This so terrified John that he would sometimes hide in a closet.

When John was a young child the family lived on the first floor of a small, two-family pink-shingled house owned by his maternal grandparents. The house was in the old part of town at 211 Robinson Street, two blocks from the river and the railroad station. His grandparents lived at 224 across the street. The rooms were small and there was a back door into a yard and an alley next to his bedroom. Their neighbors were immigrants, mostly Polish, a couple of Italian families, a few Irish and Germans, even a couple of Jewish families. There was a marsh by the river where all the duck hunters went. John remembered the smells in the spring and fall, especially the lilacs in the spring, and one incident in particular. He was about seven years old and was standing in his grandmother's backyard when a woman appeared. His Aunt Mary, who gave piano lessons, lived in his grandmother's house, so strangers often came and went. There was a big, fragrant, lilac bush in the yard. This woman stood near the bush and spoke his name. "Johnny," she said, smiled, and was gone. That's all there was.

Corapi was shy as a child and felt rejected by his father, whose idea of teaching his son to play baseball was to stand him fifty feet away and fire fastballs at him. John was introverted and scared of other kids. He would get beaten up regularly and at times had to be forced to go to school. When he showed up at home bruised and in torn clothes his parents would give him a hard time because he wouldn't defend himself.

When John was thirteen and still gaining self-confidence, his father divorced his mother. He entered high school soon thereafter, was a B-student, played football, and was elected first treasurer then vice president of his class. In the fall of 1965, he went to the State University of New York in Albany, but got off to a poor start academically. Corapi quit school, returned to Hudson, and hung out for a while with an ex-soldier who had served in the Eighty-second Airborne Division. They went skydiving together, which inspired Corapi, who was drifting with no idea of what to do next, to enlist in the army in the early spring of 1967. He signed a commitment to serve in the Special Forces, but in a helicopter accident in the Canal Zone he reinjured a shoulder that he'd originally hurt playing football and ended up in Heidelberg as an administrative assistant. He was released a month or two early from the army in 1970 and began attending Pace University in Pleasantville, New York. Within a week of arriving at Pace where he planned to study accounting, Corapi met a married student named Joe Zerga. Corapi and the older, more sophisticated Zerga, who had lived for two years in England and Austria, quickly became friends. The two young Italian-Americans hung out together, hunted, and went to field trials for hunting dogs.

Corapi was not thrilled with accounting, nor was he very good at it, but he stuck it out. Zerga, on the other hand, who seemed driven at least in part by his father's success as a businessman, was the best student in the class. When they were graduated from Pace in 1973—Zerga, summa cum laude and Corapi in the middle of the pack—Corapi took a job at Coopers & Lybrand in White Plains, New York, and Zerga joined a firm in Las Vegas. Two months later Corapi quit his job, which he found stultifying, and joined Zerga in Las Vegas at the firm of Harris, Kerr, Forster. Corapi and Zerga were the only non-Mormons in their accounting firm. To spare the Mormons from having to work in the casinos and hotels they did all of the hotel and casino auditing. The Mormon partners were delighted because they could send the Italians from New York into the dens of iniquity and still collect the fees. Corapi audited the Flamingo, Bugsy Siegel's original Las Vegas hotel, the Tropicana, and a small club downtown that was "owned by a mob guy," Corapi said, "who had nine beautiful daughters."

In 1975, Corapi left Harris, Kerr, Forster to become assistant controller of the Tropicana. His job was to make sure that nobody was skimming money from the gaming tables. These were the days in Las Vegas when Joe Louis was working as a host at Caesars Palace and Johnny Weismuller, the Olympic swimmer and movie Tarzan, was doing the same at the Tropicana. Corapi had a key to the dressing room at the Folies Bergere. All he had to do was ask and he would be comped into any casino's gourmet restaurant or show in town. Even if three hundred people were waiting in line the maître d' would take him in and bring him to a front table. The operative term in Las Vegas in those days was juice. Corapi had juice.

Nevertheless, after about a year he left the Tropicana to take a job as an investigator with the Nevada Gaming Control Board. Zerga also went to work for the board at about the same time. Corapi said later that he saw the job as a stepping-stone to a bigger job with a casino.

Their work as Las Vegas auditors and their experiences as investigators had made Corapi and Zerga, who were both still in their twenties, wise beyond their years. They were exposed to greed and sexual license daily and violence was a hovering presence in their world, all of which hardened them. They also learned that lying and scams were commonplace and that corruption was simply a part of the human condition, which prompted them to be cautious, pragmatic, and analytical.

While working for the gaming control board, Corapi had some bookkeeping clients on the side. One of them, who might have had mob connections, owned a restaurant. When he couldn't come up with the money to pay Corapi for his work, he gave him half the restaurant. This, plus the fact that Corapi was dating a secretary who worked for the board, led to Corapi's resignation under pressure. But he was ready for a change. He spent about a year in an accounting practice in Bullhead City, Arizona, but he wasn't doing well and wanted to make more money faster. He had read a couple of books, including *Winning Through Intimidation* by Robert J. Ringer, which whetted his appetite for big money, possibly in real estate.

Those were boom days in Los Angeles, so in 1978 he moved to Marina del Rey, got a real estate sales license a month later, and landed a job with a large firm that specialized in apartment buildings. About a year later he got a broker's license and opened two offices, one in Century City and the other in Encino. In his first year he made little or nothing. In the second year he made about $50,000. Then, in his third year, Corapi got involved in condominium conversions, which was the ticket he'd been waiting for. He bought apartment buildings and converted the apartments to condos, selling them off as individual units, which was extremely profitable and later became illegal because it was eliminating the rental housing stock. Corapi said he could double his money in twelve to eighteen months. By the early 1980s, he was making hundreds of thousands of dollars a year.

Corapi bought a house on the water in Oxnard about forty miles north of Los Angeles that was cedar on the outside and oak on the inside with three wall-to-wall native-stone fireplaces. It was about 5,500 square feet with a 2,000-square-foot bedroom and cost a bargain $650,000 because the builder had gone broke. Corapi parked his sixty-foot Hatteras yacht at the dock and his Ferrari and Cadillac in the garage. He was hanging out with real estate hustlers, people wanting to make big scores fast. They snorted coke and liked to show up at the best clubs and have the valet guy park their cars in front. He worked seven days a week, eighteen hours a day with no high or noble aspirations. His only goal was to win; make big bucks. Like everyone else he knew he aspired to run with the fast crowd, but somehow he never quite succeeded. Buying a house in distant, unfashionable Oxnard was emblematic of his inept efforts.

Nonetheless, Corapi, who was dark-skinned and ruggedly handsome, was living a version of the high life, maybe on the fringe, but still driving fast, expensive cars, getting invited to places where celebrities were sometimes seen, and dating hot, expensive women. After he had been in Los Angeles about a year and a half he attended a party at a mansion in the Hollywood Hills. Chevy Chase was there and an exotic dancer jumped out of a cake to celebrate his birthday. Corapi went to the party with a young model he had been going out with and her equally beautiful mother, whom he had also been dating. He met another beautiful young woman at the party and they talked for about twenty minutes while having drinks together, at which point she said to him, "I'm going to have to introduce you to my best friend." Corapi took it literally, and said, "That's fine." They walked to an empty bedroom in another part of the house and talked a while longer. When no one appeared, Corapi asked her, "Where's your friend?" She laughed and said, "Oh yes," and produced a small vial filled with white powder. She had a spoon, which they used to snort the coke.

"It was a seductive moment," Corapi said. "This was an actress, not a well-known actress yet, but an actress. And she was certainly good-looking. And she was a definite insider in the Hollywood scene. So there were two things, there was the business dimension of getting in with the in crowd and making money with them. And there was also the sex side of it. She was good-looking. It didn't occur to me to say no, thank you, I don't do that. I just went with the flow and that was the beginning of my end."

Six months to a year later Corapi met Ike Turner through the mother of the young girl with whom he had attended the Hollywood Hills party. Turner was in dire financial straits. He was a freebase addict and was reduced to selling whatever he could to support his habit, even, according to some accounts, the platinum records off the wall of his recording studio. Corapi was introduced to Turner to help him sell the studio. When he went to see it, Turner took Corapi upstairs to his party pad above the studio. The entrance was through a set of tall, narrow doors that led into a room with fuchsia-colored shag carpeting on the walls. It was furnished with a large glass table, a sofa, a coffee table and a few chairs. Turner asked Corapi if he liked it, and Corapi, not knowing what else to say, said, "Yes." Turner said, "I furnished it myself, in early nigger."

The door to Turner's pad was six-inch-thick steel. A video camera was focused on it so that anyone inside could see the police when they were coming. Periodically the police would break down that door, but Turner would always see them first and consume the coke or flush it down the toilet. After a while, Turner produced some high-quality Peruvian cocaine and began smoking it in a glass pipe. "I tried it," Corapi said, "and that was it. They take the cocaine and mix it either with ether or baking soda. That night, I think, it was ether based—the kind that blew Richard Pryor up. For people who tend to be shy or introverted it is the Holy Grail. Your personality changes almost immediately, no inhibitions, you're not scared of anything, worried about anything. It's an intense euphoria. But, of course, what goes up must come down. And it does, hard. Because the high doesn't last very long, you have to keep doing it, or you are going to come down, and it is extremely unpleasant."

Corapi dates his drug period roughly from late 1979, when he bought his new red 308 GTS Ferrari with beige leather interior, until sometime in 1982. He attended a party in the Hollywood Hills that John

Belushi was at the night he died later at the Chateau Marmont. He said that his last year in Los Angeles twelve people he knew died, half from heart attacks and half from suicide. He attributed all of their deaths to drug use. The days were growing short for Corapi, too. One night he went to a Halloween party at a club hosted by Elvira the Witch. That began a three-day drug binge that almost killed him and ended with his on-and-off girlfriend trying to take him to the hospital. Several hospitals refused to take him before she finally brought him to the Los Angeles VA hospital. They didn't want to take him either, but when she said, "I'll just leave him on the steps," they agreed to admit him.

A week or two after he was admitted, Corapi got angry and fought with a member of the hospital staff. They took him into a white examination room, strapped him to a table, and shot him up with Thorazine and left him there. He was looking up at the ceiling, helpless, wondering, "How can I be here? I was a nice little kid, I wasn't a criminal." Later a nurse entered his room, bringing the scent of lilacs with her. It evoked the memory of his childhood experience in his grandmother's backyard. The nurse stood at the foot of his bed, shook her head, smiled a kind of mysterious smile, and said, "Johnny." Then she left the room. Corapi understands that she could have been wearing lilac perfume, that she could read his name off the chart and could conceivably have used a diminutive. Nonetheless, for anyone inclined to believe in mystical things this was certainly that kind of experience. He had been panic-stricken, strapped down to a table, and it gave him a sense of great peace and consolation. He had no religious thought in his mind at the time.

After almost a year in the hospital the doctors decided that he was ready to leave. But by this time his house, cars, and boat had been repossessed and the doctors would not let him go without a plan. His mother agreed to lend him or give him—he can't remember which—money to help him get started in the real estate business again. When he was discharged he took a small apartment in Encino, a block or so north of Ventura Boulevard, and rented a small office in a bank building nearby. He got a copy of the apartment directory and began cold calling owners trying to drum up a listing. He made his first commission quickly and bought a car. Soon thereafter he took a four-day trip to Las Vegas to visit his old friend Joe Zerga. During the entire time Corapi lived in Los Angeles he had maintained virtually no contact with Zerga, who had left the gaming control board around the same time he did. After leaving the board Zerga expanded his accounting practice, which he had kept on the side, but did not invite Corapi to join him. Zerga never had thought Corapi was the world's best accountant. He said that Corapi could never pass the CPA exam because he never did his homework.

One day not long after his trip to Las Vegas, Corapi was having lunch in the little coffee shop in the building where he worked when an absolutely drop-dead gorgeous young woman, maybe twenty-one or so, walked in. She came over and asked if he minded if she sat with him. He said later, "She was the emissary from hell." She said it was Friday— party night—and she really liked to get high. He said, "One thing led to another and I was back in it." He thinks he got some cocaine, went somewhere with the girl, and spent the night. Within a month, he was in desperate shape again.

He called his mother and she came out to try to help him. A few days later, when she was about to leave, he panicked. He told her he didn't have a friend in the world and he felt like an idiot. His mother was afraid he might attempt suicide and called the police. Corapi said later that he did want to die, but suicide was not something he had contemplated. The police tried to arrange an intervention with a social worker, but Corapi wouldn't let the social worker into his apartment. They then called a SWAT team to get him out. Alone in the apartment, he took out a gun and put it under a towel on the table. His idea was that when the police broke in, he would uncover the gun and they would kill him. Two cops came through the door, and one of them drew, fast. But he didn't shoot and Corapi didn't touch the gun. The police took Corapi to the hospital in handcuffs. He stayed in the hospital for a few days until the police decided he was okay and released him.

Within a few more days, he was on the street, homeless. He didn't know what to do and didn't care. He was just waiting to die. He survived by eating out of garbage cans and slept under the trees in a park in Encino. His mother was able to get in touch with a friend of his she had met, a Lebanese known as A.J. She sent a letter to A.J. for John and A.J. drove around looking for him. He finally found him in the park in Encino and delivered the letter. (Subsequently, A.J. blew his brains out after coming down hard from cocaine.) In the letter, his mother recommended that John pray. She enclosed a prayer card and every day after that he said a Hail Mary. A few weeks later he called his mother and asked her for a ticket to return home. She sent it to the post office box he had for his office and he went home to Hudson just before his thirty-seventh birthday.

Corapi felt like he was suffering from a combination of depression and acute anxiety. His old Robinson Street neighborhood was now very rundown and he found the view from the back porch profoundly depressing. He had lived in a house on the beach with big balconies, a boat in the water, and fancy cars in the garage, and now he was looking at ramshackle, old, dirty buildings. "I'm thirty-seven years old and I'm a loser," he thought. "I don't have anything; I'm destitute. I had to seek refuge with my poor mother. I'm a middle-aged man with nothing."

He remained in this general state of despondency for several weeks, saying his daily Hail Mary, but not seeing his life going anywhere. Then, very early in the morning of June 24, he was unable to sleep. At his wit's end, he sat up in bed and cried out to God, "If you are real—and I don't know if you are or not—then you've got to help me fast, because I'm pretty sure this is it. I'm at the end. I'm going to die pretty soon. This can't go on." He lay back down in bed. There were no visions, no voices. But a profound peace came over him. He couldn't move. There were no thoughts, just a pervasive, penetrating peace. Around six in the morning he came out of that state with a deep awareness that God loved him. He felt sorrow for his sins out of love for God. The theological term he eventually found for it was "perfect contrition." The experience crystallized for him in the phrase "God's name is Mercy." He also knew that he was called to be a priest.

He got up and got dressed and went out into the hallway where he met his mother. He said, "Mom, I want to go to confession," and his mother responded simply, "Okay." Without knowing why, he told her that he did not want to go to confession locally. She said that wasn't a problem, that she knew where to go. She took him to the Shrine of the North American Martyrs in Auriesville, New York. They drove up later that morning and walked to the Jesuit church, a very large, round log structure that holds 10,000 people. An old priest dressed in a cassock heard his confession. Corapi began: "Father, I have sinned, I haven't confessed in twenty years." He said later that despite his colorful past, the confession didn't take as long as you would think, because there are only Ten Commandments. The priest gave Corapi absolution and then looked at his watch. "Amazing!" he said. "It's exactly three o' clock in the afternoon, the hour when Jesus died. You can be forgiven of your sins." The priest said that he sensed something else, but that he didn't know what it was. Corapi said he knew. "I'm called to be a priest," he said, to which the old priest responded, without noticeable irony, "Well, you know, all things are possible with God."

Corapi and his mother went home to Hudson. The next day they went to mass; and they went every day after that. He read the Bible and prayed each day. Corapi followed this routine for more than a year. He had almost no contact with anyone other than his mother. He read from the big, white family Bible, beginning with chapter one, verse one of Genesis. He would read with a ruler, moving it down from line to line as he read, and he went through the entire Bible that way. He also rediscovered Archbishop Fulton Sheen, the charismatic bishop in the red cape and white skullcap whom Corapi saw on television as a child in the 1950s.

When Corapi finally began looking for a place to study formally for the priesthood, he found the experience somewhat unnerving. It seemed to him that there were strange things going on in the church. It was almost as if there were two churches, two religions. He was interested in the Franciscans, but the vocation director he visited spent most of his time telling him things like "We don't have to wear habits anymore, we can go to the movies." "Here I was, an ideological revert to the faith," Corapi said, "and he was almost apologizing for what they were. It really turned me off. And he's smoking a cigar while he's doing it." He had a succession of similar interviews. Many of the seminaries would not have taken him because of his age, but, he thought, "I wouldn't have taken them because they were so screwed up." Finally, he phoned a priest who had come to his attention through his reading and asked him where he would go if he had to choose a seminary. The priest suggested Holy Apostles Seminary in Cromwell, Connecticut.

Two years later, after spending some time in a monastery in Maine, Corapi was admitted to Holy Apostles Seminary where he studied for four years and earned a master's degree in scripture studies. In his first month there, he met Father Jim Flanagan, founder of a little-known Robstown, Texas–based order called the Society of Our Lady of the Most Holy Trinity. Father Flanagan's idea was to have priests, religious, and laypersons work together in the areas of greatest need. Flanagan met Corapi while he was recruiting for the society and asked him, "Would you like me to tell you your vocation?" When Corapi didn't object, he said, "You know, you're a preacher." Corapi was convinced that Flanagan was not guessing or simply telling him what he wanted to hear. Flanagan told Corapi specifically that he was called to follow Bishop Sheen and that he would get the same education that Sheen had in his day. Later, during Corapi's years in Cromwell, an Opus Dei priest named John McCluskey gave a presentation at the seminary. He talked about the University of Navarre, the Opus Dei institute in northeastern Spain. As he was talking Corapi had a powerful feeling that he would go to Navarre and indeed follow in Sheen's footsteps.

Joe Zerga, who kept up with Corapi's whereabouts by calling his mother, knew that he had attended a seminary and was studying for the priesthood. Although Zerga was born a Catholic, he actually never had been baptized in the church. He greeted the news that his friend was becoming a priest with a mixture of shock and amusement, remembering some of the very wild times they had had together in Las Vegas. He said years later that they "weren't exactly virgins in the whorehouse." He also said that as much as he respected Corapi, they differed on many issues such as gay marriage, with which, he said, he had no problem at all. While Corapi was in Spain for three years Zerga would from time to time "assess" his gambling clients a couple of hundred dollars to send off to his friend studying to be a priest.

It was only after Corapi arrived in Pamplona that he learned that Navarre did not accept American degrees, which meant that he had to take a set of examinations in Spanish to qualify for the program leading to a degree in sacred theology. After a summer of dawn-to-dusk language cramming he passed the exams and began to study philosophy and theology. It was the first time he ever thought he had a gift for anything. "I was good at it," he said, "right out of the gate." Aquinas and Augustine were his favorites. He completed his doctoral degree and was ordained in Rome by the pope. It was during the ordination ceremony in St. Peter's Basilica that his third experience with women and lilacs occurred. After the three-hour ceremony, in which Mother Teresa stood behind him as he waited to kneel before the pope, Corapi and the other new priests began to file out of the basilica. The families were standing on the left and the College of Cardinals was on the right. Just behind them, a dark, Semitic-looking woman, quite beautiful, smiled enigmatically, shook her head and said softly, "Johnny," as he passed her. There was an unmistakable smell of lilacs.

*   *   *

In the fall of 1993, now a full-fledged priest, diploma in hand, Corapi returned to the States to follow his calling. In the beginning he would accept offers to preach somewhere; the parish priest would give him a couple of hundred dollars from the collection plate and he would go home to his mother's house where he was living. Then fairly early on, he preached in northern California and the collection brought in about $18,000. "The pastor had never seen anything like that," Corapi said. "It was the feast of Corpus Christi. They had over five thousand people. It was a weekend, Friday night, all day Saturday, and part of Sunday. He was an old monsignor, a good man. I saw it register on his face. He was like many a parish pastor, interested in the collection. He asked, 'How much, how much.' You could see the calculations racing through his mind instantly. He was trying to figure out how to divide it up now. You know, the deal changed." At a couple of other appearances they forgot to pass around the collection plate. After that Corapi, who was trained as an accountant, after all, decided to charge a fee for his service. He began with $2,500 and then moved up to $3,500, which remained his fee for years. He figured that when he spoke the collection always brought in $8,000–$10,000, so the church came out ahead.

As the speaking invitations increased, and he began taping his sermons, Corapi hired a couple named Kurt and Sandra Schirmer to manage his business affairs. The problem, he said, was that eventually they were taking 90 percent and he was getting 10 percent. At one point Zerga warned Corapi that the Schirmers had control of all of his business operations, the inventory, the sales, the cash, and the deposits. Corapi told Zerga that they did not get any cash sales, that they were all credit card sales. But Zerga told him that he knew statistically that 25 to 30 percent of sales were always in cash at that level. The Schirmers contended that because they were instrumental in videotaping Corapi's major work on the catechism of the Catholic Church they were the producers and therefore entitled to a piece of the action.

Corapi eventually decided he could buy a tape recorder and a couple of high-speed duplicators and do it himself. He would take the tapes home, copy them, and send out orders. In 2003, he set up his own little company. With the proceeds, he said, "I support the Society of Our Lady and other works in the church. I have a secular corporation. I'm in charge of it. I make the decisions. They look at the fruits; there's a passage in the Bible, 'By their fruits ye shall know them.' I get nothing for the shows that I do. EWTN [Eternal Word Television Network] pays nothing. The deal I have with them is that I give them programming and I get a tag at the end of my show where people can get my material or contact me. It's a million-dollar deal, at least. The website [Corapi set up to sell his DVDs and tapes] has been bringing in over $100,000 a month. It will be $2 million a year in sales very quickly. Someone will figure that out sooner or later, and decide that they want some of it. But they won't get it."

Corapi's spiritual message, not unlike his personal fiscal policy, was unapologetically conservative, which put him out of step with the hierarchy of the American Catholic Church and, he believed, unless he was careful, could threaten his livelihood. "Things are strange in the Catholic Church," he said. The same disasters that resulted in the [sex] scandals have resulted in other disasters, doctrinal disasters. There's a permissiveness that was allowed to run amok for a long time. You don't know who your friends are or who your enemies are." Corapi said that a long time ago he decided not to let himself get backed into a corner where the church could manipulate him with threats like denying him a pension or a home or an assignment.

He worried that it would be a real test of faith for him if the church asked him to go live in a monastery and give up his worldly goods. "Hopefully, I would do it," he said years later, with an inflection in his voice suggesting that he might not. When pressed, however, he conceded that he had superiors like everyone else and if they said, "You're finished," he'd be finished. But when really pushed about what he would do if ordered to turn over his assets, he said he had concluded that because of his status—somewhere between a member of a religious order and a parish priest—canon law was ambiguous on this question.

Before leaving the diocese of Sacramento, Corapi completed what to date is his magnum opus, a series of fifty one-hour lectures explicating the entire catechism of the Roman Catholic Church. With this project done, it was time to move on. He headed north and settled in Lake California, a new gated subdivision not far from Cottonwood, just south of Anderson on the border of Shasta and Tehama counties. He bought a modest white brick and gray frame house with a deck backing onto the lake and a dock for his little boat, which he used to fish for bass and blue gill. He also rented a small house in town for Tamra, his office manager, who helped run his business, arrange his travel, and generally look after anything that needed looking after. It was the perfect place. For one thing, it was only a fifteen-minute drive to the airport. It was also far enough away from Redding, and sufficiently isolated and protected, so that he could remain invisible, which he wanted to do partly because of his desire to avoid the nut cases he seemed to attract, but also because it was his nature.

Despite his profession, and the obvious ease he felt in front of a congregation of thousands, he was a private man and uncomfortable with people he didn't know, even devoted fans and followers. There was something incongruous about this uneasiness with people given Corapi's psychological and physical presence. Although he was only five feet seven inches tall, he cast a longer shadow. He was thickly built and carried himself with a fighter's confidence, wariness, and spring-loaded tension. He was olive skinned with an oval-shaped face, a slightly pronounced nose, and very dark eyes, and he wore a three-day growth of beard not unlike Steven Spielberg's. But what was most striking about him was his voice, which Cecil B. DeMille might easily have cast as the voice of God.

Corapi did not seek out friends among the other residents of Lake California, a number of whom were doctors who practiced in Redding. He did, however, strike up a friendship with his next-door neighbors, Linda and Nick Costanzo, an older Italian-American couple. Nick's family was from a small town in the arid interior of Sicily and Linda's was from a village near Rome. Linda even worked for Corapi for a while taking phone orders. Corapi liked Linda Costanzo's Italian cooking and he would have meals with the Costanzos often. For the next two years he lived quietly on the lake, traveled the country and even occasionally abroad speaking to large groups of Catholics often numbering in the thousands, and he looked after his business. He went hunting and fishing when he had time. He rarely went to Redding. Most of what he needed from there Tamra brought him. He was content and he was aware that given his tumultuous past he had a great deal to be thankful for.

6

An Error in Judgment

On May 16, 2002, a celebratory dinner was held at the Riverview Country Club to honor Redding Medical Center's heart team for performing 104 cardiac surgeries the previous month. This was a record for the hospital and would have been an impressive pace for a much larger academic medical center. A big crowd turned out to pay tribute to Drs. Moon and Realyvasquez and their colleagues. The team's April performance was referred to glowingly in the invitation as an "awesome endeavor," and appeared to be just another example of the big-league stature of RMC's California Heart Institute. And the blowout at the club was typical of the pride the hospital took in its heavily advertised heart program.

No one can say for sure how many of those 104 patients chose Redding Medical Center because of its ubiquitous advertising. But neither can anyone argue that RMC's ongoing campaign on radio, television, in the newspapers, at hospital-sponsored health fairs, and by direct mail was anything less than robust and effective. One especially powerful direct-mail piece prepared at Tenet's administrative headquarters in Dallas provided some sense of the impact the hospital and its owner were after. The mailer, promoting $39 cardiac screening exams, said on its front cover: "EVERY MINUTE a husband, father, or son dies of cardiovascular disease in this country." On the reverse side, against a background of gray granite, large engraved capital letters asked: "Where is it written in stone that guys over 40 should consider a cardiac screening?" Inside, the answer to this ominous question was framed in a dramatic photograph of a cemetery. The large tombstone dominating the foreground was engraved with this simple epitaph: "Beloved Husband, Father, Son John Doe, 1955–2002." Subtle it was not.

Soon after the self-congratulatory dinner at Riverview, Nick Costanzo noticed that his neighbor John Corapi seemed unusually tired. He recommended that Corapi see the Costanzo's family physician, Daniel Alcala, who was chief of staff at Redding Medical Center, for a routine checkup. Corapi agreed to do so. The priest had paid little attention to the RMC ads, even though there was one at the airport featuring a picture of Moon. Corapi had just turned fifty-five and his father had suffered from heart disease. He went to see Alcala, who examined him and found nothing wrong. But because of his symptoms, exhaustion, and shortness of breath, Alcala recommended that Corapi see Moon.

Nick Costanzo, who had a stent in one of his coronary arteries that had been inserted by Moon, advised Corapi that Moon's bedside manner left much to be desired, but that he was a first-rate physician. Corapi, a bit nervous about seeing a cardiologist, discussed his plans with Joe Zerga, who also had a stent in one of his coronary arteries that had been placed several years earlier after a routine cardiac checkup. Zerga encouraged his old friend to have his heart looked at because of his age and family history. And Zerga's girlfriend, Christine Mody, a cardiac critical care nurse, sought to put Corapi's mind at ease by telling him that in case he didn't like the doctor to whom he had been referred he could always find another cardiologist. None of them knew that Corapi was under considerable stress, which could have contributed to or even caused his symptoms. Right around that time the Schirmers had filed a civil lawsuit against him seeking a share of the proceeds of his business. Moreover, Corapi was extremely upset by the sex scandals then sweeping the Catholic Church.

In any event, Corapi did go to see Moon in his office at 1555 East Street across a parking lot from the entrance to Redding Medical Center. Moon administered a standard exercise stress test in which Corapi's heart rate was measured while he walked on a treadmill at an increasing pace for about twenty minutes. Moon reviewed the results right away and told Corapi in his typically blunt fashion that they were normal, but that it was a useless forty-year-old test, which made Corapi wonder why he had to take it and pay for it. The possibility that it might be just to bill for an extra test never occurred to him. He asked no questions and agreed to go to the Women's Imaging Center on Court Street in Redding to have a heart scan, also known as a calcium-scoring test. A heart scan measures the calcium content of the coronary arteries and is viewed by many cardiologists as an index of the likelihood of future coronary artery disease. Corapi took the test and went home somewhat apprehensively to wait for the results. On June 3, he received a call from Moon's office telling him that his test score was 75, which was somewhat elevated, and that Dr. Moon wanted him to have an angiogram, for which, although Corapi didn't know it, a bill at Redding Medical Center might run as high as $30,000. Corapi was surprised and upset, but he said, "If that's what the doctor thinks I should do, that's what I'll do." The procedure was scheduled for June 11 at 6:30 a.m.

Corapi's office manager, Tamra, picked him up at his house around six in the morning on Tuesday, June 11, and drove him to Redding Medical Center. The morning air was still cool, but the day promised to be hot, probably over a hundred degrees. Weather was the last thing on their minds, though. Neither knew what to expect from the angiogram and they were worried. Tamra and Corapi stopped at the front desk and were directed to the admitting office to fill out forms, including a release accepting the risks of the procedure. Then they were taken to a plain white room where Corapi put on a hospital gown and was hooked up to an IV drip. They waited there for three hours until Tamra, who has a short fuse, especially when it comes to Corapi's welfare, was past being irritated.

When Tamra heard loud voices outside talking about shopping at Kmart she headed for the nursing station bristling and demanded to know why they were keeping Corapi so long without telling him anything. She said he was nervous and cold. A nurse said they would bring him a warm blanket, which only made Tamra angrier. She asked the nurse why they had him come to the hospital at 6:15 in the morning if he was not going to be taken to the cath lab until 11:00. The answer seemed arrogant to Tamra. "Because Dr. Moon likes to stack his patients," the nurse said. She said that when there were cancellations Dr. Moon wanted to have patients available to fill the openings in the cath lab. Had Michael Stewart, a cardiologist from Red Bluff, been there, he would have told Tamra that doctors as well as patients often had to wait for the RMC cath lab because Moon regularly bumped other doctors, usually by insisting that his cases were emergencies. For Moon it sometimes seemed the words emergency and ordinary were synonyms. He once bragged to John McDermott, a cardiac surgeon at Mercy Hospital, that 90 percent of the cardiac surgery at RMC was done on an emergency basis.

Finally, around 11 a.m., Corapi was taken to another room, prepped, wheeled up to the catheterization laboratory on a gurney, and placed on a table under a battery of X-ray machines and monitors. Moon did not keep him waiting. He came in immediately, gave him a shot of Xylocaine, and began the procedure. While injecting the fast-acting anesthetic Moon asked Corapi, "What do you do?" Corapi, who had not identified himself as a Roman Catholic priest, said, "I lecture." Moon asked, "What do you lecture on?" Corapi replied, "I lecture on ethics." Moon and the two technicians who were assisting him burst out laughing. One of the technicians said, "Well, Tenet ought to know all about that." At the time Corapi had his own worries and it wasn't until much later that he began to wonder what the laughter had been all about.

After giving the anesthetic a few minutes to take effect Moon made a quick incision in Corapi's groin, introduced a catheter into his femoral artery and threaded it up into his coronary circulation. When the tip of the catheter was in place he injected a bolus of contrast dye and took X-ray moving pictures. Corapi saw the dye flow in on an overhead monitor. He noticed that there was another monitor as well. Moon had introduced a second catheter and was also doing an intravascular ultrasound test, known in the trade as IVUS, something few cardiologists used at that stage of diagnosis. Moon, however, said it gave him valuable information and he used it frequently. The previous year he had done 266 IVUS procedures, which involved threading a tiny ultrasound transmitter into the coronary circulation to generate an image of the full 360-degree circumference of the arterial wall. IVUS is riskier and costlier than angiography and is used by most other cardiologists only to confirm the precise location of a lesion, typically in the left main coronary artery, that has already been determined by angiography to require interventional or surgical treatment. The screen on which the angiogram was visible was in front of Corapi and the intravascular ultrasound screen was to his right. Corapi was tense, but felt only a bit of discomfort and no real pain.

From his prone position, Corapi saw Moon point to the ultrasound screen and heard him say to the technicians, "You see this? This is not good." Then, surprisingly quickly, the procedure was over. Almost immediately after withdrawing the catheter, while slipping out of his gown, Moon leaned over Corapi, and said, "I'm sorry; there is nothing I can do for you. You need a triple bypass tomorrow morning." And then he was gone, leaving Corapi in a state of semi-shock. Corapi asked one of the technicians, "What does that mean?" The technician said, "It means that you need bypass surgery tomorrow morning." Corapi was totally unprepared for the possibility of emergency surgery and no one had explained to him why he needed it. No one had told him anything about the location of the blockages in his arteries or the extent to which they limited blood flow. Was it more than 70 percent, which is usually the case when surgery is indicated, or less? He did not know whether they were in major vessels such as the left main and left anterior descending coronary arteries, which feed the left ventricle, the main pumping chamber of the heart, or in the right coronary artery, the main conduit to the right side of the heart. And they had not told him whether the ability of his heart to pump blood to the rest of his body had been compromised, an important indicator for coronary artery surgery.

Corapi was now both frightened and confused. He had been thinking ahead to an important address he was scheduled to deliver at a conference in Norfolk, Virginia, the following week. Even though he had just been told he needed triple-bypass surgery the following morning, he reflexively asked a technician whether he thought it might be possible to postpone the operation. The technician said the only way would be to check himself out against doctor's orders.

Meanwhile, Tamra was still sitting nervously in the room where Corapi had waited before his angiogram. Her cell phone was ringing almost nonstop because EWTN, the Catholic television network, was reporting incorrectly that Corapi had had a heart attack. Between calls Moon appeared at the door and said sharply, "John Corapi." Tamra looked up, expecting him to come in and sit down and talk to her, as she had seen other doctors do while she was waiting, but he didn't. Instead, he brusquely motioned to her with his finger to come into the hall. She guessed from his peremptory behavior that something was seriously wrong. As soon as she was close enough, Moon thrust a handful of pictures at her chest and said, "Triple bypass." She tried to catch hold of the pictures, but they fell to the floor and she bent to pick them up. By the time she was upright again Moon was twenty feet down the hall. A gray-haired candy striper who had seen what happened told Tamra that Corapi would be wheeled past the room they were in and that she would be able to go with him.

Five minutes later a male nurse appeared, pushing Corapi on a gurney and Tamra joined them. While walking to the elevator, she pointedly asked the nurse, "How many of these do you do a day and is anybody monitoring this?" Corapi, thinking about his upcoming surgery and not wanting to antagonize any hospital caregiver, found the question unnecessarily accusatory. He said, "Tamra!" in a tone meant to end the interrogation. But the nurse replied, "Yes, we have a monitoring system, all hospitals do."

On the way to the recovery room, Tamra asked some additional but more benign questions, including when the surgery would be and the nurse told her it would be either the following day or the day after that. Corapi then said to Tamra, "I need you to do some things for me. You need to take care of my will, get a signature card from the bank, and call the people in Norfolk." Tamra left to take care of these chores and another nurse came into the room and began to tell him some of the routine he would need to know before the operation. Even though he had been told he needed immediate surgery and that there was no chance that Moon would let him go, he asked her whether Moon might let him travel to the conference in Norfolk, which was very important. She agreed to find Moon and ask him. She left the room, returned in about five minutes, and, to Corapi's great surprise, she told him that Moon had said it would be okay for him to go. She said they would admit him to the hospital at two o'clock the following Monday, June 17. Corapi immediately called Tamra, who had been gone less than fifteen minutes. He reached her at the Bank of America branch on Hilltop Drive and told her to come back to the hospital because he was going home and they would be going to Norfolk after all.

When she got back, Tamra, who was worried that Corapi unwisely might have talked his way out of the hospital, asked the nurse, "Are you going to take responsibility for us? You realize he is going to be flying all the way to Norfolk and back. He's going to be speaking Friday night and all day Saturday. It's a very hectic schedule." The nurse said definitively, "The doctor says it's okay."

By the time Corapi was able to leave the hospital it was three in the afternoon. Tamra drove him home to Lake California and he went to bed immediately. He felt sick and worried to the point of depression. Then the phone rang. It was Joe Zerga. Tamra took the call and spoke to him out of Corapi's hearing. She told him Corapi needed triple-bypass surgery and that she thought Corapi might have talked his way out of the hospital. Even though both Corapi and the nurse had told her that Moon was allowing him to go, she still believed that Corapi, whose trade is persuasion, had convinced them to let him go against their better judgment. But she was wrong about this. Corapi, like most anyone facing major surgery, was afraid, confused, and in no condition to challenge a doctor's orders. Zerga suggested to Tamra that Corapi might want to have his surgery in Las Vegas. He said that Christine, his partner, knew all the doctors and could arrange things. Zerga also told Tamra that he would speak to Corapi about it and that they could stay at his house until he had recuperated sufficiently and was ready to return to California. Tamra then went home to Redding.

The next morning, Zerga woke his girlfriend from a sound sleep around six in the morning and said, "Can you talk to Father?" Mody had done a twelve-hour shift in the ICU the day before, but she woke quickly, which comes naturally in her profession, and said, "Sure." Zerga said, "Try to talk him into coming to Las Vegas to have his surgery." Zerga then called Corapi and they spoke briefly. He told Corapi that given Mody's contacts he should come to Las Vegas for his operation. But Corapi told him that Redding Medical Center had a great cardiac program and that they advertised themselves as one of the ten best in the country. Zerga, who is suspicious both by training and inclination, found it curious that a relatively small hospital in a small city in rural northern California would have such a highly ranked heart program, but the thought passed as quickly as it had come. He told Corapi that Mody could get the very best cardiologist and surgeon in Las Vegas to do his work-up and surgery and that they would look after him during his recovery. Then he put Mody on the phone.

Mody thought it would be difficult to convince Corapi to come. She said, "Why don't you come to Las Vegas, Father John? I'll get the best doctors and nurses for you, you'll come and stay with us and we'll take care of you at home." She was surprised but pleased when Corapi put up no resistance at all. He told Mody, a strongly believing Maronite Catholic of Lebanese extraction, that he had had a dream the previous night in which Mody's grandmother told him that he would be all right, and he agreed to come to Las Vegas as soon as possible. Mody told him, "Get on a plane with your toothbrush and your film, you don't need anything else."

As soon as he got off the phone Corapi called Tamra to ask her to get plane tickets to Las Vegas because he had decided to have his surgery there. He told her that she would have to go to the hospital to get his records so that he could bring them with him. He also had Tamra cancel the trip to Norfolk. The subject of the Norfolk conference, which was for naval officers and Pentagon officials, was the post-9/11 world. Tamra called and suggested to the sponsors of the conference that they show Corapi's videotape "New World, Old World," a spiritual interpretation of the events of 9/11 in which Corapi used analogies from combat and military training to talk about spiritual warfare. She also asked that the military officers and others who attended pray for Corapi's recovery. Between June 11 and June 14, Tamra canceled about six months' worth of events. Among other things, this would mean that the sponsors would lose deposits on the reservation of convention centers. Also, because EWTN got the story wrong, reporting that Corapi had suffered a heart attack rather than that he was going to have triple-bypass surgery, they received dozens more telephone calls asking whether he was okay. Tamra was swamped for a couple of weeks handling this fallout.

That afternoon the hospital faxed a release form for his records to Corapi, which he signed, and faxed back, and the next morning at eight o'clock, Tamra was at the hospital to get the records. When she told the two women at the front desk that she had come to pick up Corapi's medical records, both women looked distressed. One of them made a brief phone call and then she conferred with the other. Finally she said to Tamra, "There's no one to escort you down there." Tamra, impatient by then, responded, "Well, I think if you give me directions, I'd probably find my way." The woman said she supposed that would be all right, and told Tamra where to go. Tamra found her way without difficulty to a door that said "Records." A woman told Tamra that the records were not ready. Tamra said she had been told to come at eight o'clock. The woman offered to give her the written report, but not the angiographic and IVUS images. When Tamra persisted, she said, "If you wait here, someone will come down."

A few minutes later a nurse named Tamara Caudle came into the room. She took Tamra to another room and told her that the copies of the images were not ready yet. Caudle asked Tamra if she could return later to pick them up, but Tamra said she had a flight to catch in the afternoon and would wait for Caudle to make copies. It took about forty-five minutes, but then Caudle returned with a VHS videotape and a CD-ROM. The angiogram was on the disk and the intravascular ultrasound was on the videotape. Caudle continued to hold on to the materials. She said to Tamra, "You know, my stepfather had the same thing. If this were my father, or my stepfather, I would have him admit himself today and have this procedure." Tamra noticed that Caudle's hands were shaking. She thought it might have been because she was being harsh with her and had upset her. Caudle finally handed over the records to Tamra.

As they walked out, Caudle tried again to convince Tamra to have her "father" admitted for the surgery. Tamra asked Caudle why she felt that way if Moon had given his approval for Corapi to travel to Norfolk. She said, "I don't know, but if it were my father, I would have him come here for the surgery." Caudle asked Tamra where Corapi was going for a second opinion. Tamra told her that he was not going for a second opinion; he was going to have the operation. He was going to Nevada because he had a friend there who was a cardiac nurse. Tamra also told Caudle that she really didn't like Moon's bedside manner. Caudle responded, "Well, he comes off that way, but he is a really good doctor." Tamra then left the hospital with the records and went home. A few hours later she and Corapi flew to Las Vegas.

When Joe Zerga picked up Corapi and Tamra at the airport that evening he thought Corapi seemed unusually subdued. Zerga also noticed that his friend looked older and that his body language suggested that he was carrying an enormous weight on his shoulders. But when they arrived at Zerga's art-filled house at 1222 Weatherwood Court just fifteen minutes from the Strip, Mody, a tall, slim, slightly lugubrious-looking woman with a warm smile that changes her face completely, thought Corapi looked completely normal. He was hungry and Mody went to the kitchen and made sandwiches for him and for Tamra. She had called Richard Shehane, a cardiologist, and Nancy Donahoe, a cardiac surgeon, to arrange for Corapi's records to be reviewed and to schedule his surgery. She asked Corapi if she could look at his report. She said she was afraid to put the CD in her computer because she might damage it, but Tamra handed her the report and she began to read it.

A minute or two later she came across Moon's previously unmentioned diagnosis of spontaneously dissecting arteries, which shocked her. "Spontaneously dissecting arteries!" she said. "This is an emergency! I've never seen a spontaneously dissecting artery." She said she couldn't believe that they had let him on a plane with that diagnosis. When arterial dissections do occur they are almost always fatal. In anyone other than a young woman, however, they are almost never spontaneous and almost always are caused when a catheter breaks through the plaque and the inner lining of the artery as a result of the way the physician has manipulated it. This results in blood entering the space between the inner and outer walls of the artery and slicing through the tissue in a spiral pattern.

But then, aware that Corapi was already frightened, she belatedly tried to soften her alarmed reaction. She added, "What do I know, I'm only a nurse." At the same time, she was thinking that it didn't make any sense. Corapi looked good, he didn't appear to be in any acute distress, and when she asked him how he was feeling he had no complaints. She specifically observed that he had good color and his breathing was not shallow. He seemed fine. They looked at the still shot of Corapi's arteries that he had brought with him and they looked pretty good to her, too. She said she didn't see any occlusions. But again, she said to herself, "I'm not a doctor. I'm missing something here." Finally, she went out of the room and called Shehane again. She read him Moon's diagnosis and asked him whether he thought Corapi should be taken to the hospital immediately and possibly put on an intra-aortic balloon pump. Shehane asked her how he looked. She said, "Fine," and he said, "Stay calm and bring him to the office in the morning." When she hung up Mody took Tamra aside and told her not to be surprised if the surgeon wanted to send Corapi directly to the operating room.

The next morning they got up while it was still dark and had a breakfast of bagels and coffee. Their first stop, before going to Shehane's office, was St. Thomas More Roman Catholic Church where Mody had arranged for Corapi to go to confession. Corapi jumped out of the car and explained the situation to the waiting priest, Father Michael Keliher, who immediately led him inside the church, heard his confession, and gave him the anointing of the sick, which used to be called extreme unction, and prepares the seriously ill for death. Mody then drove Corapi in light traffic to Shehane's office on Maryland Parkway near Sunrise Hospital.

Shehane, whose olive complexion and droopy mustache make him look vaguely Mexican, laid a hand on Corapi's shoulder and asked him how he was feeling. Corapi said he was nervous, but otherwise okay. He answered Shehane's questions about why he had gone to Moon and told him about his family history of heart disease. Shehane then took the disc and tape into another room and shut the door. Mody found this behavior a little odd, but then she remembered that she had tipped off Shehane about the spontaneous dissections. When he returned ten minutes later, he said that both the angiogram and the intravascular ultrasound looked completely normal. Mody was stunned and asked, "Do we have the right film? Is his name on there?" It was. Shehane then did a basic physical examination of Corapi and scheduled a series of cardiac diagnostic tests for the next day.

Shehane had been using intravascular ultrasound for years. He explained later that the flap from a coronary dissection was very easy to see and that he didn't see one dissection, let alone the three indicated in Moon's report. He said he only used IVUS to evaluate lesions that were of questionable significance. In the past the technique had been used frequently for stent deployment, he added, but now cardiologists don't need it unless the stent is not fully deployed or there is in-stent restenosis, a buildup of smooth muscle cells that curtails blood flow. Shehane had never heard of anyone using IVUS the way Moon used it. He also said that spontaneous dissections were not only extremely rare, but usually fatal and that "You can't transfer someone with spontaneous coronary dissections from Redding to Las Vegas." Shehane called Nancy Donahoe and told her that she could take Corapi off the surgical schedule, but that he would still like her to review the records and pictures. He told Corapi that if those were his images he was normal and that "he didn't even need a cath to begin with because he didn't have any symptoms." A calcium score of 75 was normal for a man his age.

Mody then drove Corapi to Valley Hospital to see Donahoe, who is tall and slim and exudes the bright-eyed alertness and self-assurance common to surgeons. Donahoe and Mody were good friends. Mody not only had worked with Donahoe as a nurse, but she also had sold her a house in her other life as a real estate agent. When Mody had told Donahoe that a good friend of Zerga's needed a bypass operation and that he had decided to have the surgery in Las Vegas because Mody could handpick the physicians and nurses, Donahoe said that she was

honored and flattered. She had rearranged her schedule to accommodate a meeting with Corapi the next afternoon and surgery the following morning.

They were waiting for her when Zerga called to find out what was
happening and Mody said, "Are you ready for this? Father has normal
coronary arteries. He has no coronary occlusions." Zerga couldn't
believe it. Mody then paged Donahoe and she met them in a hallway and
took them to a room near the cath lab where they could view the
angiogram together. They only looked at the angiographic film because
Donahoe, like most surgeons, did not read IVUS. Donahoe also told
Mody, Corapi, and Tamra that in the ten years she had been doing cardiac surgery she had never seen anyone with spiral dissections in both
the left and right coronary systems. She slipped the disc into a computer
and when the moving images appeared on the screen she stopped them
every few seconds to get a good look. Donahoe pointed to an area of the
screen—Corapi thought it was the upper left—and said, "This artery
has a 20 percent narrowing, but it is not necessary to treat it." She asked
Corapi, "Do you see anything, do you see any narrowing in these arteries, do you see any point where there's a constriction?" He didn't. Donahoe then told Corapi that he did not need bypass surgery. She said, "I
would not operate on you if you were my relative."

Corapi remembers Donahoe saying that his arteries were as big and
wide open as garden hoses. "If there's nothing wrong," he asked, "why
do I need a triple bypass?" "You don't!" Donahoe said. Corapi then
asked her whether medical science is so imprecise that based on the same
diagnostic information you could get diametrically opposed conclusions? "No way! It's not possible," Mody said, "Thank God, we were
here. We could have been away. You could have gone ahead and had
that surgery."

Later, when they were walking down the hall together, perhaps sens-
ing that Corapi was still worried, Donahoe said to him, "Listen, don't
worry, there's nothing wrong with you." But as much as he wanted to,
he did not totally believe her. Both Tamra and Mody also kept telling
Corapi to stop worrying. But Corapi wasn't ready to concede that easily. By that time the others had begun to conclude that a fraud might
have been committed, but Corapi, whose groin still hurt from the
angiogram and who had been under great stress, was not so sure. He
thought it was almost too good to be true. When he returned to the

house that afternoon after having blood drawn for the tests Shehane had ordered, he seemed to Zerga to be very much in turmoil. After all, if the Redding physicians were right and he did nothing about it he was going to die. On the other hand, if he went back there and had the surgery, he might have his chest cracked open for nothing.

Unlike Corapi, Zerga, a bull-chested man with spiky iron-gray hair and a thick, neatly trimmed black mustache, had a personality and temperament consistent with his appearance. He was both incisive and decisive. And when he wanted something he was not easily deterred, either professionally or when pursuing his other interests, such as history and art. On this occasion, seeing Corapi's anxiety, Zerga did what came naturally to him; he took charge. He asked Corapi to give him a detailed chronology of what had happened when he went for his angiogram in Redding, which the priest did. With this account in hand Zerga drew on his experience as an accountant with ample courtroom experience, as a gaming board investigator, and as someone who had had his own bout with coronary disease. He found the fact that Moon had allowed Corapi to leave the hospital inconsistent with the dire diagnosis. He asked Mody how many times in her twenty-five years as a nurse she had seen spontaneously dissecting coronary arteries. She said "Never." Zerga, who had studied statistics and understood the laws of probability, said he "knew when he came to Las Vegas that there were only six ways to roll a seven." Moreover, he thought about an evening six or seven years earlier when he was having dinner at Nancy Donahoe's house. In the course of conversation, Vincent Siragusa, a cardiologist who was there, suggested that he have an exercise treadmill test. Zerga said he was in good shape and didn't think it was necessary, but Siragusa convinced him. He took the test and it indicated that he might have a problem. Siragusa told him that the next step would be a thallium stress test, to rule out a false positive on the exercise stress test. As it turned out, Zerga's thallium stress test was positive, so he had an angiogram, which showed a 95 percent blockage in his left anterior descending coronary artery. He was treated with angioplasty and a stent. His course of care, which he remembered in detail and applied to the case at hand, made him wonder why Corapi had not been asked to take a thallium stress test.

That night, Corapi, still uncertain and apprehensive, wanted to go out for dinner. He suggested that they go to Prime at the Bellagio, Las Vegas's premier steakhouse, where they had celebrated Zerga's sixtieth birthday. They got a good table because the maître d' was a friend of Mody. To begin Corapi ordered a seafood platter for the table that cost about $100. Mody, who smiles easily and speaks softly, was somewhat taken aback at the price and she began teasing Corapi. She said, "I could be feeding you Jell-O now." She also made a buzzing sound imitating the saw used to split the sternum for bypass surgery and asked Corapi, "Tell me what this is?" Corapi laughed resoundingly. She then said, "You were so lucky, this was God's work. He put us here for a reason," meaning herself and Zerga. Mody also urged Corapi to call his mother and he said he would.

John, Joe, Christine, and Tamra happily washed down their oysters, clams, mussels, and shrimp with white wine. Corapi then dug into a large steak flamed in bourbon as they marveled over what had happened in the past seventy-two short hours. It was finally beginning to crystallize for all of them, even Corapi, that they might not be dealing with an accident or an aberration. As they talked it through over dessert and coffee on the restaurant's patio, they began to ask questions. How could there be a major cardiac center in Redding, California? How is that demographically possible? The word fraud might even have been used. Before they got up to leave, Zerga said decisively, "John, we are flying back up to Redding. I want a meeting with Hal Chilton," the hospital's CEO. Corapi was emotionally and physically worn out and was in no mood to pursue the matter, but it was fast becoming Zerga's show. Corapi picked up the check and they drove back to Zerga's house for the night.

The next morning Mody took Corapi back to Shehane's office for a nuclear stress test, which measures blood flow at rest and during exercise, and for a carotid ultrasound to determine whether there were blockages in the carotid arteries, which carry blood to, among other sites, the brain. These tests and the blood tests, including a lipid panel, all turned out to be negative.

Zerga, who had seen more than a pot full of corruption in his professional life in Las Vegas, did not need to hear anything more. He was convinced he knew what was going on. Tenet Healthcare, the company that owned the hospital, was bottom-line driven like most corporations and the message was delivered from corporate to the hospitals. People like Moon and Chilton who generated very high and escalating revenues became golden boys. "These guys did it for money," Zerga said. "These people prostituted their profession in order to make money. And they did it by cracking people's chests open." Corapi was still not totally convinced, but he didn't want to hear about it; he just wanted to get away from it all. He and Tamra stayed on in Las Vegas for a couple more days, just relaxing around the house. They didn't even answer their cell phones. Mody answered their other calls, but there were few of them because almost nobody knew where they were. The much-needed rest was good for Corapi, who after returning to Redding relented to pressure from Zerga to try to arrange a meeting with Chilton.

Zerga planned the strategy. He instructed Corapi to call the hospital and set up an appointment, but not to tell them that he, Zerga, would be coming to Redding for the meeting. Tamra called Chilton whose secretary said that he would not meet with Corapi and that whatever had happened was between Corapi and the physicians. He said the hospital only provided a place for them to operate and had no responsibility for their diagnoses. Corapi told this to Zerga who asked Mody, "If something like this had happened at Sunrise Hospital would the hospital have been interested?" She answered, "Absolutely!" Zerga then advised Corapi to call Redding Medical Center again and leave a message: He, Corapi, would be in the lobby of the hospital at two o'clock the following afternoon and he hoped that they would accord him the courtesy of a meeting. Zerga then flew to Redding.

Meanwhile, Corapi also began looking on the Internet for information about Redding Medical Center and Tenet. One link led to another and he soon found himself looking at Medicare statistics, mortality rates, and so on. While going through the data on RMC he remembered the big sign with Moon's picture on it at the Redding Airport promoting the hospital's heart program. By the time he finished his Web search Corapi believed that it was "logically, statistically, and demographically impossible that Redding Medical Center could be doing this many cardiac procedures." He compared the mortality rates at Redding Medical Center with those at a couple of dozen other hospitals. The rates at RMC were lower than at the other hospitals, from which he reasoned that a likely explanation might be that they were operating on healthy people. And the fact that RMC was the most profitable of all of Tenet's 115 hospitals aroused even more suspicion. Corapi and Zerga had already decided that Corapi's case could not be an aberration because it was so cut-and-dried. Since it was not a borderline case they were convinced that it had to be part of a criminal pattern of behavior. Corapi's Internet research seemed to support this thesis.

The next day, Thursday, June 27, Corapi and Zerga went to the hospital and Tamara Caudle met them in the front lobby. Zerga said that she glanced at him and did a bit of a double take, but didn't say anything. She took them to a small conference room and Chilton was already there. Jan Chicoine, the director of Outcomes Management and Health Information, was also there and took notes. Chilton sat at the head of the table, Caudle and Zerga were facing each other across the table and Corapi sat to Zerga's right. Chilton began the meeting by asking, "Why are we here?" Zerga told him they were there because of serious concerns over Moon's diagnosis of Corapi. Chilton referred to Corapi as Mr. Corapi, apparently unaware that he was a Roman Catholic priest. Zerga passed to Chilton some material on Corapi that he had downloaded from the Internet. Chilton looked at it and seemed a bit baffled. Zerga noticed that Chilton was sweating.

Caudle then very confidently told Corapi, "I've spoken to two other cardiologists. They concur with Dr. Moon, and you're going to die. You have to have this surgery right away." Caudle was holding a black-and-white picture in her hand. Zerga asked her whether she was a cardiologist. When she said, "No," he asked, "Then what are you?" She said, "I'm a nurse." He asked her to show him where the arteries were dissecting. She held up the black-and-white picture and made circular motions in front of it with her hand. "Right here," she said. She then placed the picture facedown on the conference table and said, "Of course, they can heal, you know."

Zerga, astonished by this performance, asked her, "Do you do bypass surgery prophylactically at Redding Medical Center?" Chilton by then was looking very uncomfortable. But Caudle pressed ahead trying to convince Corapi, using the same example she had used with Tamra, to have the surgery as soon as possible. She said, "If you were my father I would urge you to have it this afternoon. Let us do it this afternoon." When Corapi asked whether anyone other than Moon had reviewed the angiogram and IVUS, Caudle said, "Yes, two other cardiologists reviewed it." Corapi and Zerga asked her to give them the names of these cardiologists, but she refused to do so. Corapi asked if the two cardiologists had put their findings in writing, but he never got an answer to his question. Chilton offered to have Moon come in to explain things to them, but, Zerga said, "Why would we want to talk to Moon? Why would we care what he has to say at this point? He is only going to defend what he already said." By this time, Zerga was completely convinced that they were dealing with possible criminal fraud, at least on the part of Moon and Realyvasquez. But Corapi was still frightened and wavering. Caudle had just told him again that he was going to die.

Chilton and Caudle tried to impress upon Zerga and Corapi that RMC was more sophisticated and more aggressive in treating heart disease than most hospitals. They also emphasized that Moon was a highly skilled cardiologist who had done more than 35,000 caths even though he was only fifty-five years old. Zerga asked Chilton, "Do you think that John and I are stupid?" Chilton said, "No." "Then why are you treating us as if we were stupid?" Zerga asked. "We're not stupid." He asked Chilton, "Why did you charge him for a stress test?" At this point, Zerga later said, Chilton was shaking. Zerga then asked, "Why did you even do an angiogram? Does everyone who comes into this hospital get an angiogram? You gave him a stress test and then went straight to an angiogram without a thallium stress test." He told Chilton that the thallium test cost $3,500 whereas the angiogram cost $30,000. Zerga said Chilton did not respond to any of these questions.

Despite his own experience and research, and even despite Chilton's and Caudle's unconvincing performance, Corapi left the forty-five-minute meeting shaken and still not sure that he didn't need the surgery. On the one hand, he had seen the statistics, he understood the demographics and the logic of the situation, and therefore, rationally, it was easy to believe that something very wrong was going on. On the other hand, he found it extremely hard to believe that doctors were sawing open the chests of people who had no disease. Also in the back of Corapi's mind was the fact that his father had undergone bypass surgery twice, as well as valve surgery. And not long before, following a routine checkup, Zerga was found to have a 95 percent blockage in his critically important left anterior descending artery even though he was asymptomatic.

After the meeting, seeing Corapi's continuing fear and uncertainty, Zerga told him that they had to fly back to Las Vegas and get one more opinion. At first, Corapi resisted. He said, "I can't take much more." But Zerga told him that he really had no choice. He said he was going to call Mody and ask her to make an appointment with another cardiologist. That evening, Corapi, Zerga, and Tamra, hoping to have a relaxing dinner away from Redding, went to a restaurant called the Tail O' the Whale on Shasta Lake, fifteen miles north just off of I-5. As soon as they were seated, Corapi looked up and saw Moon and his wife absorbed in conversation at the next table. Moon almost certainly had to have seen Corapi, but if he recognized him he did not acknowledge his presence.

Corapi returned to Las Vegas with Zerga on June 30. The following day they went to the office of Allen Rhodes, the cardiologist Mody had arranged for them to see at Sunrise Hospital. Rhodes looked at the angiogram and the IVUS, although he told Corapi that he didn't think it was necessary to look at the IVUS because it was not a primary diagnostic test. Afterwards, Rhodes reassured Corapi that there was absolutely nothing wrong with him. He also said a small spot on an artery that Donahoe had noticed probably had been caused by a catheter sheath hitting the vessel's wall. He said, "If I thought there was anything wrong with you we would take other steps."

Zerga then asked Rhodes what he thought about a fifty-five-year-old cardiologist who had done more than 35,000 caths. Rhodes said, "I'm fifty-five years old, I have a very busy practice, and I've only done seven or eight thousand caths." Zerga asked him for his opinion about a diagnosis of spontaneously dissecting arteries. Rhodes said that he had only seen a spontaneous dissection once in his career. Such dissections were extremely rare and associated with young women. They also were almost always fatal, with about 70 percent of them detected postmortem. Zerga asked him what he would do if he saw such a case, and he said, "You have to call the ambulance right away," adding that the patient probably would not make it. Zerga said, "John, that's it" and Rhodes added, "It's a justice department problem," seeming to suggest that he thought Moon had been guilty of fraud, not just malpractice. Zerga asked Rhodes if it were possible to misdiagnose something this badly and Rhodes said, "No. This is not a case of two physicians recognizing a common ailment and differing on the treatment. This is black and white."

The next day Rhodes gave Corapi a physical examination and reviewed the reports of Shehane's diagnostic tests. Rhodes then showed the angiogram to his partner, John Bedotto, who concurred with Rhodes's opinion that no invasive treatment was necessary. Corapi was finally convinced. He and Zerga returned to Zerga's office and called Hal Chilton. Both men were on the line. At the other end Chilton and Tamara Caudle were on the line. Zerga told them that they now had two more board-certified cardiologists who had said definitively that there was "no basis for Moon's diagnosis and recommendation." Chilton said, "Well, so what do you want to do about it?" suggesting that they could come up to Redding again and meet with a cardiologist. Corapi said, "We've met with a number of cardiologists and we're well past that. Don't you think you should look into this? Don't you think you should have an investigation?" Chilton answered, "No, we have absolute confidence in Dr. Moon. We're quite comfortable with our position. If you want to seek counsel, go ahead."

Chilton had every reason to be confident. For more than twenty years Moon had been delivering remarkable results. There had been occasional minor problems, usually related to his personality, but no serious challenges to his preeminence among Redding cardiologists. The only major exception, the case of Charles Kenneth Brown, who had suffered a stroke, was abandoned by Moon in unstable condition, and then died three weeks later, seemed to have been successfully swept under the carpet by the Mercy medical staff and administration. And because Moon was RMC's rainmaker, generating far more revenue than any of his colleagues through his own practice and his referrals to Realyvasquez and the other cardiac surgeons, the cardiologist knew Tenet would back him to the hilt if Corapi filed a malpractice suit. At the same time, Chilton must have recognized during their meeting that Zerga was tough and smart—Corapi spoke little if at all—but it is not at all clear that Chilton understood the trouble he was buying when he decided not to just quietly settle the matter. He did not know that Corapi and Zerga were both accountants, that both had been investigators with the Nevada State Gaming Commission, that Corapi had seen more of the seamy side of life than most men would in three lifetimes, and that Zerga was born with a double dose of tenacity and focus.

Although Corapi was now convinced that he had been the victim of an unnecessary invasive procedure, he was not eager to get into a situation that would attract media attention. Besides, he was already involved in a lawsuit with Kurt and Sandra Schirmer and he didn't want to get involved in another. But Tamra said to him, "You have to do this, you know too much; you can't just walk away from something like this. You aren't the only one they're doing this to." He told her, "You've been listening to me too much." But in the end he concluded that there was a moral imperative to follow through because people were probably dying as well as being physically and emotionally traumatized. He discussed it further with Zerga and they decided they would have to hire lawyers. They also found out that the FBI investigates Medicare fraud and, if Corapi's case was not unique, there almost certainly was Medicare fraud involved. They decided to contact the California State Medical Board, the fraud division of Blue Shield, Corapi's insurance company, and, most important, the FBI.

7

The Investigation

Toward the end of the first week in July, Joe Zerga picked up the phone and dialed information. To his surprise, he learned from the operator that the FBI had an office in Redding. He called the number and reached Mike Skeen, a compact, conventionally handsome, disarmingly soft-spoken forty-two-year-old who was the senior resident agent. Skeen was an army brat who had followed his father into the service, where he flew helicopters, then served briefly as a Washington State highway patrolman before joining the FBI. He had requested assignment in Redding under a seniority program in 1999 and unless he asked for a transfer or the bureau needed him elsewhere he could remain there for the rest of his career. Skeen liked it in Redding, as did his wife, Roxanne, and they had no plans to leave.

Zerga identified himself as a forensic CPA with investigative experience and in condensed form told Skeen what had happened to Corapi. Skeen listened carefully without interrupting as Zerga tried to convince him that Corapi had been a victim of criminal fraud. But despite Zerga's insistence it sounded to Skeen like a typical malpractice case, not a pattern of criminal behavior that would justify FBI involvement. Besides, at the time Skeen was alone in the office—his partner had been transferred to the FBI training academy and his replacement had not yet arrived—and he had more pressing matters on his plate. Skeen, who speaks deliberately, enunciating each word carefully, in uninflected Middle-American English, told Zerga politely and not at all dismissively that the first anniversary of 9/11 was coming up and his priority was terrorism. Although Redding's surroundings were not obvious targets to those unfamiliar with the area, Skeen's concern was not idle. The big dams and power plants nearby, Shasta, Keswick, Lewistown, Trinity, and

Whiskeytown, supplied water and power to a significant portion of California. Shasta Lake alone held 4.5 million acre-feet of water and was a major irrigation source for the farms of the Central Valley that supplied America with two-thirds of its produce. It also contributed substantially to the drinking water supply of twenty million Californians.

On the other hand, in the almost three years since he had arrived in Redding, Skeen had heard more than one version of a wisecrack about the hospital that had been making the rounds for almost a decade. A common variant went like this: "Don't have a car accident in front of RMC or you'll end up with a zipper in your chest," which everyone knew meant a bypass operation. He'd also heard another one-liner that was well known in legal and medical circles in town: "If there's a woman in Redding who still has her uterus, she's a tourist." Skeen knew from experience that in his line of work jokes like these, while proof of nothing, should not be completely ignored. But for the moment at least he saw nothing that would justify initiating an investigation, and he said as much to Zerga.

Skeen also knew that if the government were to bring a fraud case against Moon the defense would introduce expert testimony that his diagnosis of Corapi amounted at most to malpractice, but certainly not fraud, that it was only a single case, and that there was no smoking gun. He told Zerga this, too, but he also said he would be willing to take a look at the medical records anyway and talk to Corapi personally. The Las Vegas accountant, who boasted that he numbered among his clients five of the world's leading high-stakes poker players, then said to Skeen with a calculated edge, "That's fine, but I want you to know this: I'm also contacting the California State Medical Board." He wasn't bluffing. He notified the board on July 9, which was the same day he sent Corapi's medical records to Skeen.

When Skeen hung up and thought about the conversation, he found the matter intriguing. Zerga sounded knowledgeable and intelligent. As soon as he got off the phone he did a Google search on Moon. He came up with a three-part series about him that had appeared in the *Record Searchlight*. The series was flattering, but something about Moon's ego and contempt for government oversight caught his attention. Along with the information Zerga had provided, the series convinced Skeen that the allegations were worth looking into. He decided it would make sense to talk to Maline Hazle, the reporter who had written the articles on

Moon. Hazle, a talented journalist who had been a reporter for the San Jose *Mercury News* and had come to the Redding area with her husband planning to retire, couldn't stay away from the news business. She told Skeen what she could and also put him in touch with a potential source. After talking to Hazle and weighing what he had learned, he decided that the basic story of Corapi's experience probably was enough to begin an investigation and formally open a case.

Skeen, who had kept a fairly low profile in Redding, phoned a number of people he knew looking for leads. He also called the source Hazle had recommended, a life and health insurance broker named Marge Beck who for years had been concerned that unnecessary surgery was being performed at RMC. Beck had been quoted in another series of articles, published in the *Record Searchlight* in April 2002, about the rising costs of healthcare and why HMOs had left northern California for more profitable places. Skeen went to see Beck at her office at 1348 Market Street in Redding on July 29. Beck grew comfortable with Skeen during their conversation. When he told her he needed help in interpreting the information and records he had gathered, she decided that she could trust him and that he was serious about the investigation. She told him that it was common knowledge in Redding that too many heart procedures were being done at RMC, and she provided him with copies of statistical data she had collected over the years.

Beck told Skeen she would call a couple of doctors she thought might be willing to help him, one of whom had been on a quiet crusade to put an end to the unwarranted procedures for several years. She did not disclose their names because Redding is a small town and she believed Moon, Realyvasquez, RMC, and Tenet were powerful enough to threaten any physician's livelihood. The first doctor she called did not want to talk to Skeen. The second was the crusader, a slightly eccentric, somewhat disgruntled and occasionally disheveled family practitioner named Patrick Campbell. Among other things Campbell was a former professional classical violist and an accomplished amateur photographer. Campbell, who had begun his career in medicine when he was ten years older than most of his colleagues, joined a practice in Redding in 1993. He had collected evidence for several years that he believed proved Moon and Realyvasquez were performing unnecessary procedures, including bypass and valve surgery. Although he was initially hesitant because his previous efforts to have Moon and Realyvasquez investigated had been frustrated,

Campbell thought it over and agreed to tell Skeen his story and answer whatever questions the FBI agent might have.

Campbell had noticed soon after he arrived that the Redding Medical Center was doing an unusually high number of heart procedures for a hospital of its size that was situated in an underpopulated part of the country. But the relatively high numbers were not nearly enough to make him think that Moon and Realyvasquez might be systematically disregarding the guidelines of the American College of Cardiology. It would be another couple of years before he began to believe, based mainly on the experiences of his patients who had been treated by Moon and Realyvasquez, that many of their clinical judgments were so far out of line that honest doctors could not possibly disagree over them. When Campbell discreetly began raising the subject with colleagues, however, it soon became clear that some Redding doctors were unwilling to accept that Moon and Realyvasquez were practicing way outside the standard of care. Others either had no interest in blowing the whistle on their colleagues or were afraid to do so.

Campbell understood the risks involved in taking on Moon and Realyvasquez. These were not just any doctors. They were the force behind RMC's extremely successful California Heart Institute, Tenet's biggest profit center, and Redding's greatest source of civic pride. They were not only the two most powerful men in Redding Medical Center, they were two of the most powerful and highly regarded men in the city—men, Campbell thought, to be feared as well as respected. Nonetheless, over a five-year period Campbell had made sporadic attempts to warn hospital administrators, and on one occasion local and state officials, that Moon and Realyvasquez were doing risky, invasive procedures on people who didn't need them. Campbell did more than most, but his attempts were not vigorous enough to stimulate an investigation. Moreover, as more politically astute doctors might have told him at the time, he had about as much chance of producing results by going to hospital executives as he would have had of getting a hit against Roger Clemens or winning a game against Roger Federer.

Through Campbell and Bob Pick, a Redding cardiologist who practiced across town at Mercy Hospital, Skeen quickly identified another person who was very knowledgeable about the RMC heart program. He believed this person might be able to produce hard evidence of wrongdoing, that this was someone who could be his Deep Throat. However, this individual was very skittish about talking to the FBI and about being publicly identified, so Skeen moved slowly and carefully. Eventually Skeen would refer to this valuable source as CW1. Meanwhile, with additional introductions from Beck, Skeen spoke to several other doctors in town. He was beginning to accumulate evidence. Corapi had almost no disease yet he was told he was going to die. It looked like Campbell would be able to establish that there were other victims. And other doctors had similar suspicions based on patients they had seen. In less than a week Skeen was reasonably confident that his criteria for opening a new case had been met. The situation being described constituted a federal violation; the evidence appeared to substantiate the allegation, and it had the earmarks of a case the U.S. attorney's office would prosecute. His boss, Mike Mason, the special agent in charge in Sacramento, agreed, and when Skeen's request came in he signed off on it.

Skeen called Joe Zerga to let him know that an investigation was underway and that he wanted to meet with Corapi soon. Zerga had already sent him Corapi's records. Skeen also explained that if Zerga took any further action such as reporting what happened to other agencies, including the medical board, or filing lawsuits, it could alert Tenet and RMC to what was going on and they might destroy records or otherwise compromise the investigation. Skeen was careful to frame his message as a suggestion, not as an instruction or an order. He knew that as a federal law enforcement officer, he should not recommend a course of action that in any way could harm a citizen's interests. Nonetheless, as intended, Zerga sensed his urgency. He agreed to Skeen's terms with two exceptions. He told Skeen that he and Corapi already had contacted Corapi's insurance carrier, Blue Shield, and the state medical board. He said, though, that his impression, based on a conversation with a board employee named Susan Fisher, was that the board was not interested in Corapi's story. A follow-up letter from the board dated July 17, 2002, reinforced this feeling, partly because of its bland, nonspecific content, and partly because it was not signed. Zerga did not hear from the board again until October 31. A letter signed by Lynda Gentry, a consumer services analyst, said that Corapi's complaint had been sent to a medical consultant for review and evaluation. Between July 12 and August 14, Corapi received four brief letters from Blue Shield signed by three different employees promising to address his concerns. None did.

*   *   *

July 30, 2002, like every July day in Redding as long as anyone could remember, began sunny and hot. Mike Skeen arrived at his small, unidentified, nondescript office at 1900 Mistletoe Lane before eight o'clock. His brown hair was carefully brushed straight back, he was wearing a tie despite the heat, and his dress shirt clung a bit to his thick torso. He was drinking coffee and preparing for back-to-back interviews with Pat Campbell and John Corapi. Skeen had spoken to both men on the phone and was looking forward to meeting them. Campbell came in first at nine o'clock.

Although he had been practicing medicine in Redding for almost ten years when he came to see Skeen, Campbell, like John Corapi, was an outsider. He was not a Redding local. With his liberal political views and cultural interests—you might even say his 1960s sensibility—he was an unlikely candidate for the city's establishment. He wasn't a Rotary Club member and had not joined the Riverview Country Club. Campbell grew up in Portland, Oregon, in the 1950s and 1960s in what he himself thought of as a blue-collar lower middle-class home. His father changed jobs frequently, working in factories and later selling cars. Pat's own view of his father was that he wasn't a very good car salesman; that he probably was too nice and couldn't close the deals. In the early 1970s, a time during which there were lots of skyjackings, he wound up getting a job as an air marshal with the U.S. Customs Service. He seemed to have an aptitude for this work and he stuck with it.

As for Campbell, his interests developed differently and, it would seem, unpredictably. Although no one played or listened to classical music in his home, he heard a string quartet somewhere when he was ten years old and fell in love with the sound. He soon discovered that he had musical talent. After his parents divorced during his sophomore year in high school, Campbell floundered for a while and his grades suffered. He had no idea what he wanted to do other than continue playing music. Two years later he won a full music scholarship to Lewis & Clark College in Portland, which was considered to have the best music program in the area, and as a junior he was offered a partial scholarship to the New England Conservatory of Music. He accepted it, but in the end he got cold feet and didn't go. He was beginning to have second thoughts about a career as a classical musician. Among other things he worried about the relatively poor wages orchestra musicians earned. Money was a problem when he was growing up and he was convinced that one of the reasons his parents divorced was financial insecurity.

Campbell eventually entered the University of California at Santa Cruz where he majored in biology. He received a BS degree in 1981. He then took six months off and did an internship in Sacramento on a state assembly committee on energy, land use, and resources. In his opinion political battles often worked to the detriment of good government and were distasteful. He also concluded that news coverage of the committee's work was often distorted. This was the beginning of Campbell's political education, but it didn't adequately prepare him for what was to come. It also was during this period that he began to think that medicine might be a financially secure, morally acceptable career. With this in mind, but still in no great hurry and happy with the laid-back liberal environment, he returned to Santa Cruz and for several years took graduate courses, mostly in chemistry. Finally, at age twenty-nine, he applied and was accepted into medical school at the University of California at Irvine. He was graduated in 1988 and completed a residency in internal medicine at the University of California at Davis three years later.

After practicing in Sacramento for two years, Campbell was recruited by RMC to join the general practice of a doctor named Dinesh Mantri. Tenet Healthcare, like other for-profit hospital corporations, but perhaps more aggressively, provided inducements to physicians to practice nearby and refer patients to their hospitals. He accepted the offer, which included a salary guarantee for his first two years of $125,000 a year. After negotiating and signing a contract with the hospital's chief executive officer, Don Griffin, he moved to Redding with his wife and two young children. Not long after he arrived, however, the contract came back from corporate headquarters substantially revised and he refused to sign it. He could not appeal to Griffin because in the interim the CEO had left. One day while Campbell was discussing his contract problem with Lynn Seaburg, who handled physician relations for the hospital, Moon appeared and, as Campbell remembers it, told Seaburg something like "Just make it happen," and left. What did happen was that Campbell went to work without a contract. Within about a year he was making enough money so that it didn't much matter.

From the beginning he saw many patients who had undergone bypass surgery and still had unusually high cholesterol levels. He wondered why nothing was being done after surgery to keep their lipid levels and other risk factors in check. Later in his first year in Redding, probably in the winter of 1993, he attended a three-day meeting in the Bay Area on treating lipid disorders. The meeting and what he was seeing in his practice combined to stimulate his interest in lowering high lipid levels and in preventive cardiology generally. After giving it some thought, it occurred to him that it would make sense to set up a preventive cardiology and diabetes clinic in the hospital. Campbell went to Moon, the director of cardiology at RMC, and sounded him out about it. But Moon wasn't interested. Campbell couldn't be sure, but he speculated that Moon's lack of interest might have had to do with the fact that such a clinic at best would be revenue neutral. Money never seemed to be too far from Moon's mind.

Soon after Campbell arrived, Moon cornered him and told him he should consider becoming a cardiologist because of the money they made. He bragged that the previous year his practice had grossed more than $4 million. Campbell discussed the clinic idea further with Seaburg and Wally Quirk, an administrator, but given Moon's lack of interest, it was not surprising that the idea went nowhere. It was widely believed among the physicians and staff at RMC that Moon was more powerful than any administrator and that just before Campbell came to Redding he had engineered the departure of Jerry Knepp, a popular CEO. According to one Redding doctor, Moon had spread disparaging rumors about Knepp.

Around the same time, Campbell referred a Medicare patient named Mary Rosburg to Moon because an exercise treadmill test he administered was mildly positive. Moon did an angiogram and told her she needed a single bypass of her left anterior descending coronary artery, and that she needed to have her mitral valve replaced. Walter Schell, a cardiac surgeon in Realyvasquez's practice group, called Campbell to tell him that he didn't think surgery was necessary and recommended medical management of the problem. Campbell asked Schell to discuss it with Moon. The next thing Campbell heard was that Schell had performed the bypass and valve surgery the following morning.

A couple of months after the surgery, Rosburg asked Campbell if it would be safe for her to go to the coast for a vacation. Campbell said it would be as long as she did not forget to take her Coumadin, a blood-thinning medication that is especially important to use after valve surgery. She traveled to the coast and while she was vacationing in

Trinidad near Mendocino a clot developed in the artificial valve, possibly because she was taking too low a dose of Coumadin. She was rushed back to RMC, where Moon did an emergency catheterization in Campbell's presence. Campbell could see on the screen that the valve was filled by the clot and was hardly moving. Moon then went on vacation and left the case in the hands of his associate, Walter Fletscher. The following day Schell operated a second time on Rosburg. He replaced her defective valve with a pig valve and everything seemed okay. But one week later she suffered kidney failure and died. Based on Schell's comments, Campbell concluded that Rosburg should never have had open-heart surgery in the first place. He could not prove that her death had occurred as a direct result of the unnecessary surgery, but he believed this to be so. It was his first serious inkling that something might be wrong at Moon's highly touted California Heart Institute.

About a year later, Campbell was asked by Bob Pick, with whom he had already discussed his diabetes and preventive cardiology clinic idea, whether he might be interested in setting it up at Mercy Hospital, RMC's crosstown rival, which was owned by the nonprofit Catholic Healthcare West. At first Campbell was naïve enough to think the two hospitals might establish the clinic as a kind of joint venture, but he soon discovered that for an RMC doctor to run a clinic at Mercy would be looked upon as treason by the RMC administration and many if not most of his colleagues. There had always been competition between the two hospitals, but there was an unwritten agreement between them that RMC would specialize in treating heart disease and Mercy would specialize in treating cancer. When Mercy established an open-heart program in 1992, the competition became much more intense, at times even nasty. Campbell's defection would be especially noticed because both hospitals were eager to cement the loyalty of provider groups and Campbell's group was an important contributor to RMC's patient base. Nevertheless, he was eager to do it and was still frustrated and irritated by RMC's rejection of his proposal.

Pick, a tall, good-looking man who is built like a defensive end, got his cardiology training in the navy and began doing angioplasty in 1980 when it was still in its infancy. He said that in his judgment it was not until the establishment of the Mercy heart program in the early 1990s that Moon and his associates began performing unnecessary angiograms and cardiac operations to ratchet up their numbers. Pick had been successfully recruited by RMC to join Moon's practice, but it did not take him long to discover that Moon was arrogant and difficult to get along with. He also observed that about a third of Moon's angioplasty cases, an unusually high percentage even in those early days, were unsuccessful and the patients had to be treated surgically. He was naïve enough to offer to help Moon improve his outcomes, which, he said, led to a blistering two-hour tirade. Among many other things, Moon told him that he wanted to become a member of the elite group of cardiologists who had done at least ten thousand catheterizations and he wanted to build a highly successful heart program at RMC, both of which he later did.

Soon after Pick's approach, which resulted in an offer from Mercy, Campbell attended an annual RMC cardiology symposium hosted by Moon and Realyvasquez at the very upscale Squaw Creek resort at Lake Tahoe. Between fifteen and twenty pharmaceutical companies were represented at the meeting and also paid about half the costs, which were about $200,000. There were strict rules about how much could be spent because otherwise it would be considered enticement of physicians and therefore illegal. About one hundred physicians came for educational sessions in the morning, golf or family activities in the afternoon, and lavish receptions both evenings. The faculty members were often nationally recognized cardiologists and cardiac surgeons. Christiaan Barnard, the heart-transplant pioneer, was once on the symposium's faculty, as was Marcus DeWood, who used a technique known as selective coronary angiography to prove that most heart attacks were caused by blood clots in the coronary arteries. DeWood's work confirmed a critically important theory formulated by a Chicago cardiologist named James Herrick in 1918, but which fell out of favor because no one had demonstrated it experimentally.

Doctors who attended the symposium received continuing education credits, but the real purpose of the gathering was not education, it was to encourage referrals to RMC from doctors in the 40,000-square-mile rural area the hospital served. Susan Bisetti, who worked in marketing at the hospital, analyzed the costs and benefits of the meetings per doctor and how much business it translated into for Tenet. Hospital and corporate executives were determined to make sure that these efforts generated revenue. Bisetti had regular meetings with Steve Schmidt when he was CEO and later with Hal Chilton about planning the conferences, and then reported back to them on the payoff. For each physician who attended the meeting, these reports tracked for the next year the number of referrals, the kinds of procedures their patients had at RMC, and the amount of money earned on these procedures. Bisetti got the reports from the cath lab and the operating room, although she said often it was very difficult to identify the referring physician. Her reports circulated within the hospital administration and then were sent to corporate headquarters.

While at the cardiology symposium, Campbell approached Wally Quirk, who he thought might be able to help him. He told Quirk that Mercy wanted him and that "RMC should get off its ass." Campbell also used another channel. He complained to his senior colleague, Dinesh Mantri, who referred almost all of his cardiac cases to Moon, in the expectation that through the Mantri-Moon connection his offer from Mercy would get to the hospital leadership. Campbell's preference was to set up the clinic at RMC. But when nothing happened in the next few weeks, he accepted Mercy's offer. This, he said later, "set off a shit storm. I was called a traitor by the RMC people."

Although Campbell's relationship with RMC administration and staff was clearly strained, he continued to practice there and to wonder about Moon's standards for diagnosing coronary disease and recommending surgical treatment. Because of his interest in lipid management, he was particularly taken aback by Moon's hesitancy at the time to prescribe the cholesterol-lowering drugs called statins. He remembers Moon telling him that the drugs were too expensive. His professional contacts with Moon were limited to discussions of patient care and brief discussions of this kind, except that about two years after his arrival in Redding Moon engineered a merger between Mantri and Campbell's practice and the practice of two other primary care physicians, Bruce Kittrick and Gary Crawford.

Campbell's worries about Moon and his practice group remained relatively muted until sometime in late 1995 or early 1996 when he saw a sixty-five-year-old patient of his named Emma Jean Montgomery who was complaining of atypical chest pain. She had previously undergone angiograms and other coronary diagnostic tests and to Campbell's knowledge had no significant coronary disease. But he was sufficiently concerned to call Dr. Thomas Russ, an associate of Moon. Russ gave her a nuclear stress test, which she passed, but he wanted to do an angiogram. Campbell did not think this was unreasonable because the sensitivity of the nuclear test was only about 70 percent, which meant there was a reasonable chance of a false negative. Russ performed the angiogram and told Campbell that Montgomery had a ruptured plaque in her left anterior descending coronary artery and two other blockages and needed immediate triple-bypass surgery. Realyvasquez performed the surgery without incident and she went home.

About two months later, Campbell received a copy of the dictated cath report, which said she had some disease in three vessels, but none of it was critical and the chest pain could not be explained by the catheterization findings. This clearly meant that surgery was not needed. At first he thought, "That's bizarre, maybe he mixed up two patients." But then his suspicions kicked in. He wanted to be as discreet as possible, so he asked one of his patients who worked as a technician in the echocardiography lab at RMC to "borrow" the film. He then asked Bob Pick's partner, Roy Ditchey, to review it with him at Mercy Hospital. Campbell said to Ditchey, "Tell me what you see." "Exactly what was in the dictated report," Ditchey answered, "three-vessel nonobstructive disease. She needed medical therapy," not surgery. When Campbell told Ditchey that Montgomery had undergone bypass surgery he looked stunned.

Campbell now thought he had a smoking gun. His concern that Moon, Realyvasquez, and their associates were overly aggressive seemed to seriously underestimate the problem. He was becoming convinced that these doctors were diagnosing disease where there was none and recommending and performing unnecessary catheterizations, open-chest and open-heart surgery. He began discussing what he thought he was seeing with Ditchey and Pick and with other Redding physicians. He also talked to all the doctors in his group, but with one exception they were unwilling to criticize Moon and Realyvasquez. Dinesh Mantri said nothing and Bruce Kittrick said, "Well, we don't have a lot of heart failure here," apparently suggesting that Moon and Realyvasquez were doing prophylactic procedures that prevented future heart disease. The exception was Gary Crawford, who said, "I think Moon's a jerk and I've thought so for a long time." He thought Moon was far too aggressive and, unlike most Redding physicians, he also doubted the cardiologist's intellectual capacity. On the other hand, Crawford sometimes doubted himself and wondered whether Moon might not just be practicing cutting-edge cardiology.

By this time, Pick, who had come to Redding in 1990 from Loma Linda Hospital in Southern California, had already seen at least one case he thought was a clear-cut example of unnecessary coronary bypass surgery. It involved a patient of his who had undergone angioplasty to open a blockage in his right coronary artery. This patient also had chronic back pain. He began appearing in emergency rooms all over the area describing coronary symptoms so precisely that frequently an angiogram would be ordered and he could get opiate painkillers, to which Pick believes he had become addicted. Sometime in 1995, Pick's colleague Steven Mendelsohn did an angiogram on the patient at Mercy and found no new coronary disease. But a week or so later, he appeared in the RMC emergency room. Moon's colleague Tom Russ did an angiogram and sent him to Realyvasquez for a quadruple bypass. A couple of days later Pick wandered into the patient's room by mistake and saw him in bed with a big bandage on his chest. "What are you doing here?" Pick asked. "I had a four-way bypass," the patient said. Pick was incredulous and went to get the film. He says he asked Sheryl Hallstrom, the cardiac coordinating nurse, to look at it with him. "You look at these all the time, Sheryl," he said. "Where's the coronary disease?" According to Pick, Hallstrom, an admirer of both Moon and Realyvasquez, replied blandly, "I don't know; I just work here." Hallstrom does not remember being asked to comment on angiographic film by Pick or ever making such a comment to him, but Pick later testified to this encounter under oath.

This was the first such case Pick recalled seeing, but it would not be the last. By the mid-1990s, other doctors in town, even those who had seen no hard evidence of wrongdoing or malpractice, were beginning to be concerned about the high volume of cardiac procedures being done at Redding Medical Center. Moon was doing two hundred or more catheterizations a month. His supporters said he could do so many because he was so skillful and so fast. A more likely explanation was that instead of taking the time to do the requisite histories and physicals on his patients he had nurses doing them for him. What's more, he shot too few images and his catheterizations were often so rushed and sloppy that those he shot were useless. RMC's stunningly high catheterization and cardiac surgery numbers had even attracted the attention of the editors of the *Dartmouth Atlas of Health Care*, a highly regarded academic compiler of healthcare statistics. Campbell also asked a few out-of-town cardiologists who had provided second opinions on cases diagnosed by

Moon what they thought of Moon's pattern of practice. These conversations supported his suspicion that something very bad was going on.

At the time Campbell was chairman of the medical-care committee at RMC and in this capacity received monthly reports on patient complaints. It became obvious after a couple of months that Moon and Russ were getting an unusually high number of complaints. Even though what he knew firsthand was limited to two cases he felt he should do something. In the summer of 1996 he ran into Stephen Corbeil, RMC's CEO, in the Redding golf course parking lot, and told him about the patient complaints. Corbeil's unambiguous response was "Mind your own business." The subtext of this cryptic answer was that Redding Medical Center—by virtue of its high cardiac volume, its saturation advertising of the heart program, and its 24/7 Medevac service delivering patients from outlying areas—was riding high and you'd damn well better not mess with it. Around the same time Bob Pick had a similarly unsatisfying conversation with Corbeil in the hallway at RMC. Pick had already begun to shift his entire practice to Mercy because of his concerns about the unnecessary procedures and because cardiac referrals from the RMC emergency room were all going to Moon's group.

Corbeil left RMC in September 1996, and was replaced by Ken Rivers, one of seven CEOs at RMC during the 1990s. Campbell took advantage of the change in leadership to prod his partners, Bruce Kittrick, Dinesh Mantri, and Gary Crawford, into a meeting with Rivers in the spring of 1997 to discuss their growing concern that too many heart procedures were being done at RMC and that some of them might have been medically unnecessary. Everyone in the Redding medical community knew that Moon and his surgeon of choice, Realyvasquez, were doing an extraordinarily high number of procedures relative to RMC's patient base. The 1999 issue of the *Dartmouth Atlas of Health Care* reported that in 1995–96 Redding Medical Center had the highest bypass surgery rate in the country.[14]

To Campbell's surprise—because he thought Kittrick was a "go along to get along" kind of guy—his partner acted as spokesperson for the group at the meeting. He told Rivers without mentioning any names that the group had heard that some cases were inappropriate and that they were worried about patients getting proper care. He suggested to Rivers that a review be conducted by independent cardiologists of about ten randomly selected angiograms. Campbell hadn't known that Kittrick planned to make this proposal, but was pleased that he did. Rivers's response was polite, even cordial. He defended the program by citing praise for it from Medicare and HealthGrades, the online rating service, but he seemed sincere and genuinely concerned to Campbell and he said he thought a study could be done as long as patient confidentiality was protected. Rivers said he would have to consult with the hospital's lawyers, but to Campbell at least it seemed as if the review would take place. Campbell's group was a major source of referrals for the hospital, which, he reasoned, was a strong incentive for Rivers to respond favorably to their request. But five or six months passed and Campbell heard nothing more about it.

Then, in October 1997, Campbell was invited to meet with Morris Eagleman, a cardiac nursing supervisor, and Rivers in Rivers's office, to discuss the possibility of moving his preventive cardiology clinic from Mercy to RMC. Rivers asked Campbell what he was being paid by Mercy to run the clinic, which was $4,000 a month for a day a week on-site, and offered to pay him the same amount. But when Campbell asked for the same staff he had at Mercy, two full-time nurses and a full-time dietitian, Rivers turned him down. Campbell rejected the offer, but before leaving the meeting, he asked Rivers, "By the way, what ever happened to that study you were going to do?" Rivers seemed flustered and didn't answer immediately. Then, he said, "Oh, oh, that study. The lawyers are still looking at it." A few days later, Campbell sent a counterproposal to Rivers asking for twice what Mercy was paying him, which was his way of telling him to go to hell. The following spring, Campbell spoke at a diabetes meeting run by RMC, where he continued to refer most of his patients. When Rivers left the meeting he stopped and shook Campbell's hand and gave him what Campbell thought was an "I know that you know smile." Campbell took this to mean that Rivers and other RMC administrators knew Moon and Realyvasquez were performing unnecessary procedures. Rivers left RMC a few weeks later for Lake Medical Center, a Tenet-owned hospital near Long Beach, California.

During Ken Rivers's brief tenure as CEO of Redding Medical Center a forty-year-old executive named Greg Gibson joined the management team as chief operating officer. Because of a known drug problem, his contract required him to undergo monthly testing. A big, handsome outgoing man who lived out on Texas Springs Road near Chae Moon, Gibson appeared to be a very different kind of administrator from most of his colleagues at RMC. For one thing, he came down to the emergency room on a regular basis to check on how the nurses and technicians were doing and to find out if all their needs were being met—even small things like whether they were getting enough time for lunch or whether they were getting breaks. According to one of the nurses, Kacie Carroll, who had been a California Highway Patrolman until she injured her back, he truly cared about quality of life for RMC employees and about the quality of patient care. "He was very charismatic," Carroll said, "just a very nice man."

One of the things Gibson learned immediately in his new job was that the pressure to produce income for the hospital and for Tenet was enormous. In a sense he was lucky his first year there because the hospital generated unusually high revenues. This was not only because of the booming cardiac business, but because of a flu epidemic that year, which kept the emergency room extremely busy. Hospital admissions were so high that there weren't enough rooms for all of the patients. Many of them were lying on beds, gurneys, and cots in the hallways. From a business perspective, it was a chief operating officer's dream year. But because of Tenet's insatiable demand for profits Gibson's good luck coiled around and bit him in the back. Tenet executives told him that they expected the same amount of revenue from him the following year. He told his bosses that it couldn't be done, but they insisted not only that it could be done, but that if he knew what was good for him, it would be done. It was. Pretax net income the following year increased by almost $4 million.

Another thing Gibson learned quickly at RMC was that Moon and Realyvasquez both seemed to be completely untouchable and were the beneficiaries of a great many expensive perks. Moon, for example, used the hospital aircraft to go to golf tournaments. The rules didn't apply to them. Both men were lax about dictating their charts, as are a great many doctors, but Moon was notorious. Normally a doctor would be sanctioned or suspended for falling as far behind as he typically did, but Gibson was told that Moon was to be left alone. Gibson also observed that the primary responsibility of Ellen Read, a good-looking blonde whose title was director of nursing, was to keep Realyvasquez happy. Bill Browning, who ran the pharmacy, said the same. When asked about her relationship with Realyvasquez years later, Read said, "Fidel and I became the very best of friends," but Read denied that the relationship was intimate.

One of the things she did for him in her dual role as professional colleague and friend was to try to get him to dictate his patient notes. His response when she bugged him to get them done was "I don't need a mother." They were close enough so that Realyvasquez confided in her that Moon drove him crazy, but he added that he didn't think he was dangerous. From 1998 until 2000 when she left the hospital, Read and Realyvasquez had coffee together between his first and second case almost every day behind closed doors in her office. She said they used to talk about things like mortality statistics and what was going on at the rural hospitals. Gibson intimated to Kacie Carroll, though, that Realyvasquez's relationship with Read had another dimension and that Read was known around RMC as the "head nurse." But Bill Browning disagreed. He did not believe they had a romantic relationship. On the other hand, he disparaged Read's medical knowledge and said he thought Realyvasquez was comfortable with her mainly because she was totally nonthreatening. Gibson said Read was exceedingly well compensated, including six-figure bonuses, and a housing supplement.

Although Ken Rivers was formally his direct superior, Gibson actually reported to Dennis Brown, Tenet's regional vice president. Rivers spent a good deal of his time building business, which in practice meant driving beautiful, winding mountain roads through the vast, pine-forested hinterland surrounding Redding to recruit for and service the network of rural primary care doctors on whom the heart program depended for referrals. High-ranking Tenet executives, including Tom Mackey, head of hospital operations, and Neal Sorrentino, who was in overall charge of Tenet's western division, often conferred privately with Moon and Realyvasquez about this all-important "cardio-network." As a result of Rivers's frequent trips away from the hospital, Gibson was left in charge much of the time. Brown traveled to Redding twice a month for meetings and Gibson sometimes went to the regional headquarters in San Francisco to confer with him.

Gibson was particularly struck by the close watch Tenet executives like Brown kept on RMC's financial performance. Every month Joe Nowicki, the chief financial officer of RMC, and his counterparts at other Tenet hospitals were required to produce reports that included narrative sections detailing key events that influenced each hospital's financial performance, and a statistical section that, among other things, analyzed the contribution of individual doctors to each hospital's bottom line. There was a point during Gibson's tenure at which a decision was made to separate these accounts for individual physicians from the main report. After that they were handled with secrecy; these reports were never sent by email. Brown hand carried them to corporate headquarters in Santa Barbara for the monthly meeting, which was attended by Tom Mackey. Gibson sometimes received phone calls from these meetings and was asked questions like "Moon's off a little bit, what's up?" And while Gibson was at RMC, Tenet executives sent daily email messages pressing for ever-greater profits from the heart program. Gibson also heard comments at board of directors' meetings to the effect that the already prolific Moon and Realyvasquez had to increase the number of procedures they were doing because Tenet was giving the heart program tens of millions of dollars annually for building and equipment.

Among the sensitive matters Gibson was privy to while Rivers was CEO was the negotiation of a new contract for Realyvasquez. More than a year before the expiration of Realyvasquez's old contract, which Gibson said was in clear violation of the Stark Law* because the compensation was pegged to revenue he generated for the company, Rivers received a set of demands from the surgeon. His job, rather than the normal task of negotiating an equitable agreement linked to the value of Realyvasquez's service, was to tailor a contract to meet the surgeon's demands, which included compensation of more than a million dollars a year for nine or ten years. This was a complicated chore because both Moon and Realyvasquez were compensated in a variety of ways, some of which were not meant to be transparent. These included salary, bonuses based on exceeding budgeted profits, stipends for medical directorships that in the mid-1990s were worth $120,000 a year to Moon and $180,000 to Realyvasquez, emergency room on-call pay, subsidies for rent and salaries for employees, and fringe benefits such as the use of hospital-owned aircraft. But Rivers filed Realyvasquez's draft contract in his desk drawer rather than dealing with the surgeon's technically and legally complex demands. Whenever Realyvasquez asked about the status of the contract, Rivers made excuses to string him along.

---

*This legislation, named after Rep. Pete Stark of California, is designed to eliminate corruption in healthcare.

When Realyvasquez eventually realized what was going on, he became furious. He went to Tenet management and threatened to quit, showing them letters from other hospitals offering him what he wanted. This dispute contributed to Rivers's transfer. Rivers was replaced as CEO by Steve Schmidt and after that the contract negotiations with Realyvasquez progressed fairly rapidly with the help of Dennis Brown and others. Gibson said great care was taken to give Realyvasquez what he wanted while structuring the contract to avoid violating the Stark Law. After several meetings a contract was drafted that met Realyvasquez's approval, although its details were kept confidential. According to Gibson, a similar process was followed with Moon soon thereafter, also leading to a lucrative new contract whose terms were also kept confidential. Gibson said what Tenet wanted—and got—from Moon in return was three hundred caths a month, a number far higher than could be justified by the disease rate in the local population or very likely anywhere. And it was a pace that no cardiologist could maintain with a professional level of competence, not even Chae Moon, the fastest catheter in the West. But more caths begat more bypass surgery, which would appear to have been Tenet's goal.

Greg Gibson left RMC abruptly in 1999, not long after Steve Schmidt became CEO. According to Kacie Carroll, Gibson and Schmidt did not get along. She said Gibson came down to the ER one day, sat down, and said, "Well, I've come down to say good-bye. I'm being transferred out to Phoenix, Arizona." Bill Browning, who knew that Gibson had a drug problem, said Schmidt asked him to document a pattern of drug abuse by Gibson, but he refused to do it on the grounds of medical confidentiality. Browning told Schmidt that he, Schmidt, was contractually responsible for monitoring Gibson's drug use. Schmidt's and Gibson's offices were side by side and Browning asked Schmidt why he hadn't noticed Gibson's frequent sweating and other symptoms. When Schmidt said he thought Gibson sweated a lot because he was such a big man, Browning asked him how long he'd worked in medicine, which might have been the straw that broke the camel's back. A few months later Browning was fired over an allegation of forgery that he denied and that was never proved. He considered suing, but true to his army background he dropped the idea in part, he said, because "management serves at the pleasure of the company."

* * *

During the years Rivers and Gibson ran RMC, Campbell continued to refer patients to them if he thought they had acute problems despite his strong belief that Moon and his partners were subjecting patients to unnecessary invasive procedures, and that some of these patients wound up having unnecessary surgery. He was not yet firmly convinced that Moon was willfully diagnosing nonexistent disease and that Realy-vasquez was operating on patients who clearly did not need surgery. Besides, Campbell said, expressing a point of view that helps explain why so few doctors are disciplined by their professional societies, "The etiquette is that unless the patient expresses some reservation about returning to that cardiologist, I can't say I don't want you to go back there. That's just the way it works in reality and practice."

Then around the beginning of 1999, a second patient Campbell had sent to Moon went to surgery and died a short time later. She was a feisty, vigorous woman of about seventy-eight who had type 2 diabetes. She came to Campbell complaining of chest pain. He thought it might be cardiac pain and administered an exercise treadmill test in his office. It was mildly positive and he advised her to see a cardiologist. It was not an emergency. Her husband asked her whom she would like to see. He had undergone heart surgery and was under Moon's care. "Well, isn't Dr. Moon the best?" she asked. "I'd like to see Dr. Moon." At their request, Campbell referred her to Moon. Soon afterwards she had bypass surgery and returned home.

About six weeks later her husband flagged Campbell down in the hallway and said his wife was in the hospital. Campbell went to see her, looked at her chart, and saw she had undergone the surgery and was doing poorly. She was on glucophage, a medication used to reduce blood sugar, when she was rehospitalized. Campbell recognized that this was not a good medication for someone who had recently undergone surgery and wrote an order to discontinue it. He then saw on her chart that her ejection fraction was in the 30–40 percent range, which meant that her heart was not pumping blood efficiently, although it had been normal before her surgery at 60 to 65 percent. She was discharged and Campbell took over her care. She began losing brain function almost immediately, went steadily downhill, and died shortly thereafter. Campbell felt that the patient had been in good health for a seventy-eight-year-old and that the surgery had been inappropriate.

Not too long after this patient died Campbell saw a Medi-Cal patient in her mid-fifties on whom Moon had done several caths and placed a couple of stents. She had chest pain and he sent her back to Moon. The next day, when Campbell was visiting her hospital room, Moon arrived waving a Polaroid picture of an artery showing a little flap and said, "See, Campbell, you were right. She has a dissected plaque." Campbell didn't disbelieve him. However, Moon subsequently told the patient that the problem was not her heart and that she should go back to Campbell. Campbell asked her if she wanted to see another cardiologist. She said friends were telling her she should, so he sent her to Ditchey. In the meantime she showed up at the Mercy emergency room. Ditchey admitted the patient, did a cath, found that her coronaries were wide open, and sent her home. Ditchey then got her earlier films from RMC, reviewed them, and wrote a letter to Campbell saying she never had any obstructive disease, no indication for stents or repeat angiograms. He also wrote that Moon's studies were of poor quality, which at the time was a bold thing to say. Ditchey believed Moon took too few views and the ones he took reflected an inadequate understanding of the patient's coronary anatomy and the equipment he was using. He also found Moon's written reports superficial.

Soon thereafter Campbell met Ditchey in the corridor at Mercy and Ditchey told him that the patient had not needed any invasive treatment. Campbell told him about the flap and Ditchey said it was a contrast-streaming artifact, which results from blood diluting the contrast dye, thereby distorting the image. Campbell found it hard to believe that something that looked like that could be an artifact, but at the time he knew little about dissected plaques, which are different from and less immediately threatening than dissected arteries, although Moon appears to have sometimes used the terms interchangeably.

By early 1999, Campbell was sending Moon only those patients who had previously been under his care and those who insisted on being seen by him. Of course, given the size of Moon's practice and his renown in the community, this was a significant number of patients. Campbell still did not feel he had a large enough and conclusive enough body of evidence to tell patients he suspected that Moon and his partners were performing unnecessary procedures and making specious diagnoses. One reason for this was that the random study of ten angiograms that Kittrick had proposed had never been carried out. Moreover Campbell worried that anything negative he said about Moon would find its way back to the powerful cardiologist and lead to retribution. But finally, in a state of anger and frustration after failing to prevent Moon's practice associate Tom Russ from performing a catheterization on a patient he believed didn't need it, Campbell put together a package of four cases and in March retained a local lawyer named Jerrald Pickering. Campbell asked Pickering to find out, without disclosing Campbell's identity, how he could put an end to what he now felt certain was a pattern of medically unnecessary invasive treatment.

Over the next two weeks, Pickering made a series of discreet inquiries. He told Campbell that he had conferred with a lawyer in the office of Shasta County District Attorney McGregor Scott and persons in the fraud divisions of Medicare and Medi-Cal. According to Pickering, the lawyer in Scott's office said he had heard rumors about medically unwarranted heart procedures at RMC, but that without more information than Campbell had provided he could not open an investigation. He said the Medicare and Medi-Cal officials told him essentially the same thing. At the suggestion of a Medicare employee Pickering spoke to an assistant U.S. attorney in Sacramento and once again was told that he did not have enough information to initiate an investigation. Pickering also spoke to persons associated with both hospitals, but because he would not identify Campbell or provide medical records, they said they would not pursue the matter either. He later said in a sworn deposition that he "concluded that a strong case could be made, not only for potential criminal charges, but also for civil fraud and other actions as well." Nevertheless, he wrote Campbell the following in a letter, dated April 1, 1999, that—despite its typos, grammatical errors, and odd emphases, not to mention its menacing, apocalyptic, and archaic language—shaped Campbell's understanding of the situation he was seeking to get involved in and the risks that involvement could entail.

> Dear Dr. Campbell:
> . . . We have examined the documentation provided and reviewed it with an out-of-town medical doctor. We have made discrete inquiries and contacts locally. We have discussed it internally. All of which makes a strong case for not only potential criminal charges, but civil fraud and other actions, as well.
> . . . [T]his particular case is just the tip of the iceberg, as the same motivations and practices are present to a lesser and/or greater extent at both hospitals.

Each hospital is not so secretly delighted with any and all problems the other institution may suffer. Each is quite willing to stand behind (way behind) and privately encourage anyone who wants to blow the whistle on the other. All of this you already know. What you do not know is, that the public authorities are basically either not interested or judge the political correctness or profit first, then the merit (i.e., What does it do for me?).

Consequently, as your objective and very experienced legal adviser, I set the information aside for a while, came back and on[c]e again reviewed the situation. The conclusion is inescapable: Do not blow any whistle! Period. Rationale for this is: (1) you would be very alone, (2) there is too much money involved, (3) except for the victims and/or their families, no one cares, and (4) you would instantly find yourselves with a bunch of new vigorous enemies.

Sincerely,

PICKERING LAW CORPORATION
Jerrald K. Pickering

Pickering charged Campbell just under $1,000 for his services, which Campbell resented, and, Campbell said, he failed to return patient records Campbell gave him. Nonetheless, Campbell followed Pickering's advice for the next three years.

Soon after, in April 2000, Campbell and his wife began trying to adopt a child abroad. They eventually succeeded, but the process was expensive and emotionally draining and it involved two two-week trips to Russia in October 2001 and April 2002, when they brought the child home. What with keeping up his practice, exploring the possibility of filing a whistle-blower or what lawyers call a qui tam* lawsuit, and the adoption, Campbell felt himself under tremendous pressure. Neverthe-

---

*Qui tam is short for the Latin phrase *qui tam pro domino rege quam pro se ipso in hac parte sequitur,* which means, "who pursues this action in our Lord the King's behalf as well as his own."

less, he pushed ahead. In late 2000, while waiting for data from Ditchey and Pick, he was treating a fifty-three-year-old diabetic male with no evidence of coronary disease. After an office visit in December, Campbell scheduled a follow-up visit for six months later. He did not see the patient again until May, when he ran into him and his wife in the supermarket. He was shocked when they told him that his patient had undergone multivessel bypass surgery on March 24, 2001, at RMC.

Neither Moon, who had diagnosed the patient with coronary disease, nor Realyvasquez, who had performed the surgery, nor anyone else at RMC, had notified Campbell. When the patient came to Campbell's office for his follow-up visit he explained what had happened. The patient had told his wife, a surgical nurse who worked with Realyvasquez, that he was having chest pain. She arranged for him to see Moon, who talked to him for a few minutes, checked his pulse, and ordered an angiogram. Moon diagnosed multivessel disease and recommended bypass surgery. The patient gave Campbell permission to review his medical records and angiographic film, which he did with Bob Pick, who confirmed Campbell's impression that the patient had no significant coronary disease.

That summer, Campbell also discussed the RMC situation with a patient of his named Leon Malcolm, who had been an insurance fraud investigator. Malcolm asked Campbell before they met whether it would be okay if an FBI agent listened in on their conversation. Campbell agreed, but because he was feeling somewhat paranoid about word getting back to Moon, Realyvasquez, and Tenet, he arranged to meet Malcolm at a Mormon church in south Redding, where they spoke for about an hour and a half. The FBI agent did not show up. Malcolm suggested that Campbell report the doctors to the state medical board. Campbell asked him if he would give the board the information without mentioning his name. Malcolm agreed, but nothing came of it.

Then, out of the blue on July 29, 2002, Campbell received a phone call from his insurance broker friend Marge Beck asking whether he would be willing to speak to Mike Skeen of the FBI. With that call, seven years of increasing suspicion, confused or contradictory reactions to it, and growing frustration with his inability to act on what he knew were about to enter a new phase. The next morning for three hours, from nine o'clock until noon, Pat Campbell sat face-to-face with Skeen and unburdened himself. When he left he gave Skeen copies of all the information he had painstakingly collected about Moon, Realyvasquez, their practice associates, and their patients, as well as a long list of potential sources of information. About a week later, Campbell and Bob Pick, who knew nothing of Campbell's visit to Skeen, were talking and Pick asked rhetorically, "Why didn't *we* think of calling the FBI?"

Campbell's conversation with Skeen was an opportunity to focus his thoughts about what had happened and why it had happened, but he remained conflicted. He continued to believe that at times Moon was acting in what he thought were the best interests of his patients. But he also believed that was not the whole story, that Moon was a complicated person who sometimes knowingly did things that were not in the best interests of his patients. Campbell seemed to be still working through the contradictions, trying to decide what to think about what happened and the men who made it happen.

He thought Moon had an incredible need to be the best, the most powerful, the top dog, the ultimate alpha male. He thought there were times that Moon sincerely cared about his patients, but other times when he showed thoroughgoing contempt for them. He recalled Moon sitting in the medical staff lounge and pontificating about Medi-Cal patients, welfare people in general, those good-for-nothing people he had to take care of who were nothing but scum. People who worked hard were good people in Moon's book. Part of his railing against Medicare and Medi-Cal recipients was that they didn't work, they didn't contribute to society. Campbell also thought Moon did things to patients he knew to be unnecessary because of his megalomania. He had worked himself, both psychologically and professionally, into a position where he not only thought he could do no wrong, but in fact nobody would question him. The goal was to make more money; more money meant more power; the higher the numbers the greater their power with Tenet. It was no more complicated than that.

But Campbell still pondered whether it might not have been more complicated. Perhaps Moon really had a fundamental belief that cathing people was the only way to find out what was really going on with them. He had certainly persuaded a lot of people locally of that. Campbell believed Moon had a mill going with nuclear treadmill stress tests. He asked people to come back every year for another test at $1,600 a pop. Eventually he'd tell them there was a problem and do a cath.

Campbell's thoughts about Moon and Realyvasquez might not have fully jelled, but at least he had finally found someone outside his small circle of colleagues and friends in Redding who would listen to him. More important, it was someone who conceivably could do something to stop the cardiologist and cardiac surgeon from performing unnecessary procedures on credulous patients. Campbell felt good about Skeen and thought he would do his best to do the right thing. But since he had first begun to suspect wrongdoing he had grown deeply cynical. He believed that most of his colleagues had let him down, that Pickering had not done all he could, and that the officials Pickering had approached were either uninterested or, worse, possibly complicit with Tenet, a corporation he believed was politically powerful in California. Still, he found it a great relief to unburden himself. Now only time would tell whether the information he provided would do any more good than that.

8

The Investigation II

About an hour and a half after Pat Campbell left Mike Skeen's office on July 30, 2002, John Corapi walked into it wearing jeans and a polo shirt. The priest and the FBI agent were alike in a number of ways. Both were fit, compactly built men who had served in the military and liked guns and the outdoors. And both were men whose lifework was closely linked to their traditional moral vision. They went directly to their business with little small talk. Corapi began telling his story with Skeen politely interrupting from time to time to clarify a point or to ask a question. Skeen, who was amply endowed with the skepticism appropriate to his profession, was impressed. He found Corapi intelligent, logical, with a good grasp of the facts, and an almost verbatim memory of conversations. Skeen had already spoken to Corapi on the phone and had heard part of his story. Corapi repeated it that afternoon with almost no variation.

Corapi was not only consistent, he seemed genuinely angry about what had been done to him—the instilling of the fear of potentially fatal disease and major surgery even more perhaps than the relatively minor physical violation of the unnecessary angiogram. He was not only credible but passionate when he said that his sole motivation was to stop such behavior so that others would not be subjected to the same thing or worse. The fact that Corapi was a Roman Catholic priest meant little or nothing to Skeen, except it occurred to him that if he were a prosecutor he would love to have as a witness someone like Corapi, an upstanding clergyman whose sole motivation was to put an end to this outrage without hoping to gain financially. Eventually however Skeen would revise his judgment. He would come to question Corapi's value as a witness largely because of his substantial and at least partly self-interested financial dealings, which, at a minimum, were unusual for a priest and could lead to questions about his character in court.

Corapi told his story to Skeen without reference to Joe Zerga. He said that he went to a physician on his own because he was concerned about his family history of heart disease. Corapi told him that Moon administered and interpreted the treadmill test—although his medical records indicate it was a doctor named Sander Saidman who did it—and then told him that it was worthless forty-year-old technology. Afterwards Corapi described the details of Moon sending him for a calcium-scoring test, and someone from Moon's office telling him he had scored badly and that Moon thought he should have a catheterization. Corapi continued fluently recounting his entire experience from the cath lab at RMC to his decision to contact the FBI.

Corapi also told Skeen about RMC's CEO Hal Chilton telling him to get a lawyer. Corapi remembered Skeen's response: "If we're going to conduct an investigation, work with us. Don't file any lawsuits because it's absolutely imperative that no one have a clue that there's anything going on. Don't talk about it with anyone except your counsel." Skeen listened to everything Corapi said with a trained ear and when Corapi left a couple of hours later he thought to himself that what he had heard that day added up. There was something especially compelling about hearing a doctor's account and a patient's account consecutively. Even though he was alone in the office with the 9/11 anniversary closing in on him and there was the usual press of other cases, he knew for sure that this was something he could not ignore, though he also realized that it would be unusually time-consuming. Skeen had no experience with medical fraud cases and he knew little or nothing about treating coronary disease, its prevalence, or mortality rates. The learning curve was going to be very steep.

A day or two after interviewing Campbell and Corapi, Skeen placed a phone call to Dan Linhardt, an assistant U.S. attorney in Sacramento with whom he had worked on many investigations. Skeen did not need permission from the U.S. attorney to open an investigation, but it is generally considered good practice to get an opinion from the prosecutors before going too far down the road. If they are unimpressed with a case there is good reason to question whether the man-hours and expense of an investigation would be justified. Skeen and Linhardt, a short, olive-skinned lawyer with a lot of experience who was close to retirement, talked for forty-five minutes. Linhardt told Skeen at the beginning of their conversation that medical fraud cases were hard to make and that those involving unnecessary procedures were the hardest. He said they tended to turn into expert-versus-expert cases that confused juries, and U.S. attorneys usually tried to avoid them unless they were black-and-white, which was rare. But Skeen explained that this case was different because there was plenty of hard evidence. He told Linhardt that there were angiograms for each patient, which identified any blockages in their arteries, and that these could be enlarged and shown to juries. Linhardt was soon persuaded and by the time they finished talking the two men had agreed that Skeen should continue his investigation and draft an affidavit designed to convince a judge to issue a search warrant. A warrant would allow the FBI to seize records from the hospital and from the doctors' offices. It normally took a couple of days to complete an affidavit and get a warrant issued. But this time was different. The final sixty-seven-page document had gone through nine drafts and took three months to finish. The acting U.S. attorney, John Vincent, wanted it to be "bulletproof."

While making contacts, setting up and conducting interviews, and keeping up with his other work, Skeen tried to learn as much as he could as quickly as he could about heart disease, cardiology, and cardiac surgery. He did extensive Internet searches, read books, and talked to doctors he could count on to be discreet and who were willing to help him. One, Roy Ditchey, had heard rumors about inappropriate treatment in RMC's heart program even before he moved to Redding from Eureka up near the big redwood forests on the coast in 1996. He was particularly helpful, answering Skeen's questions about what a cardiologist could tell from angiographic images and how they were taken and how and where they were stored. Ditchey also sent him to the right sources for additional information and drew diagrams to help him understand coronary physiology and how medical devices worked.

When Skeen read about coronary disease and treatment in a book, he did not always understand it. He would then go to a source, usually Ditchey, to get further explanation. He learned that the coronary arteries fed blood to the heart muscle and that when an important artery was totally blocked the result could be a major heart attack. He also learned that the left anterior descending coronary artery (LAD) was a key vessel because it fed blood to the left ventricle, the heart's main pumping chamber. And he learned that most heart attacks were caused by rapidly forming, relatively fragile blood clots, not by a slow buildup of calcified, stable arterial plaque.

Skeen also needed to learn important statistics: About half a million Americans die each year from coronary artery disease, thirteen million Americans have it, and more than seven million living Americans have suffered heart attacks. Moreover, between 1950 and 1999, because of better treatment and lifestyle changes, the death rate from coronary artery disease declined by 59 percent, although the actual number of deaths declined far less sharply because of America's increasingly aging population. More important, Skeen needed to know how often cardiac procedures, including diagnostic catheterizations such as angiograms, angioplasty, and bypass surgery, were being done around the country. This would give him a sense of whether they were being done too often at RMC. The actual figures for 2002, which could only have been estimated at the time, were 1,463,000 diagnostic catheterizations, 1,204,000 angioplasties, and 306,000 bypass operations. And when he needed to look up medical terms, he used the online medical encyclopedia on the University of Maryland website. Within six months he had grasped the basics, but the learning process was ongoing.

During this time, Skeen was developing a source inside the hospital and learning about the layout, physically and logistically. He asked the doctors he interviewed where various kinds of records were kept. And once Skeen won the confidence of his anonymous source CW1 (to whom I will refer with female pronouns for the sake of convenience), she explained how patients flowed through the system. She also drew maps for him of the floor plan and told him where records could be found. Because Skeen socialized almost exclusively with a small group of friends, most of whom were law-enforcement officers and their families, he was not well known in town. He was able to go into the hospital himself without being recognized and develop a mental picture of his own. He did this a couple of times just to get a general sense of the place, but stayed in the public areas. He did not visit the cath labs or the cardiac operating rooms.

During these visits, Skeen was able to learn the location of the CEO's office and also where medical records were kept. His inside source told him where records were being stored outside the hospital, which was important because search warrants were only good for the specific locations described in them. He was told by a local cardiologist about the jukebox-like machine that contained records including angiograms on disc. He needed to know where the cath lab and cardiac operating rooms were and what various sets of initials stood for such as CCU (cardiac care unit) and CVOR (cardiovascular operating room). All this took time, and always there was the risk that there would be a leak, the investigation would be blown, records would disappear or be destroyed, and the entire effort would be wasted.

Skeen had asked Campbell to ask Pick and Ditchey if they would talk to him, and they both agreed. He interviewed them separately, first Ditchey and then Pick, a day or two apart at their offices in a complex of single-story buildings adjacent to Mercy Hospital. Ditchey told Skeen he first began to suspect that there were problems in the RMC heart program as far back as 1996. He was still practicing in Eureka, which is about 100 miles from Redding, when he heard about a patient who had undergone unnecessary bypass surgery after a diagnosis by Moon. Over the next couple of years, based on his own examination of numerous patients, he concluded that Moon frequently had done uncalled-for catheterizations. He also told Skeen that Moon had performed angioplasty on and placed stents in some patients who did not have significant coronary artery disease. Moreover, he told Skeen that Realyvasquez accepted Moon's recommendations uncritically and performed bypass operations on patients who did not need surgery.

Ditchey also told Skeen that some patients who came to him for a second opinion after having seen Moon said that Moon did not do the standard noninvasive workup designed to eliminate the need for a relatively risky, invasive catheterization. Often, they said, he would not take a personal history, or administer an electrocardiogram, an exercise treadmill test, a nuclear stress test, or tests for elevated cardiac enzymes, all of which provided information that could make catheterization unnecessary. This practice pattern was consistent with the belief that catheterization was the only way to definitively diagnose coronary artery disease and therefore it was a waste of time and money to do anything else. It was also consistent with the extraordinarily high number of catheterizations Moon boasted he had done, and with doing unwarranted procedures.

Ditchey told Skeen that Moon frequently misused intravascular ultrasound to persuade patients that they needed bypass surgery. He explained that the IVUS image showed areas of differing contrast because of normal differences in density in the lining of the artery and because of areas of plaque. These plaques might be minimal and stable and require no treatment, or they might be obstructive, or fragile, indicating that they could break loose, form a clot and block the artery, causing a heart attack. Ditchey learned from patients that Moon would often point to these dark areas, as he did in Corapi's case, and tell the patients that they had spontaneous spiral dissections.

Ditchey said that in the spring of 2002 he was invited to see Hal Chilton, CEO of Redding Medical Center. Chilton and other RMC chief executives periodically invited Mercy cardiologists to visit so that they could sell their program and encourage referrals and admissions. During this meeting Ditchey told Chilton he thought RMC was a good, physician-friendly hospital, but that he was convinced that Moon and Realyvasquez were performing invasive heart procedures on patients who did not need them and urged him to investigate. Chilton expressed disbelief and told Ditchey he had no reason to think anything like that was going on, but Ditchey did not believe him. By then he had come to believe that the RMC administrators knew exactly what was going on and did nothing about it because of the tens of millions of dollars annually Moon and Realyvasquez were generating for the hospital and for Tenet Healthcare. He even wrote an editorial for a medical journal focusing on RMC's excessively high rates of bypass surgery and other cardiac procedures. To allay his wife's fears about a potential libel suit, however, he had a lawyer review the editorial. In the end the lawyer's suggested revisions resulted in a version of the article that he couldn't live with and he never submitted it for publication. Ditchey also gave Skeen the names of three patients and two medical professionals he said were able to corroborate his information.

Skeen next met with Pick, who was trained as an osteopath before becoming a cardiologist and practiced in Eureka and Loma Linda before coming to Redding. Pick told Skeen that he first became aware of Moon in 1987 when he went to RMC to perform some cardiac procedures. He said he had neither heard nor seen anything at the time that raised suspicions about Moon or his practice. This was the year RMC's open-heart program got underway and the year Realyvasquez began doing cardiac surgery full-time at the hospital. When Pick moved to Redding in 1990 to join Moon's practice, the cardiac program was growing quickly and

RMC was gearing up a major advertising campaign to promote it as one of the nation's best. But Pick, who at the time practiced at both hospitals, as did most cardiologists in town, became concerned before the end of his first year that Moon was diagnosing and treating outside the standard of care. It was around this time too that a number of other doctors in town began saying to one another that Moon and Realyvasquez had become too aggressive in their diagnosis and treatment of patients.

Pick told Skeen that he had learned of a patient whose artery Moon had scored with a catheter, causing a spiral dissection. The patient's artery had collapsed and Moon had tried to repair it with a stent, but failed. Pick said the patient was rushed to surgery and subsequently died as a result of the dissection. Pick also explained to Skeen that a catheter is much more likely to cause a dissection in a healthy artery because the wall of the vessel is not protected by the layer of calcium that forms inside a diseased artery. This means that the risk of injury or death increases when catheterizations are performed on patients who don't need them.

Like his partner, Roy Ditchey, Bob Pick had collected data on his own patients who had been treated by Moon and Realyvasquez. He told Skeen that nineteen of them did not have coronary disease that would warrant any type of surgical intervention. He also told Skeen that in 1998 or 1999 he told Steve Schmidt, then the CEO of Redding Medical Center, that he believed unnecessary heart procedures were being performed and that it was a serious problem that needed to be corrected. When nothing happened by the summer of 2001, he went to Hal Chilton, by then the CEO, and his chief financial officer, Richard Phillips, and told them much the same thing he had told Schmidt. He said Chilton told him somewhat enigmatically, "We have heard that, but we're not sure how to handle it." Although Chilton never said so, Pick got the impression that he thought the problem should be dealt with by doctors, not administrators. In any event, once again, no action was taken. Pick, like Pat Campbell, told Skeen that he was worried that if word of his investigation leaked to RMC administrators, or to Moon or Realyvasquez, they might destroy or alter records. Shortly before his meeting with Skeen, Pick had asked the hospital for angiographic film on a recent patient of his and was told that the film had been destroyed, even though Medicare required hospitals to retain these records for six years and three months. He also left with Skeen detailed information on the nineteen patients who were subjected to invasive treatments by Moon and in some cases by Realyvasquez.

One other thing that Pick told Skeen indicated a surprising lack of oversight and concern on the part of the federal government. One of Pick's colleagues had discussed his belief that unnecessary coronary procedures were being done at RMC with a Medicare representative in Stockton, California. Pick's colleague also told the Medicare representative that some echocardiograms at RMC were being interpreted by technicians, not physicians. However, the Medicare official seemed uninterested and took no action.

Of all the non-physician sources Skeen interviewed, Bob Pick's close friend CW1 was almost certainly the most valuable. CW1, a tart-tongued East Coaster from near Newburgh, New York, who had worked at Mercy Hospital for four years before transferring to RMC in June of 2000, knew about Moon's overly aggressive practice by 1998. While working at Mercy as a cardiovascular clinical nurse specialist she became quite friendly with Pick, who by then was deeply concerned about Moon. Pick showed CW1 angiographic film of a thirty-eight-year-old woman who had undergone bypass surgery at RMC. She said, "She doesn't have coronary disease," to which Pick replied, stating the obvious for emphasis, "Well, she had bypass surgery." Pick told CW1 that what Moon was doing was insane. Just before she left Mercy for RMC, Pick said to her, "Wouldn't it be great if you went over there and you caught this guy?"

About a year and a half later, CW1 learned that B.V. Chandramouli, an associate of Moon who was managing the care of one of Moon's patients while the senior cardiologist was away, had read the patient's angiogram and told him that no treatment was necessary. However, when Moon returned he reviewed the film and told the patient that Chandramouli didn't know what he was doing and that the patient needed surgery. When CW1 heard that the surgery had been scheduled, she became incensed. She went to Chandramouli and pressed him to tell the patient that he had to get out of the hospital. The cardiologist eventually did so. She believes the patient checked out and did not have the surgery, but she is not absolutely certain.

CW1, who has a master's degree in nursing from the University of California at San Francisco, had been taught to read angiographic film by several doctors at St. Mary's Regional Medical Center in Reno, where she had worked before coming to Redding. There was a cine-film reader in a storeroom just behind the cardiac surgery intensive care unit at Redding Medical Center and CW1 used it to look at angiographic images of cardiac surgery cases. In September 2002, for the first time, she saw film at the hospital of pristine native arteries in a patient who had undergone bypass surgery. Forgetting about the films Pick had shown her in 1998, CW1, speaking carefully, told Cindy Gordon, the cardiac nurse supervisor, that "Before I came here, I heard a number of stories that suggested that patients were having surgery and didn't need it. I have a concern that this patient didn't need surgery." Gordon's face tightened. She took a step backward and said in a constricted but cutting whisper, "We're aggressive here, but we'd never do surgery on a patient unless they needed it. Do you understand?" Confronted with this response by her immediate superior, CW1 backed off. After CW1's conversation with Gordon, a note was placed on the cine-film reader saying, "This machine is for doctors only." But CW1 kept using it anyway because she believed it was important to have a thorough understanding of the condition of the arteries of the patients she was caring for. Sometime in the next couple of months the machine was reported to have been broken and then it was removed from the storeroom.

Nobody raised the subject of unnecessary surgery again, but it wasn't forgotten. There was retaliation. CW1 applied for several jobs in the hospital and never even got interviewed, despite the fact that her educational and experience levels qualified her for the positions. Rumors were circulated that she was a pathological liar and that her nursing credentials were suspect. Two friends regularly told her what was being said about her. This was unnerving, but she persevered. For a long time she felt that someone was out to get her. There were phone calls and email messages. Other nurses said things like "We're going to get you." One day Riaz Malik, the RMC surgeon, drove up to her house, which is way out in the country about thirty miles from Redding and not easy to find. She was up in a tree trimming branches when he arrived. She came down and asked him what he was doing there and how he had found her. He said he'd just been driving around. She couldn't explain what he was doing there and found his presence somewhat menacing. CW1 was afraid for a time, but after a while things seemed to quiet down and her mind eased some.

CW1, who had a suffer-no-fools approach that could easily have been mistaken for a superior East Coast attitude, said disdainfully that most of the nurses at RMC were from Redding families with lumber and mining backgrounds and that they were Rotary Club types and very cliquish. She said when they came on their shifts they would socialize for forty-five minutes before taking care of patients. Many of them were trained in Redding at Shasta College, a two-year program, and few had bachelor's degrees.

CW1 considered most of the locally trained nurses mediocre at best, a view shared by several other nurses who came to Redding from larger cities and medical centers. She said they were promoted to the level of their incompetence because Tenet and RMC wanted people who were easy to control in mid-level positions of authority. She also thought that RMC hired dysfunctional people who were loyal because they couldn't get work elsewhere. CW1 cited her own experience applying for a job as a heart-failure nurse at RMC. The position was posted for someone with a master's degree. Tamara Caudle, Cindy Gordon, and another nurse named Georgia were conducting the interview. When it was Gordon's turn to ask questions, she said she didn't have to ask any. She said, "Well, I'll just have to let you know all about [CW1]. I know her very well." CW1 did not get the job. It went to a nurse with a two-year associate's degree.

CW1 ordered a course on compact disc from which she learned to read IVUS. Ironically, she also received instruction from Moon's associate and one-time partner, Thomas Russ, who had been trained in IVUS. But he told CW1 that he did not use it as a primary diagnostic tool because it was experimental and too easy to misread. He also told her that he had expressed concerns about this to an RMC administrator in 1996, soon after Moon began using it, but the administrator was unresponsive. After learning how, CW1 read IVUS images whenever she had the chance. She saw numerous cases where the dissections and plaques mentioned in the written record were not visible to her on the film. At one point she showed one of Moon's ultrasounds to Russ and asked him whether he could see the dissection Moon had noted in the patient's record. Russ said he could not.

There were also other sources of information available. RMC compiled data for the National Registry of Myocardial Infarction and for a database kept by the Society of Thoracic Surgeons. These data were kept at a storage facility owned by Genentech, for whom CW1 sometimes gave lectures on cardiac care. She had access to and would sometimes look at these databases. CW1 found Redding Medical Center patients coded as having had acute myocardial infarctions who did not meet the diagnostic criteria for acute MI. These patients were being put on a waiting list, sent home, and then brought back to the hospital for bypass surgery. She told Mark Eliason, who worked in quality assurance and was in charge of national registry data collection at RMC, that there were patients listed in the database who did not meet the criteria. He told her to take them out. But even after that, CW1 continued to find records of patients who did not meet the criteria. And after some of them were admitted for surgery, she was able to review their angiographic stills. No one tried to stop her because they knew she was extracting data for the NRMI registry. During one month-long period in 2002 she estimated that 75 percent of the patients who had undergone bypass surgery at RMC didn't need it, and over three months she identified what she believed to be 165 unnecessary surgeries.

CW1 observed a number of cases she thought were not only unwarranted, but especially egregious, including a forty-three-year-old marathon runner and a thirty-one or thirty-two-year-old whose mother had undergone bypass surgery three months before him. But what finally put her over the edge was when Realyvasquez seemed exultant about having done a triple bypass on a twenty-eight-year-old man who CW1 believed had disease needing treatment only in his right coronary artery. She was also convinced that the proper treatment would have been angioplasty and a stent, not surgery, for the one artery that did require intervention. She was caring for the patient postoperatively when Realyvasquez came in, obviously excited, and said to her, "Can you believe it? We did a triple bypass on a twenty-eight-year-old!" She replied coldly, "And you're proud of yourself? Did you ever think of getting a lipid profile, seeing if he has homocysteine problems, finding out whether it's hereditary?" He was furious, and growled "Get whatever lab you want," to which she said angrily, "Don't get mad at me. Give appropriate care." His response was to shout "What, you're the doctor? Order it!" and stomp out of the room. He didn't talk to her for two weeks.

Around that time, Ricardo Moreno-Cabral, Realyvasquez's partner, was about to leave RMC to return to his family in Southern California. He was friendly with CW1 because he liked her homemade salsa, and one day he stopped by to talk to her while she was caring for a patient. He asked her what she was doing. She told him she had just ordered two units of packed blood cells for a patient who had a hematocrit of only 23, which meant he was low on hemoglobin and therefore his body's cells were not getting enough oxygen. Moreno told her pointedly, "You need to be very careful here. Don't do anything you don't have a written order for. I'm leaving and I want you to hear what I'm telling you. I know you're really smart and you know what I'm talking about. Don't do anything without a written order." Moreno-Cabral's comments were indirect, even enigmatic, but CW1 had no doubts as to what he was talking about. She believed Moreno-Cabral left because he was afraid that what was going on in RMC's heart program would lead to disaster and that inevitably he would be caught up in it. She did not believe that Moreno-Cabral himself had done unnecessary surgery.

Not too long thereafter the NRMI and STS data at RMC disappeared from where CW1 normally was able to gain access to them. She was told that Tenet no longer wanted to pay Genentech for the NRMI data and was building its own database, and that there was no one available to enter the STS data. But by then she had compiled a list of sixty-nine coronary bypass patients, all of whom died, that she had gleaned from these databases. In her judgment their angiographic still pictures clearly indicated that they had not needed the surgery. She gave this list and the accompanying X-ray images to the FBI. The bureau advised her for her own safety not to keep copies.

CW1 was not the only nurse who had concerns about Moon and Realyvasquez based on personal experiences and observations. Another was Mary Rose Roach, who began her nursing career at Redding Medical Center in 1978. Roach worked with Moon in the cardiac care unit beginning around 1986. Later she worked with him in the cardiac ICU, and, from 1990 to 1995, in the cath lab. Before she got to know Moon better, she had the impression that he was quiet and professional. But after she began working with him her opinion changed. She came to believe that Moon's emphasis on speed and his short temper caused anxiety for the nurses and technicians that sometimes led to critical errors. When asked for an example under oath she described a patient who was having a heart attack and was being transferred from the emergency room gurney to the cath lab table. Medications that were being administered intravenously had to be transferred from the ER pumps to the cath lab pumps. "Dr. Moon was really revving up to go before we were ready," Roach said, "and he was already starting the catheterization and yelling at people to get going and get out of the room. And one of the medications [was accidentally] emptied into the patient, entirely in the patient. The patient had a seizure and cardiac arrest [and died]. And I can't say that that was his fault at all. I can just say that the speed at which the nurse was being required to work was made more stressful by his screaming at us."[15]

Roach had often experienced verbal abuse by Moon, sometimes in front of patients. But this abuse did not seem to affect her opinion of his skills as a cardiologist. She thought he was very proficient technically; that he was extremely quick and had a very retentive memory. She was amazed how much he could remember about a patient and his disease. When she was working in the cath lab, however, Roach did notice that there were many more normal caths than would be expected. This suggests that patients without objective indications of coronary disease were being subjected to catheterization. Yet, when Sheryl Hallstrom, the cardiac coordinating nurse, showed the films to patients and their families, as far as Roach could tell, the films showed the disease.

But about six months before Roach left RMC, in 1995, Moon began using IVUS, and that changed everything. Nurses and technicians working in the lab were not comfortable with the new technology. They learned to set up the equipment and they knew that it was intended to help with stent deployment, but, with one possible exception, they could not read the images. They also knew that most cardiologists did not use IVUS as a primary diagnostic tool, which is the way that Moon was using it. When he pointed to where he said there was a blockage they could not see it. He would point to what appeared to be a shadow or a crack, which they could see, but they had no way of knowing whether it was disease. "He defined what we were seeing," Roach said. People came in with symptoms suggestive of coronary disease, but they had normal blood flow. Based on the IVUS, Moon would send them to surgery. "That's when he became very crazy and abusive to all of us and that's when I left," she said. She also said that his once smooth handling of the catheter became rougher and jerkier. In retrospect, Roach believed that Moon became more hostile in response to challenges from personnel in the lab after IVUS was introduced. She said he would rant and rave at the nurses and technicians with the patients in the room, telling them they were "a bunch of fucking idiots." She said that in this environment, no one questioned Moon; they just did what he said. Roach went through the full chain of command, including the corporate ethics committee, to make complaints about Moon, but she never got anywhere.

Marie Rua, an ER nurse who worked at Stanford University Hospital in the early 1990s on both open-heart surgery and transplant surgery, came to Redding in 1998 after Roach had left nursing. Rua was hired by Mercy Hospital, but not long afterwards she was offered part-time work at RMC and accepted that as well. She was the sole support of her family at the time and was working four to five twelve-hour shifts a week, three at Mercy and one or two at RMC. She was also taking night calls from Mercy to work on its fixed-wing airplane. Rua came into contact with Moon her first day working in the emergency room, which, coming from Stanford, she found somewhat old-fashioned. She was amazed at the feverish activity. She saw nurses and technicians "all over a terrified patient" on the table, putting in lines, although she could see no reason for this kind of urgent attention on the monitors. Moon was right there urging them to hurry up and get the patient to the cath lab.

Another patient came in with chest pain. He looked like a healthy male in his fifties. Someone said, "My God, he's got chest pain." Moon rushed over and said, "He's next, he's next, get him ready."

Rua said, "Excuse me!" The patient had not had any vital signs taken, no tests done, nothing. "You say you have chest pain. Well, is it relieved when you burp? Have you been under a lot of stress lately? Can you point to your chest pain?" She said patients would often point to a place that indicated a gall bladder problem. The whole time, Moon was behind her saying, "We don't have time for this, we don't have time for this!" She and the other nurses felt like Charlie Chaplin working on the steadily accelerating assembly line in *Modern Times*; faster, always faster. She said, "Their system was set up so that anyone who walked in and said they had chest pain, mind you, they could have a knife stuck in their chest, they went to the cath lab."

Rua's first-day observation was consistent with what others had been seeing all along. Bill Browning, the pharmacy chief, who was often in the ER, said "there were minimal diagnostic criteria" to get ER patients to the cath lab. There was no workup; they might have ordered cardiac enzymes, but they certainly didn't get the results. There was a pipeline to RV [Realyvasquez]."

The same day she was sitting at the bedside of a patient trying to find a vein to put in an IV line without stabbing the patient. Moon was directly behind her sticking his finger in her shoulder and telling her, "Go right there, go right there, this is what we need to do, hurry up!" Rua, who was not at all intimidated, turned around and said to him, "Hey, unless you have a diamond in your pocket, you need to back off." It was her first day at the hospital and she had no idea who Moon was or how powerful he was. Surprisingly, Moon did back off. He said it was just a suggestion. The other nurses looked on in astonishment. "Do you know who that was?" one nurse asked as he stomped off to the cath lab. Rua of course didn't, but another nurse told her, "That's who brings in the revenue for Redding Medical Center."

Later, when Rua was working a night shift, they were getting ready to send a patient to the cath lab. At that time, two new medications were being tested in clinical trials at the hospital. Moon came in and said, "I want that new drug." Rua asked him which drug he meant. Moon said, "I don't know, that new trial drug, what's the name of it?" Another nurse came up with a name and he said, "Yeah, yeah, that one." He rummaged around in a cabinet and found the drug, gave it to Rua and said, "I want you to give it to the patient." She asked him how much she should give, because she'd never given the drug before. He said, "I don't know, just read the instructions." Then she asked Moon again what dose he wanted to give because the instructions indicated a range of dosages. He looked at the vial, said he didn't know, but then said, "Oh, just go ahead and give the whole thing." Rua told Moon that she didn't feel comfortable with that because, for one thing, he couldn't even come up with the name of the drug, and because "the whole thing" wasn't one of the options on the instruction sheet. Moon then told her that she could give any dose she wanted to give. And again, Rua told him that she wasn't comfortable with that and that he should do it himself and he said, "Okay, give me the goddamn thing. I'll do it." Rua said that no one said a word because it was Moon. "He was God."

Rua said that no one else in the emergency room would complain about what was wrong and that she was told to keep her mouth shut. Like CW1, her impression was that some of the nurses who came out of nursing school and went straight to work at RMC simply didn't know any better. She found the responses of the RMC nurses to her complaints almost robotic. They used little pat phrases, all the same, to justify what they were doing. Two nurses she knew well, Ted Blankenheim and Terry Brushett, were like that. She said they would criticize Mercy, while she thought that Mercy did a far better job with cardiac patients than RMC. She said that Moon never even took his stethoscope out of his pocket to listen to the patient's chest and that he never asked patients about their risk factors or looked at their EKGs. The emergency room doctors would often call Moon before getting patients' lab work back. Sometimes patients would ask Rua, who was supposed to get their consent for the procedure, why they needed a cath. Instead of getting the consent, she would tell them to ask the doctor. When they did ask Moon why they needed the procedure, he would say, "Because you're going to die without it!"

In 1997 or 1998, Terry Brushett, who was by then Rua's husband, saw a woman who was about ninety years old arrive at the ER experiencing chest pain. Her cardiac enzymes were checked and were normal, indicating that she was not having a heart attack. She was given some nitroglycerin to get rid of the chest pain and would have been sent home except that it was late at night. So the doctors decided to keep her in the hospital overnight and monitor her until the morning. She was Brushett's patient throughout the night and she had no problems, so he was surprised to find her there the next day when he came to work. He asked why she was still there and was told that Dr. Moon had come in late at night, saw her, and wanted to cath her. He did the angiogram that day and sent her to surgery. The woman died a few weeks later, never having made it out of the hospital. Brushett said he was upset by the incident, adding that a lot of people at Mercy Hospital were saying "Dr. Moon would cath a turnip." Brushett also said that time and again he'd seen Moon send elderly, very high risk diabetic patients to surgery. He said these patients would do poorly afterwards and he thought that was wrong when they could have been treated medically. Some of the nurses called these surgeries kimchees, by which they meant rotten CABG. Kimchee is a spicy, malodorous Korean cabbage dish and CABG (pronounced cabbage) stands for coronary artery bypass graft. Yet, despite what he saw and heard, Brushett just could not bring himself to believe that Moon and Realyvasquez were doing unnecessary invasive procedures.

Another nurse, who asked not to be identified and whom I will call Linda, said her experience with Moon went back to 1992 when she worked in the cardiac care unit at Mercy Hospital. She said Moon talked a lot about his children in those days and was very family oriented. He laughed a lot, in quick bursts, and she found him to be very friendly. She also said he was generous and offered the following anecdote as evidence. A low-paid environmental services employee of Redding Medical Center won a Jeep in the Ducky Derby, an annual event sponsored by the Redding East Rotary Club to benefit the Rotary Clubs of Northern California Foundation Against Substance Abuse. Tens of thousands of yellow plastic ducks, each with a number, were dropped from a crane off the Diestelhorst Bridge. The first one to cross the finish line a hundred yards down the fast-flowing Sacramento River about a minute later won the first prize for the employee who held its number. The winner was delighted, but he wasn't sure he could keep the car because he couldn't afford to pay the tax that was due, so Moon wrote him a check. Linda remembers the amount as being about $1,000.

Moon once told Linda, "Hell is where there are no cigarettes." According to Ted Blankenheim, when Moon "left the hospital in his Cadillac all you would see would be his hands on the steering wheel and smoke barreling out of the windows." Other nurses and technicians, including Brett Larsen, recall having heard Moon say that it was all right for him to smoke because he was Korean, and his blood chemistry was different. Larsen also said he saw Moon smoking in the cath lab near open oxygen. Linda teased Moon about his smoking and asked, "What are you going to do when you come in [with heart disease]?" Moon answered, "Oh, I'll cath myself! It's not difficult, they can prep me, and I'll cath myself." Linda said, "I didn't dislike the guy at that point, and there was no reason to distrust him at that point." Moon obviously had a sense of humor about his personal health habits because when Bill Browning, who had an office across the hall from his, asked him if he always ate cheeseburgers and french fries for lunch he replied dryly, "No cheese, I'm lactose intolerant." Browning also periodically stole Moon's ashtray to discourage him from smoking in the hospital, but someone else would always replace it.

Linda said she was relatively new to cardiology at the time and had no reason to think that Moon was any different from any of the other cardiologists in the community. She said he was not difficult to work with. "If you called him you usually got what you needed from him." She did not know that he was not board certified in cardiology or anything else for that matter. Almost no one did, although in 1996 Moon mocked board certification at a gathering of patients and said publicly that he was not board certified. He said the board certified cardiologists in town didn't know how to put in a stent and he was living proof that the system didn't work. "Who shakes and bakes?" he asked in his own unique mode of English expression. "Onassis, this and that, he never had an education. Did Kennedy have an education, the original Kennedy? No, he was a bootlegger. But he knew how to achieve things."

But Linda also had personal knowledge of a troubling case involving a woman who was about forty-two years old and was on her way to the cath lab at RMC with Moon. She was having chest pains. This was during a short stretch during which there were a couple of HMOs operating in Redding and an RMC nurse called the woman's managed care company, Hill Physicians. The reviewer at Hill said they couldn't approve the procedure yet because Moon was not one of their contract physicians. She said the patient would have to be seen by one of Hill's physicians. She then called Steven Mendelsohn, who practiced at Mercy. He dropped what he was doing and went over to the RMC emergency room to see the patient. After examining her, Mendelsohn said the patient did not need a cath. When asked why, Mendelsohn said there was another explanation for her chest pain. She was bruised midline to midline and neck to waist on the left side, the result of a dirt bike accident the night before. Apparently she had not had a physical examination until he arrived and performed one.

Commenting on Moon much later, Linda said, "I don't think that he's malignant, I think he's crazy. I think he has an ego so large that it would never occur to him that he could be wrong. I don't think he's motivated by money, I think he's motivated by power. I believe that he in his heart probably really believes that he's saving everyone's life. I think he believes in his heart that he's right and the rest of the world is wrong." She said patients believed he was saving their lives because he told them that he was. He would say, "You want to die, you want to die? You want your mother to die?" He would shake his finger at them as he spoke. Afterwards, he would come back and say, "I saved your life!" She said that it never occurred to people in the generation in which most of his patients fell to ever even question what he was doing because of the respect they thought they owed to doctors. She said that elsewhere in the country people who have elective caths do not go straight to surgery. They are stabilized, put on nitrates, and sent home until the operation is scheduled. In Redding, however, primary care physicians were fed the notion that if patients diagnosed with coronary disease didn't have immediate surgery they would die. As a result it was widely accepted in Redding that a patient should go straight from the cath lab to the operating room.

Like CW1 and Mary Roach, Linda speculated that one reason so many of the nurses and technicians remained supportive of Moon was that they had never worked elsewhere. If Moon were to point to an angiogram and tell them you can't see it, but this is a ruptured plaque on the IVUS, who were they to challenge him? She added that there were many people who wouldn't say anything anyway because they were getting paid to do a job, not to question whether the doctor doing a procedure was ethical or treating appropriately. She saw this as comparable to a nurse who would take care of a patient postabortion even though she herself did not believe in abortion. Linda also remembered talking to Pat Campbell back when he first thought about becoming a whistle-blower. She said, "We are all conditioned by the movies, but I told him, 'Think carefully before you try to do something like that because people have been shot for less than this. This is a multibillion-dollar empire probably that you would be taking on. This is Tenet's cash cow.'" She told Campbell that he would be dealing with an angry community as well as the two doctors and Tenet. She said blowing the whistle in these circumstances wasn't something that she would want to do because it was the stuff of John Grisham novels and no one knew what might happen.

Rocky Milligan, a nurse at RMC who now works for the *Record Searchlight*, saw Moon with patients and their relatives because she used to go to the cath lab to do cardiac blood tests. She said his manner with patients was atrocious. What she remembers most of all, though, was an encounter with Moon in an elevator. She was telling Moon about a child with brain cancer to whom she had grown attached. His name was Mikey. He had fallen in a Wal-Mart store and was experiencing headaches so he was brought to the hospital. While they were doing the CT scan on him that identified his cancer, Rocky took his blood and she fell in love with him. She said he was too wise for his years. Rocky visited him frequently, bringing him pizza, coloring books, anything he wanted. When she met Moon in the elevator one day, she asked him, "Dr. Moon, isn't there anything we can do to save this baby? I love this baby. I want him to be okay." Moon's reply was "There's no money in the cure, there's only money in the treatment." "This is what made me leave the medical field," she said. "That shocked the shit out of me. It killed me. It made me leave. I couldn't handle that anymore."

9

Poor Patient Selection

Mike Skeen generally did not bring his work home. It was not his practice to discuss cases with his new wife, Roxanne. A slim, pretty woman with warm brown eyes and an easy smile, Roxanne was not a local girl, but she had been living in the Redding area for more than twenty years when she met Skeen. She had married Stephen Mansell, a lawyer in Redding, and moved there in 1992. Roxanne and Stephen had a daughter, Emily. But soon after Emily was born Mansell was killed in an airplane crash. In 2000, when Emily was six years old, friends introduced Roxanne to Mike. They were married April 13, 2002, in a house Roxanne and her brother had built together. It was a small wedding with friends and some bluegrass fiddlers.

Roxanne was not aware of any problems at Redding Medical Center in the summer of 2002 and knew little or nothing about Mike's investigation. Her first real awareness of possible problems involving the hospital was when Bob Simpson, the law partner of her late first husband, went for an angiogram there on July 25. Simpson, who had been graduated from the highly rated Boalt Hall School of Law at the University of California (Berkeley) and was considered to be one of the two leading trial lawyers in Redding, had felt his heart skip a beat during a bout of anxiety the day before and he wanted to check it out. He went to see a local physician named Randy Silver because his family doctor, Rich Malotky, was out of town. Silver did some tests, including an electrocardiogram. The EKG was slightly equivocal, showing T-wave inversions, a possible indication of heart disease. Although Silver did not think Simpson had any serious heart problems, Simpson requested a referral to Moon for an angiogram, anyway. Silver agreed to call, but he told Simpson he was only doing it because he was unfamiliar with Simpson's cardiac history. Simpson asked to see Moon because of his reputation in Redding as a world-class cardiologist and because of the formidable number of procedures he had done. The cath was scheduled for the next day.

When Moon, whom Simpson had met socially several times, came into the cath lab, he went to work immediately, injecting an anesthetic, inserting a sheath, and pushing the catheter through it. He then injected dye and viewed moving images of Simpson's arteries on the screen. Within seconds after the images began to appear, Moon, in his typically crude fashion, said, "Look at all this shit in there. I need to do the IVUS." Simpson thought he said "vivus," and didn't know what he was talking about. But "vivus" sounded like the Latin word for life to Simpson and he didn't like the sound of it. Then Moon inserted the IVUS catheter, threaded it up into Simpson's coronary arteries, and essentially repeated himself. "Look at this shit," he said, "look at this shit, this shit is really bad, you need bypass; four-way." Simpson asked, "What's the matter?" And Moon responded, "That was no anxiety attack, young man, you're about to have a heart attack," and walked out of the cath lab.

Moon went straight to the waiting room to speak to Simpson's wife, Michael, and said: "I'm going to admit him now. He needs to have bypass surgery." Michael asked him "When?" and Moon said, "Right now!" Moon showed her still pictures from the angiogram and said, "This is where the blockages are." Simpson was taken to a hospital room and was told that Moon had found a "widow-maker flap" in his right coronary artery and that he had several spiral dissections. It never occurred to Simpson that he should get a second opinion. He requested that Realyvasquez do the surgery because of his reputation. Moreover, a couple of years earlier Simpson's mother had had successful bypass surgery performed by Realyvasquez and Moon was her cardiologist. But he was told that Realyvasquez was out of town. Simpson elected to stay in the hospital and wait for him to return.

Meanwhile, Simpson's partner, Russ Reiner, had reached Malotky, Simpson's primary care doctor, who was in Las Vegas watching his son play basketball, and told him what was going on. Malotky called Michael at home and told her to be sure to get a second opinion. Malotky, who had had suspicions about Moon for some time, then called Simpson in the hospital and told him, "I'm not comfortable with those guys cutting on you. I know your heart! Get out of there!" Simpson answered, "Richard, that's easy for you to say, but I've just been told I'm having a heart attack or I'm going to have a heart attack and I can die if I leave. It's not so easy for me to say that." Malotky said, "At least get another opinion." Simpson agreed and Malotky called Roy Ditchey, who said he would review the film. Ditchey went to RMC, read the cath report, and viewed the angiographic and IVUS pictures. He saw no flap and no dissections and told Simpson, "Your arteries are better than normal. You have large arteries with a lot of flow." He also explained to Simpson that if his native artery, which had excellent blood flow, was bypassed, the bypass graft would collapse from lack of adequate flow. Simpson then showed Ditchey a still image that Moon had given him pointing to an area that Moon had said was a spiral dissection. Ditchey told him there was no dissection; the artery was normal. He also told Simpson he would have Bob Pick review the records.

Meanwhile two nurses hinted strongly that he should get out of the hospital. When one of them checked his heartbeat, she said, "Oh my God, it's great to hear a healthy heart like this. We don't hear heartbeats like this. You hear a lot of funny heartbeats, but it's good to hear that thump, thump, thump, thump." But Simpson, a trained litigator normally tuned in to the finest nuances of language, didn't get the obvious message she was trying to deliver. His anxiety level was too high.

That evening, Simpson was heavily sedated and fell into a deep sleep. When he woke in the morning at about 8:30, he was unusually groggy. Moon, who was standing by his bed, berated Simpson for getting a second opinion and told him that he had better have the surgery. Simpson's head was still full of cobwebs and he had to strain to follow what Moon was saying. He told Simpson that Ditchey didn't know what he was talking about and "those Mercy boys" were using fifty-year-old technology. He said IVUS was new and they didn't know how to read it. "Those boys at Mercy don't even know what it is. I don't care if you don't have the bypass. Do what you want. You are going to have a heart attack." Moon also told Simpson that he had studied under Dr. Yock at Stanford and Dr. Yock had invented IVUS. Simpson told Moon to calm down, and that while he wanted a second opinion, he hadn't ruled out surgery. Moon said, "Okay, it's your decision," shook Simpson's hand, and left for a vacation.

When Moon left the room, Simpson, for the moment, at least, thinking like a lawyer, told a nurse who had been there the whole time that if

Moon had studied with Yock, he would like Yock to review the films. The nurse left the room and returned shortly. She said she had phoned Stanford and that they had never heard of a Dr. Yock. Simpson, puzzled, asked the nurse to get a clarification from Moon. She left and returned again, this time to tell Simpson that Moon said Yock was a technician, not a doctor, and actually he had studied under a Dr. Fitzgerald. This sequence of events convinced Simpson he was being lied to. (In fact Paul Yock was a distinguished cardiologist and medical entrepreneur on the Stanford faculty who once served as acting chief of cardiology.) Simpson then called Kacie Carroll, who had left RMC and was now working as a legal nurse on the law firm's staff. He asked her to get his records to Fitzgerald at Stanford for a second opinion as quickly as possible.

At about 10:30 that morning, at Ditchey's request, Bob Pick went to see Simpson and told him that he had reviewed the cath report and films. Pick, who had seen minor irregularities in Simpson's arteries, but no obstructive coronary disease or dissections, told him, "You don't need bypass surgery or angioplasty. You need to go home. There is nothing wrong with you." "This is all unnecessary?" Simpson asked, to which Pick replied, "Take your film to Stanford or UCSF and I'll guarantee you that ten out of ten cardiologists will tell you the same thing." Simpson, at that moment thinking more like a patient than a lawyer, asked Pick, "What can I do?" to which Pick responded, "You have the power to bring this to an end." Despite this obvious appeal to his professional qualifications, Simpson, who is normally a combative and aggressive lawyer, did not snap out of patient mode. He said nothing, but thought to himself, "I know exactly what you mean, but that's your fight, buddy, not mine. I just want to get out of here."

In fact, though, Simpson was still not so sure what he wanted. Instead of asking to leave the hospital, he asked a nurse to tell Realyvasquez, who had returned, that he would like to speak to him. He still hadn't entirely ruled out surgery. A short time later a nurse named Sue came to Simpson's room and told him that Realyvasquez did not want to involve himself directly in Simpson's case because there were already too many doctors involved. Sue explained to Simpson the risks associated with the "flap," or dissection, that Moon told Simpson he had in his right coronary artery. She also told Simpson that Realyvasquez had reviewed the film and agreed with Moon that Simpson should have the surgery. Simpson asked whether Realyvasquez had read the IVUS, but Sue told him that was Moon's job. Simpson was not satisfied and told Sue he still wanted to see Realyvasquez.

While all this was going on, Suzanne Ramsden, Simpson's paralegal, called her friend Roxanne Skeen to tell her that Bob was in the hospital and needed quadruple-bypass surgery. Roxanne told this to her husband, who was in the room. "Who's Bob's doctor?" he asked. Ramsden said, "Moon." Roxanne relayed that to Skeen, noticing that he stiffened and seemed upset. As soon as Roxanne hung up, Mike told her, "There's a problem going on with this doctor." It was the first she'd heard anything about it. Although she found the news troubling, like many other people, she did not want to jump to conclusions. She had never heard anything else bad about Moon. Skeen then called Ramsden back and said: "Hey, I can't say anything, but call Bob and tell him he needs to get a second opinion. Tell him to be very careful what he's doing there; there are problems there that I'm looking at." Meanwhile, Carroll had reached Fitzgerald and he had agreed to review the films.

Later that day, unexpectedly, Realyvasquez came to see Simpson. This was not something he had been eager to do, but his associate Maja Sandberg, a vascular surgeon who knew Simpson socially, had heard that he was in the hospital and asked Realyvasquez to visit him as a courtesy. He walked into the room without knocking and asked brusquely, "You want to talk to me?" Simpson could see that he was irritated. He said, "Yes," and getting straight to the point, asked him to explain why he needed bypass surgery. Realyvasquez showed him an X-ray still picture, pointed to an artery on the left side of the heart without identifying it, and said, "This is a significant lesion." Simpson then asked about his right coronary artery, which was where Moon had told him he had a dissection. Realyvasquez said he could not bypass it because there was too much blood flow. However, he told Simpson he would have problems there someday because the vessel was diseased. "Look at that," he said, "it's all lumpy. I guarantee you that if we opened that artery it would be like toothpaste in there."

Simpson was puzzled by Realyvasquez's comment and didn't respond directly. Instead, he told Realyvasquez that the artery on the left side of the heart to which he had pointed looked like it had good flow, too. Simpson asked how good blood flow would be maintained in the bypass graft if there was still good flow in the supposedly blocked artery. Realyvasquez seemed surprised and said, "That's a very sophisticated question. Where did you get that?" Simpson told Realyvasquez he was a personal injury lawyer and he had a registered nurse on his staff. Realyvasquez retorted that in this instance his profession was a drawback, not an advantage. He said, "If you were a farmer you would have already had this surgery and would be out tending your cows."

But Simpson was not easily put off. He pressed Realyvasquez again about the risk of competitive blood flow in his native artery and the graft. He asked whether the graft wouldn't collapse because of lack of adequate flow. Realyvasquez, now obviously angry, said, "Then I'll use a vein. Veins are stupid. They don't care what the flow is." Simpson, who didn't understand what Realyvasquez was talking about, took the still image and asked Realyvasquez to show him again where the blockage was. Realyvasquez pointed to a diagonal branch of the left anterior descending coronary artery and said, "Here, you have a significant lesion and blockage." He then pointed to the right coronary artery and said, "Someday you will need bypass surgery on the right side, too." Simpson asked, "You can't do that now?" to which Realyvasquez replied, "No, not now, someday." Realyvasquez then left the room without saying another word.

Simpson tried to reconcile the different diagnoses he had heard from Moon and Realyvasquez, but he couldn't. Moon had told him loudly and clearly that his chief source of danger was a spiral dissection in his right coronary artery and without immediate bypass surgery he would die of a heart attack. And Realyvasquez had just told him that he needed immediate bypass surgery because of a serious lesion in a diagonal branch of his left anterior descending coronary artery. Realyvasquez specifically told Simpson that although one day he *would* need bypass surgery in his right coronary system he did not need it yet. What was he to make of that?

The answer came, as far as Simpson was concerned, when Kacie Carroll called and delivered this message from Peter Fitzgerald: "I don't see anything beyond his needing to check out and go home and take an aspirin. Some doctors see facts and some doctors see artifacts. All I'm seeing is artifact on the IVUS. I'm not seeing anything that looks like a lesion that needs revascularization. I certainly do not see a widow-maker. He needs to check out of the hospital." When Carroll passed on this opinion to Simpson, he followed Fitzgerald's advice. He went home to his big new house in the hills west of Redding, with its panoramic view of

Mount Shasta, Mount Burney, and Mount Lassen, to Michael, their daughter, Jenna, and son, Tony, and to their three golden retrievers. Meanwhile, without telling Simpson until after the fact, Rich Malotky reported the case to the state medical board, saying, "Although I am not a cardiologist, I am not an idiot either, and I could drive a Mack truck down Bob Simpson's coronary arteries."[16]

A few days later, during the first week in August, Mike Skeen came to the house to interview Bob Simpson. The two men talked in Simpson's bedroom. The lawyer, with his taut, broad face, intense brown eyes, and receding hairline, looked controlled and alert. But he was still not himself. His manner was still somewhat tentative; he was having difficulty calculating the magnitude of what had been done to him. Simpson, normally tough-minded and analytical, wasn't sure what the criminal part of it might be, if indeed there was one. The possibility that his case was not anomalous—that Moon and Realyvasquez were systematically doing angiograms and bypass operations on healthy people with no indications that they needed these procedures—never even entered his mind. He knew there was such a thing as clinical judgment. He was a personal injury lawyer, after all, and was sophisticated about medicine. He understood that doctors often disagreed about diagnoses and, even more frequently, about the appropriate treatment. But unnecessary surgery for profit? That simply did not compute, not in Redding, not with these doctors. He told Skeen, "I know Chae Moon; he may be an egotist, he may be a lot of things, but he's not a crook. He's got a God complex." Skeen, whose clean-cut, all-American face is free of artifice, but gives away nothing, and who had already interviewed Corapi, Campbell, Ditchey, and Pick, among others, said in his cool, flat, understated way, "You are certainly a lot nicer to him than I could possibly be."

Coincidentally, Simpson's wife, Michael, began playing golf with Moon's wife, Sun, around this time. They also were working together planning a Christmas party for their children's school. Michael did not discuss Bob's treatment with Sun Moon, nor did she know if Mrs. Moon even knew about it. But she did think about the fact that her first husband, Dino Jeantet, had been diagnosed by Moon and had undergone valve surgery. It made her wonder. And in mid-October, the Simpsons met the Moons at a cocktail party at the home of mutual friends. Bob Simpson wanted to reassure Moon that he was not going to make anything of the situation that had developed between them. He wanted to

do it in a lighthearted way, so he repeated to Moon a funny, slightly rib-
ald story his wife Michael had told him about playing golf with Moon's
wife, Sun. Moon dissolved into laughter and Simpson figured he had
accomplished his mission.

During this period, because he was busy and alone in the office, additional agents from Sacramento came up to Redding periodically to help
Mike Skeen, and he would invite them home for dinner. The Skeen's
mustard-colored frame house, which sits at the bottom of a winding
country road on five rolling acres dotted with scrub oaks, is made for
entertaining. In back there is a wooden deck with a hot tub and below
that a kidney-shaped pool, which, Skeen said dryly, is mainly for their
Rottweiler puppy, Gretchen. The single-story house has a state-of-the-
art kitchen with a green granite-topped island and an old butcher block
built into one corner. The kitchen is open to the living room so that Roxanne can cook and join in the conversation. But the agents, men and
occasional women, who came to Redding to assist Skeen, rarely talked
business, so Roxanne's knowledge of the investigation remained limited.
They liked to talk to Emily, a bright, freckle-faced eight-year-old who
read incessantly. Although Roxanne understood that the RMC case was
potentially a big one, she did not differentiate it from other big cases
that Skeen was working on at that time, such as the killing of a Red Bluff
police officer. As far as her husband's safety was concerned, at least in
the beginning, she wasn't worried. The RMC case was not like the one
involving a man who was embezzling millions of dollars from the Trinity Lumber Company. When they had trick-or-treated at his house with
Emily, they had seen a gun leaning against a wall near the door. This was
the sort of thing that Roxanne worried about.

It was only when the results of the interviews conducted by Skeen
and his FBI colleagues began to come in that Roxanne realized that this
case might be unusual. She found the bits and pieces she was hearing
about cutting open healthy people unsettling, even scary, and began to
wonder how it could have been going on without doctors or nurses turning in the culprits. What she was unaware of at the time, or at least failed
to take account of, was the pervasive, self-protective culture of medicine. Nurses, with rare exceptions, had been acculturated not to question
the clinical judgment of doctors, and doctors, like other professionals
but even more so, had been acculturated not to rat on their colleagues.

Moreover, doctors, for a variety of reasons, some having to do with their almost religious deference to an individual practitioner's professional autonomy, had never developed effective methods of identifying legal and ethical breaches and weeding out the perpetrators. There were signs that these behavior patterns were changing, but change comes slowly, especially in relatively isolated places like Redding.

Roxanne couldn't talk to anyone about her concerns or for that matter anything related to the situation because of the ongoing investigation. But she would have kept what she knew to herself anyway, because as many as 80 percent of the Skeens' neighbors were doctors. "The hills are covered with them," she said, "right here; dentists and doctors. . . . I didn't know where this was going and it just didn't seem like a good discussion to be having with anybody." Roxanne was concerned that it would create a problem for Emily in school. In any event, although they were neighborly, Roxanne and Mike had not become friends with any of their doctor neighbors. Another reason she would not have discussed the investigation was that even though she'd only been married to Mike a short time she had already grasped that because other people did not have access to the same information he did they might easily misunderstand what had happened.

Early in August of 2002, Mike Skeen was still a long way from having all the information he needed to deliver a thoroughly persuasive affidavit to McGregor Scott, the former Shasta County district attorney who was now the U.S. attorney in Sacramento. While Skeen's affidavit could eventually lead to the impaneling of a grand jury and, if the grand jury indicted anyone, to criminal trials, its immediate purpose was to get a judge serving on the U.S. District Court for the Eastern District of California to issue a search warrant. With this in mind, Skeen quietly continued his investigation.

By late August, around the time Skeen sent a first draft of his search-warrant affidavit to the U.S. attorney, John Corapi and Joe Zerga were checking in with him regularly and were frustrated with what they perceived as a lack of progress. Skeen told them that his office was very shorthanded and he was bogged down in preparations for the anniversary of 9/11. Corapi liked Skeen, but he was never quite sure whether he was just good at putting people off or if he was actually getting something done. He told Skeen that he and Zerga were concerned that nothing would happen and people were going to fall through the cracks and die. In fact, during this time Skeen felt enormous pressure to finish his work because CW1 kept calling to tell him things like "There are five more who got it who didn't need it. When are you guys going to do something?" In the end the affidavit included data on thirty-four specific cases of unnecessary heart procedures, all of which were provided by local physicians. Skeen found it maddening that he couldn't shut down Moon, Realyvasquez, and their associates instantly. He was also worried that there might be a computer crash that would destroy the angiograms, the government's most critical evidence. Between continuing to pursue the investigation and working with assistant U.S. attorneys to get the affidavit in final shape, he was getting very little sleep.

Corapi and Zerga were also frustrated in their search for a personal injury lawyer to represent them. Because California has a $250,000 cap on noneconomic damages in malpractice suits, which is what the lawyers they spoke to thought theirs was, they could not find anyone who would take their case. Corapi discussed the possibility of representation with his intellectual property lawyer in Sacramento, John Costello. Costello had a lawyer in his firm review the case, but they decided not to take it. Corapi also checked law firms on the Internet through the Martindale-Hubbell website, which provides a nationwide directory of lawyers. Finally, when after several more rejections a New York law firm that specializes in whistle-blower suits refused to take their case, Zerga talked to Danny Marks, a Las Vegas lawyer he had previously retained.

Marks agreed to take the case, but he said he would have to hire local counsel because he was not licensed to practice law in California. Corapi flew to Las Vegas, met Marks, and signed a retainer agreement. He also asked Costello if he knew anyone in Redding. He recommended a personal injury lawyer named Dugan Barr, a graduate of Reed College and the University of Chicago Law School, and Marks agreed that they should retain him. Tamra had heard of Barr and told Corapi that their travel agent did not like him. This rang a bell with Corapi, who remembered that this was because Barr was the house liberal on a local radio program on which he held daily mini-debates on social and political issues like abortion and teenage pregnancy with a conservative psychologist. Although Corapi is deeply conservative socially and politically, he didn't think his lawyer needed to be.

Marks called Barr and told him that his client had undergone an unnecessary heart procedure. He specified that this was a fraud case, not a malpractice case. Barr told Marks that he would be happy to help out if he could. Marks then arranged for Corapi to see Barr at his office on Court Street in Redding. Before Corapi came in, Barr discussed his case with his secretary/office manager, Sarah Dickerson, who asked, "To whom are you going to refer him?" The reason for her question was that Barr, like other Redding personal-injury lawyers, rarely accepted cases involving local physicians because they frequently relied on their expert testimony. But this time Barr told her that he wasn't going to refer the case to anyone else because he had been hearing about problems at Redding Medical Center for a long time and he wanted to look into it himself. At around the same time, Skeen told Corapi and Zerga that he had completed the first stage of his investigation and had turned over the results to Scott in Sacramento. He said the case was big, although it seems unlikely he knew at the time how big, and that they needed additional resources to complete the investigation.

Corapi arrived at Barr's office, in a small, two-story, cream-colored, more or less Spanish colonial style building, around four in the afternoon on October 1. Barr, a mountainous, pink-cheeked, gray-bearded man given to colorful and occasionally profane expressive outbursts, was not aware that the potential client coming to call was a Roman Catholic priest. And Corapi did not announce himself as such in manner or dress. He was wearing slacks, a dark shirt, and a sport coat. He brought with him a VHS tape that had his IVUS on it and a compact disc with his angiogram. He also brought Moon's report and a report from one or possibly two of the doctors he had seen in Las Vegas. Corapi told Barr about the case precisely and succinctly and Barr said, "Well, I've been waiting for this case all my life. It's a standing joke around here, 'Don't get a flat tire in front of Redding Medical Center or you'll end up with a triple bypass.'"

Because Barr had been practicing law in Redding for thirty-five years, what Corapi told him rang true. He'd heard all the rumors and black jokes that had been circulating in Redding's legal and medical circles. Barr discussed the matter with Corapi and told him that he needed some time to get an independent evaluation of his medical records. As they approached the cocktail hour, Corapi told Barr that he was a priest and he told him about his television appearances on EWTN, adding that he sometimes had difficulty walking through airports because so many people recognized him. Corapi also had Mike Skeen's card with him. This was how Barr learned that there was an FBI investigation underway. When the office staff went home at five o'clock, the two men relaxed, had a drink together, and talked some more. Corapi left the office thinking, "Dugan seems hopeful, but not convinced."

The next day, Barr called Mike Skeen to confirm that the FBI was actually conducting an investigation. During this conversation Barr asked Skeen "if filing a lawsuit would cause him any heartburn?" According to Barr, Skeen asked him politely but clearly not to do that. Skeen maintained that he never made direct requests of that sort, but did not disagree that anything as public as filing a suit might have endangered the investigation. In any event, because there was no statute of limitations problem and Corapi did not object, Barr agreed not to file suit until Skeen said it was okay. A few days later, Barr took the compact disc with Corapi's angiogram and the tape of the IVUS to Eugene Moffitt, a cardiologist in Chico to whom he had been introduced by a mutual friend. He showed Moffitt the angiogram and the cardiologist asked, 'How old is this man?" to which Barr replied, "Fifty-five years old." Moffitt said, "He has remarkably good coronary arteries for a man his age." Barr then showed him Moon's report and Moffitt asked, "Is this the same man?" Barr also showed him the video of the intravascular ultrasound. Moffitt said he could not read it as an expert, but looking at it, he did not see any indication that the patient needed surgery.

Before going to Chico, Barr had discussed the case briefly with Doug Mudford, a quiet, gentle associate in his firm, who had come to northern California as a child from Texarkana, Arkansas, and who hadn't entered law school until he was forty-two years old. Unlike Barr, he wasn't well known in town as a litigator. Mudford opposed taking the case for the same reason Sarah Dickerson expected Barr to reject it. Both men had discussed their problem with doctor friends in town and both received mixed reactions. Some were impressed by Moon's and Realyvasquez's low mortality and morbidity rates and others said that if you operate on enough healthy people you are bound to get great numbers.

Mudford's wife, Cherry, had a family history of heart disease and had been sent to Moon by her primary care physician in 1993. Moon did an angiogram, diagnosed two blockages, and put her on medication. Cherry Mudford was working in the medical library at Mercy Hospital in 1996 when Charles Kenneth Brown died after Moon abandoned him in an unstable condition. But Moon's reputation was so good and

RMC's advertising so persuasive that she did not leave him for another cardiologist. When Mudford told his wife about the possibility of taking on Corapi as a client, she was upset and asked, "What are you going to do, sue my doctor?" But once Moffitt told him that Corapi's arteries were clean, Barr's mind was made up.

After Barr returned from Chico, he and Mudford went for breakfast at Corbett's, at the corner of Butte and Pine streets, not far from their office. "It's time to make a decision on this," Barr told Mudford. "It's either all in or all out. Once we start it's going to be very difficult." For about half an hour Mudford raised all the objections he could think of to taking the cases and it became clear to him during this time that Barr was adamant that these were fraud cases, not malpractice cases. Mudford still had a hard time believing that, but if that really was so, it was worth taking a look at.

Mudford, like Skeen, was impressed with the fact that Corapi was a Catholic priest because he thought that juries would find him credible. And he was also pleased that they had asked an independent reviewer to evaluate Corapi's records. Nevertheless, he remained skeptical and he said that other lawyers he talked to were not nearly as sure as Barr was that it was a good idea to proceed with fraud cases. In the end, however, Mudford gave in because he couldn't think of a rational reason why surgery would be recommended to somebody who had a clean angiogram. It was also at about that time that Mudford told Barr that Bob Simpson, whom they both knew well, had narrowly escaped having unnecessary bypass surgery. Simpson's wife, Michael, had called Mudford's house to let Doug and Cherry know that Simpson was in the hospital.

After his first visit, Corapi went to see Barr at the beginning of each week. He was usually out of town lecturing Thursday through Sunday. At their second meeting, Corapi brought copies of his lectures and sermons at Barr's request because Barr wanted to see whom he was dealing with. "I didn't want to get into this thing and find out that under the guise of a Catholic priest he was preaching anarchy or something like that," Barr said. Although there were many issues on which Barr found he did not agree with Corapi, he did not think he was a nut case. Indeed, despite their radically different worldviews the two men came to like each other. They looked forward to their drinks and conversations at the end of the day, during which they gave religion a wide berth. If the conservative priest had elected to press the nonpracticing Protestant about his faith during one of those discussions he probably would have gotten a quasi-philosophical, theologically ambiguous answer something like this:

> If one spends a clear night up in the mountains away from artificial light and smog, it is pretty hard to believe that what you see when you look up happened by accident. At the same time, if there is a creator, it is hard to believe that he/she/it is all that concerned about a third-rate planet in the corner of a fifth-rate galaxy in a back street of the universe.

On a more practical level, the idea to file a whistle-blower suit as well as a fraud suit on Corapi's behalf was planted by Barr. During one of their weekly meetings in October 2002, very likely over a glass of Jack Daniel's Black Label at the end of the day, Barr suggested to Corapi—and afterwards to Joe Zerga's Las Vegas lawyer, Danny Marks—that it would make sense to file a qui tam lawsuit. Barr's introduction to whistle-blower actions had come five or six years earlier when a woman arrived at his office with a potential suit. He ended up not representing her, but he learned a lot about suing under the provisions of the False Claims Act.

Later Barr became aware of a section in the California insurance code that allowed citizens to file a similar type of action in fraud cases involving private insurance companies, recover damages on behalf of the state, and collect a reward. Barr had learned about this provision from a friend of a friend in San Diego who worked in the insurance commissioner's office. The relevant section of the code was under a title that had nothing to do with insurance fraud and was so obscure that virtually no one knew it existed. By the time Corapi came to see him, Barr, who had not forgotten about this provision, could not recall where in the code the relevant section was and had to call his friend's friend to find it. When he did he concluded that it applied to Corapi, who was insured by Blue Shield. Corapi and Zerga decided to pursue this potentially rich reward, too. As it turned out, the state of California declined to join them, which meant they would have to bear the substantial financial burden of bringing the litigation, but, if successful, they would get a bigger award.

10

The Raid

Throughout the afternoon of October 29, 2002, forty-two neatly dressed men and women filtered into Redding. About half of them checked into the Oxford Suites motel at the corner of Hilltop Drive and Mistletoe Lane, just down Hilltop from Logan's Roadhouse and a short walk to the FBI office at the corner of Mistletoe and Churn Creek Road. Many of the motel's regular clients were government employees who typically arrived in large groups, so the staff hardly noticed. The other out-of-towners had split up and taken accommodations elsewhere. They settled in and then, at about quarter to five, drove across the Sacramento River to the Redding Police Department's investigation center on California Street, a second-floor complex in the old downtown shopping mall that housed about a dozen offices for investigators, sergeants, and clerical staff. A day or two before when Mike Skeen requested the use of the facility and advised the local police why it was needed, the uniform reaction was disbelief. The Redding police chief, Bob Blankenship, who ordinarily would have been there, recused himself from the meeting because his wife, Jean, worked as an administrator at the hospital. If there were to be any leak of information he didn't want it to taint him. This kind of conflict was not uncommon in Redding, a small city with relatively few professional and administrative jobs, a substantial portion of which were provided by the two big hospitals.

The meeting was held in the center's briefing room, a nondescript space of perhaps a thousand square feet. Most of the agents sat at a rectangle of folding tables in the center of the room. The others stood behind them. Mike Skeen was in charge, but in compliance with FBI practice a high-ranking supervisor and a media specialist were also there. John Pikus, deputy chief of the FBI in Sacramento, was representing Mike

Mason, special agent in charge of the one-hundred-agent office, who was out of town. Bureau lawyers, an elite coterie within the elite agency, were standing by a telephone call away. Their practice was to talk only to the highest-ranking person on the scene. Two local Internal Revenue Service agents and one local agent from the Federal Drug Enforcement Agency were also present. This was not because there were concerns about tax or drug violations related to the investigation, but rather because resident law-enforcement agents help out their counterparts whenever they need extra manpower. There were also several agents from the Department of Health and Human Services who specialized in Medicare fraud, perhaps half a dozen support staff to help process evidence, and two or three FBI computer specialists.

Skeen conducted the briefing. He had done this sort of thing before, but always on a smaller scale. He explained the operation, which was formally referred to as the execution of a search warrant. Everyone there was familiar with it in general terms. A small group led by Skeen, search warrant in hand, would go to the CEO's office at RMC and explain to Hal Chilton what was happening and why. Other groups would go to the sites at which documents were kept—the hospital, Moon's and Realyvasquez's office suites, 100 and 220 respectively, across the parking lot at 1555 East Street, and in a building known as the Multiplex Information Service at 1627 Beltline Road—and secure all documents relating to the doctors' practices. The computer specialists would be detailed to make copies of electronic records. The evidence would then be carried away and analyzed. There were a few questions and the meeting broke up. It was not a routine assignment, but neither was it a particularly dangerous one. The agents knew what was expected of them and spirits on the whole were high.

Not long afterwards the group reconvened at the Skeens. Mike was eager to show his appreciation for the help he was getting, so he and Roxanne had invited the agents for burgers and beer. The gathering was relaxed, with people wandering in and out of the house, onto the deck and down by the pool. All but four or five of the agents were men, but one of the women had spent weeks in Redding helping Mike run the office during the investigation and Roxanne was particularly fond of her and glad to see her again. The agents stayed at the house for a couple of hours enjoying the food and drink and then, because they had a big day coming up, returned to their motels.

At 5:00 a.m. on October 30, John Corapi's phone rang. Corapi, an early riser, was already awake. It was an FBI agent who said his name was John. He apologized for calling so early and said, "I thought you would like to know we're about to go in." He asked Corapi a couple of questions and before hanging up, said, "Pray for a fruitful harvest, Father."

At 8:00 a.m., seven team leaders—one for each designated search site—met in Skeen's cramped office for last-minute instructions. The teams' other members headed for preplanned staging areas. At 9:00 a.m., exactly on schedule, the team members went to the seven sites where Skeen had told them records were kept. Each leader found the supervisor, explained why they were there, requested cooperation, and then waited for further instructions. At the same time, Skeen, Pikus, and agents from the inspector general's office at the Department of Health and Human Services, entered Hal Chilton's outer office and told his secretary why they were there. They were immediately admitted to the inner office, where they showed Chilton the search warrant and told him where the teams were deployed. They also said that they wanted to conduct their search as unobtrusively as possible and with minimal disruption to hospital routine.

At 9:05, using a speakerphone, Chilton placed a call to Tenet's general counsel in Santa Barbara, Christi Sulzbach, who asked a few questions and then told Chilton that Tenet would cooperate with the investigation. Skeen concluded from the conversation that Sulzbach was completely taken by surprise.* Chilton passed the word on to his supervisors and Skeen to his team leaders.

According to Skeen, all of the agents were dressed in business suits. However, a male nurse who was in the hospital at the time remembered seeing an agent in a "blue raid jacket" with FBI emblazoned on its back in large yellow letters. The agents were armed, but according to their instructions no weapons were to be displayed. The same nurse remembered seeing a holstered weapon under one agent's pulled-back suit coat. Although the agents were businesslike and did their best not to disturb patients, the raid, as it became instantly known in Redding, caused a

---

*His confidence that the operation was totally unexpected would increase when a Tenet lawyer arrived in Redding the next day and seemed less well prepared than he would have been with advance notice.

shock wave, first in the hospital and then, as word got out, all over the city. Dozens of boxes of paper records and hundreds of discs and VHS tapes with IVUS and echocardiogram images were being loaded into a panel truck from the seven initially identified sites and two more that were discovered during the day. The records were not only for Moon's and Realyvasquez's patients, but also for those of their practice associates. For Moon, these were Thomas Russ, Walter Fletscher, and B.V. Chandramouli. For Realyvasquez, they were Kent Brusett, a young surgeon who had been with the practice only about a year, and Moreno-Cabral and Kevin Miller, both of whom had left Redding for jobs elsewhere. This task was completed by early evening.

Meanwhile, the computer specialists were running into problems. The single most important type of record the agents were after was angiographic images, actual pictures of patients' arteries that would provide gold-standard evidence of the presence or absence of life-threatening blockages. Some of the film was in videocassette form and therefore easy to copy. But most of it was in digital form, stored in the jukebox-like machine. Within half an hour of the beginning of the raid, Skeen received a disturbing text message from the computer specialists. They were going to have to make individual copies of every angiogram in the machine. Short of hauling the machine away, which would have made the vital records unavailable to medical staff, the specialists would have to copy about 1,600 CDs one by one on-site. Skeen had told his experts that the machine stored the angiograms on DVDs, but he did not know that they would not be able to hook up a cable to the machine and download data electronically. Nor did he know that each DVD had bits and pieces of angiograms on it, not complete angiograms for any one individual. Only the computer that had written the data could extract them. Skeen had believed all along that the computer experts would be able to extract the information from the machine in a day without significant impact on patient care. Instead, it was going to take a week, a problem because if the agents left the premises they would need to get a new search warrant to return.

Shortly thereafter, the FBI asked the hospital to search its electronic files to locate all of Moon's patients who had undergone an angiogram between July 1, 2001, and August 30, 2002. The list was 1,600 names long. There were only two angiographic viewing stations in the hospital, one in the cath lab and the other in the cardiology area. It took three to five minutes to produce each new disc. The computer specialists worked around the clock. From time to time agents complained that hospital employees were bothering them, but when asked the administration put a stop to it. During the first five days, the FBI maintained a command post in a trailer parked outside the hospital to support the men working inside. But they removed it after small crowds began to gather, the atmosphere turned hostile, and it looked like there might be the threat of a confrontation between supporters of the doctors and the federal agents. Skeen, who knew Lon Horiuchi, the FBI sniper who had killed the white separatist Randy Weaver's wife during the violent Ruby Ridge standoff in Idaho in August 1992, was eager to avoid anything remotely like that.

It was not surprising that after the FBI raided the hospital and Moon's and Realyvasquez's offices, only a small fraction of the local population, including the rest of the doctors, believed that two of their city's most respected and prestigious physicians had done anything wrong. In the fall of 2002, few in Redding questioned their skill, commitment, or ethics. Everyone knew that both of them could be a bit abrasive—Moon perhaps more than a bit—but if this was part of the price to be paid for the best care, almost everyone in RMC's orbit agreed that it was well worth it. That these physicians had subjected patients to hundreds of unnecessary invasive procedures, including sawing open their chests to do coronary bypass and heart valve operations, beggared the imagination.

A lot of people in Redding saw the raid as still another example of an arrogant, overreaching federal government involving itself in the affairs of a local community that it knew nothing about and where it had no business. The most popular theory was that Washington was using the doctors to get at Tenet because the company was costing the Medicare and Medicaid programs too much money. No one in and around Redding seemed to know a whole lot about Tenet and its troubled corporate history. They did know, however, that it was a powerful bottom-line-oriented corporation and they had no trouble believing that its charges were too high. Wall Street, on the other hand, had been deeply involved in a love affair with the corporation that was fueled by its aggressive pricing strategies. On October 31, the breakup came swiftly and unsentimentally. Tenet's stock price dropped by almost half. Trading was stopped at the company's request.

On November 1, just two days after the raid, more than one hundred Redding citizens, many of whom were hospital employees, gathered in the cold on East Street at a candlelight rally. Some carried a large banner that said: "We Support Our Doctors." Moon came out of his office and Realyvasquez drove by. Sheryl Hallstrom, who worked as closely as any other nurse with the two doctors, led the group in "We Shall Overcome." A second rally was held in the downtown mall two weeks later. This time about two hundred people attended. Some wore T-shirts emblazoned with the slogan "Dr. Moon Mends Broken Hearts" and others carried signs bearing messages such as "When Is It Illegal to Save Lives?" Neither doctor made an appearance. Meanwhile, with the help of a public relations consultant named Brandon Edwards the hospital geared up to defend its reputation. Among other things, Edwards helped organize sympathetic community members into an organization called Friends of RMC with an initial mailing of five thousand and drafted model letters in support of the doctors to be sent to area newspapers.

Soon after the raid CW1, who was seen as a turncoat by a number of the loyalist nurses, followed the advice of some of her colleagues at the hospital and went to see Realyvasquez. She told him that she was not the one who had turned him in, which was technically true because she did not talk to Skeen until his investigation was underway. She said he started crying and she thought that he really felt bad about what he had done. Later CW1 heard from a friend whose husband plays golf with Moon that he was unrepentant, even defiant. Her friend told her that Moon thought he had done nothing wrong and had been "screwed over by Pick, Ditchey, and the RMC lawyers," but that the community believed in him and when this was all over "he would return to practice."

Hallstrom, rejecting the idea of collusion between the two doctors, wrote in a letter that Moon posted on his website shortly after the raid that she'd seen the cardiologist and Realyvasquez disagree over whether a patient needed surgery. She also wrote that she had never seen Moon pressure a patient into having a procedure. Eight area physicians, including Bruce Kittrick, Pat Campbell's partner, also wrote testimonial letters that Moon posted on his website. Kittrick wrote, "In my opinion, Dr. Moon is unparalleled in the catheter lab and the best cardiologist I know of at rescuing a patient from 'the brink of death.'" They all testified to Moon's competence, his integrity, his dedication to his patients and his profession, his extraordinary work ethic, and an unwillingness to believe that either Moon or Realyvasquez would collude to do unnecessary surgery for any sort of gain.

Ken Murray, a local radio commentator and political figure with strong anti–federal government leanings took to opening his program with the phrase "Welcome to Waco" and said on the air that the doctors were saviors. And a Redding lawyer named Jeffrey Jens, whose father had been treated by Moon and Realyvasquez, made supportive comments about Moon in the *Record Searchlight* and told the *California Lawyer* magazine that "They've taken the best doctor that I have ever come across and ruined his reputation."

11

Bad Outcomes

A few days after the raid, phones began ringing off the hook at Dugan Barr's law firm. Barr wasn't ready for them even though he had received a call from John Corapi letting him know that federal agents had entered the hospital and the other search sites. Barr had been surprised. It had never occurred to him that the government would act so dramatically. It had also made him feel better about the prospects for getting to the bottom of what for a decade had been for him the source of a vague, but troubling uneasiness. At first Barr and Mudford took all the calls themselves. They had already discussed the likelihood that once the FBI investigation became public knowledge they would hear from a few more potential clients who believed they might have been unnecessarily subjected to heart surgery. But they were not prepared for the onslaught that followed. As the volume of callers mounted, office staff members began taking names and numbers so that the two lawyers could return the calls.

Scores of calls came in. Paul Barth, the moderator of Barr's radio debates, volunteered to help out by answering media inquiries. The *San Francisco Chronicle*, the *Sacramento Bee*, the *Los Angeles Times*, the *New York Times*, an Australian medical paper, broadcast networks, the *Wall Street Journal*, all called. The lawyers were at the office from seven in the morning until six-thirty or seven at night and continued working after dinner at home. They had fifteen people assisting them, several of whom had been hired just to help handle the incoming phone traffic. The office logged a couple of hundred calls in the first week. Barr quickly developed a form so that the potential clients who called could be questioned systematically. He decided that either he or Mudford would interview every potential client.

The FBI raid was widely publicized, which meant among other things that the Redding lawyers were going to have to compete for clients with firms from out of the city and even out of state. Display ads for personal injury lawyers began appearing in the *Record Searchlight* on November 6 with headlines like "Unnecessary Heart Surgery?" and "Urgent News for Redding Medical Center Heart Surgery Patients." A firm from Arizona signed up a substantial number of clients and ended up negotiating an agreement with Reiner, Simpson to represent them. And a firm named Gillen, Jacobsen, Ellis and Larsen based in Orinda in the East Bay opened a small office in Redding almost immediately. Luke Ellis had read about the raid in the *San Francisco Chronicle* and at first found it hard to believe that the FBI would raid a hospital. The firm's ad offered a free consultation with one of the partners, Jim Larsen, at 1650 Oregon Street. The firm ended up representing 186 clients.

Meanwhile, Barr and Mudford were working seven days a week and doing interviews every thirty minutes. Mudford was struck by the consistency of the stories they were hearing from potential clients. Moon would do a cath and tell the patient that she needed emergency bypass surgery or she would die. "One after the other they were being threatened with death," he thought to himself. Many of the people who came in had gone to the hospital for other reasons, a hernia for example, in the case of Glen Aldridge, who ended up with a cath and a stent he didn't need. They were mostly Medicare patients and they were very emotional. It seemed to Mudford that some of them were almost in shock.

Neither Barr nor Mudford had ever handled a case anything like this one before and were forced to make it up as they went along. They knew they would have to get the medical records for each patient they might eventually represent, a number that could end up in the hundreds. Because the volume threatened to become overwhelming, Mudford volunteered to manage all of the RMC cases, leaving Barr free to try to keep up with the rest of their practice. Barr decided on the spot that if Mudford were willing to make this kind of effort he deserved a piece of the action. He told Mudford he was going to make him his partner and asked him to call a "sign painter" to change the shingle outside from Dugan Barr & Associates to Barr & Mudford, LLP.

While he was delighted to make partner, it quickly became clear to Mudford, who had never run a business of his own, that he would not only share in the profits, but also in the risk. Barr explained in a matter-of-fact sort of way, perhaps just a little overstated for emphasis, that "The kind of practice that we have may be the last bastion of venture-capital enterprise in the world today. We put our money on the line and if it doesn't work out we lose it and if it does we make money. In this business you don't get a big charge out of going to Reno or Las Vegas because we have enough money on the line inside these walls."

At about that time, a lawyer named Dave Case, who used to be Barr's associate, turned up and said, "I heard you might be able to use some help." They hired him and put him to work immediately on non-RMC cases. Barr's son Ben, who worked as an office manager in Barr's brother's law firm in San Francisco when he was not singing at the San Francisco Opera, came up to Redding to help them get data into the computers. It took about two hours to set up each case file, and between November 1 and January 1 they entered five hundred cases. And they had to find highly credible experts willing to work for the plaintiffs. Barr had been involved in an earlier cardiac disability case in which an insurance company hired a Sacramento cardiologist named Malcolm McHenry who, after studying the matter, wrote a report that was not in the interest of the insurance company that had hired him. Barr, impressed that McHenry's opinion couldn't be bought, contacted him and he agreed to be a consultant on their cases, but not to appear in court. Later, however, McHenry became so outraged as he continued to review cases that he changed his mind and volunteered to testify.

Things got so hectic that Barr forgot that he was supposed to take a brief golfing vacation the first week in November and had to pay for four or five nights of hotel reservations he didn't use. From then on Barr and Mudford worked twelve-hour days, seven days a week for almost a full year. Neither of them was able to get away at all. Barr canceled meetings in Ireland and Argentina and Mudford gave away a pair of Caribbean cruise tickets because he had to continue working on the cases. "It's the most depressing thing I've ever done," Barr said. Mudford on the other hand felt good about it. An introspective, emotional man, he was often both self-critical and sharply critical of his profession. What particularly galled him was the gun-for-hire mentality he found so prevalent although, he conceded, sometimes unavoidable. But this case, he thought, was going to be different.

Both lawyers discussed what they were getting involved in with their wives and, in Barr's case, his children. Barr's wife, Terry, a warm, youthful physical education major from Chico, had played tennis with Sun Moon, and his daughter Erin had been friendly with Moon's son, Christopher. In eighth grade Christopher Moon and Erin Barr had won citizenship awards together. Then they went off to different high schools, Christopher to Shasta High and Erin to Bishop Quinn. At that point Terry and Sun Moon drifted apart, although Terry never lost her affection for Moon's wife. When Barr asked his wife and children how they would feel about his suing Moon, his younger daughters, Catie, who was fourteen at the time, and Erin, who was seventeen, became very upset. Terry Barr was also disturbed because of her feelings for Sun Moon and because of the terrible impact she knew it would have on the Moon family. But in the end they all told Barr he had to do what he thought was right. Dugan, who had turned sixty in April, told Terry that this case "could go upside down," by which he meant that they would be stuck with a huge debt for a very long time and therefore he would have to continue working for a very long time. But she said she was ready to accept the risk because they could afford to.

Cherry Mudford had been comfortable with Chae Moon as her cardiologist, perhaps, she thought, because he did not tell her that she was suffering from a life-threatening disease. He also had drawn pictures to show her where the blockages were, a touch she liked. And she remembered thinking that he had been kind to her family members at the hospital. But she did not have a personal relationship with him or with his family, and, like Terry Barr, she believed strongly in her husband. She was sure Doug would not take lightly something like a lawsuit against the city's two leading doctors, a hospital that employed 1,200 Redding citizens and was revered in the community, and a powerful multibillion-dollar corporation. If he felt it was right that was good enough for her.

She also did not think the government would mount an operation on the scale that it did without a good reason. Although she was at peace almost immediately with the idea of the suit, and told this to Doug, it took her a week or two to adjust to the idea that she was going to have to get a second opinion and another doctor. She grappled with the fact that Moon had not sent her to surgery, but it also occurred to her that he wasn't about to send everyone for surgery. She wondered how he chose who should have surgery and who shouldn't. In the end she saw Roy Ditchey who told her that she had been correctly diagnosed and was being appropriately treated. With respect to the financial risk,

Cherry did not seem too concerned. She and Doug had no children and for some time she had owned her own hairdressing business. They treated the matter lightly, deciding together that if they lost everything they'd just run away to Puerto Vallarta.

Doug Mudford's dream had been to go to law school, but for various reasons after graduating from Humboldt State University he ended up pursuing a business career instead. He took a job with Kimberly-Clark in Redding in 1974 and over the next eight years he alternated between managerial jobs in personnel and production. Then, in 1982 he nearly died of colon cancer. He underwent surgery after being told that his chances of surviving were only about 5 percent and recovered. Cherry took this as an omen and told him that he'd been given a second chance to pursue his youthful goal of becoming a lawyer and he should take it, even though he would be past forty by the time he joined a firm.

Mudford took her advice to heart, but it was five years before he followed it. On the fifth anniversary of his surgery he began a four-year night-school program at California Northern Law School in Chico. For those four years he worked full-time for Roseburg Lumber, the company that had bought out Kimberly-Clark, commuted sixty miles each way from Redding to Chico, and got his degree on time. He took the California bar examination in August 1991 and joined Dugan Barr's firm in January 1992. He was forty-six years old.

Dugan Barr's decision to represent Redding Medical Center patients could provide Mudford with the professional gratification he had almost given up on achieving as a lawyer. As he began screening the first arrivals among the hundreds of prospective clients who would eventually file through their door on Court Street, Mudford was uncertain what to expect. He was aware of the case in which Charles Kenneth Brown died after having a stroke and being abandoned by Moon in the cath lab, but that distant memory didn't color his judgment. Sure, Barr's cardiologist friend had said that John Corapi didn't need surgery, but what if just a few patients had undergone operations they didn't need? After all, at that point the FBI probably knew only about a handful of cases. And maybe Moon and Realyvasquez just practiced more aggressively than their peers; maybe they were ahead of the curve, on the cutting edge. Who was he to say they were wrong?

Medicine is not an exact science. Honest, well-qualified physicians often differ about the degree of obstruction in an artery or about the correct course of treatment for a patient. Was Barr just going on a hand-ful of old rumors and his gut? The evidence seemed awfully thin to jus-tify taking on two of the most powerful men and the most powerful, deep-pocketed private institution in town. Mudford knew there was a real risk that, if they were wrong, their practice could and most likely would go down the tubes. But if they were right . . . if it were true, weren't these just the kinds of people, victims if you like, most of them lacking the resources to help themselves, that he had become a lawyer to help?

One way or the other, by then he'd signed on for the ride and despite some queasy feelings he pressed ahead. As the weeks passed more and more letters came back from the respected, independent cardiologists and cardiac surgeons, some with international reputations, who had been hired to review the angiograms and corresponding medical records. Before long Mudford saw a clear pattern emerging. The reviewers were finding that often the angiographic film and the written records didn't match. The cath report would say there were lesions blocking blood flow in major arteries and that they required surgery, but the reviewers were not finding these lesions on the film. This kind of inconsistency might occur occasionally as the result of an error. But by the time they were done the reviewers had reported that surgery had been unnecessary in 40 percent of the cases they had looked at and that in a substantial number of cases it had been grossly unnecessary. They also found that in a sig-nificant although indefinite number of cases disabling strokes, injuries, and even death had been caused by the uncalled-for surgery. The federal government, which was considering criminal charges against the doc-tors, was conducting a similar review, although they were using a statis-tical sample of cases rather than reviewing every one. The federal findings were almost identical to the ones Barr and Mudford were get-ting from their reviewers.

Mudford was beginning to see his job in a new light, the light in which he had hoped to see it as a student and again as a newly minted middle-aged lawyer. He was hearing shocking stories daily from people who had been frightened into having their chests cut open for no reason. These were not rumors, or guesses, or suppositions, or speculations based on ignorance about cardiac medicine or the nature of clinical judg-ment. They were true stories. Now there was objective evidence to sup-port the charges being made. He was emotionally drained by what he was being told, but he was convinced this was an opportunity to help people of a magnitude that likely would never present itself to him again. He also knew that once Barr had made him a partner the potential existed for a once-in-a-lifetime payoff. Of course, failure would mean raising and then dashing the hopes of their clients. And, after spending years working arduously but fruitlessly, the financial loss would leave him with debts that would take years to pay off.

Barr and Mudford realized soon after the raid that they could not finance the million dollars or more they knew the case would cost with retainer fees because most of their prospective clients couldn't afford to pay them. The fact that they would have to borrow a substantial sum of money to go forward made Mudford uneasy. For Barr the single most uncomfortable moment came when he had to ask his wife, Terry, to co-sign a $1 million line of credit, but she did so unflinchingly.

As time passed, the multitude of grim stories began to depress Mudford. They made him sad for the victims whose bodies had been violated and whose trust had been shattered, and they made him angry at the doctors he believed had done unconscionable things. At the same time each new client energized him and gave him a fresh sense of purpose, without which the long succession of twelve-hour days that would follow would probably have been intolerable. Mudford sat in his office day after day for months on end, surrounded by an ever-expanding pile of case files. He listened to these mostly elderly, but sometimes young men and women tell their painful stories and he was often moved to tears.

Mudford's compassion was of course for individuals—the patients and their loved ones—but at the same time the mountain of case files added up to what was beginning to look like a crime of almost incomprehensible proportions. As clients kept coming through the door—at Barr & Mudford, at Reiner, Simpson, and at Luke Ellis's firm in Orinda—there was no way to know how many patients had been needlessly subjected to traumatic invasive surgical procedures, but it was beginning to seem likely that the number could exceed a thousand.

In the months that followed, the demographic profile of these patients would emerge. Just about half were under sixty-five years old, and about half were over. Only 4 percent were under forty-five and 7 percent were over eighty. About 65 percent of the patients were men and 35 percent were women, 60 percent were retired and between 20 and 30 percent had suffered some kind of permanent disability as a result of the surgery.

There is no way to quantify how many died as a direct result of having unnecessary surgery, but there is virtually no doubt that some did. On the whole they appeared to have been lower middle and middle class. While half qualified for Medicare, less than 5 percent qualified for Medi-Cal, the state health insurance program for the poor.

For the most part, the patients were hardworking people like Steve Cook, an ex-railroad worker from Dunsmuir, a small town about thirty miles north of Redding, who had undergone a quadruple bypass in February 2002, when he was fifty years old. Cook had lost part of a leg years earlier when he had been run over by a boxcar. Not only was Cook's surgery traumatic and unwarranted, but the surgeon, Kent Brusett, used saphenous veins from his good left leg and one of his two internal mammary arteries to perform the operation. Because that surgery used up all the good conduits, the odds of a bad outcome, should Cook need additional bypass surgery, were substantially increased. And the uncalled-for operation made additional surgery more likely. Then there was Shirley McClaren, who was seventy-six years old when she went into the hospital for an operation to treat her recurrent diverticulitis. She also suffered from chronic obstructive pulmonary disease, a symptom of which was shortness of breath. Nevertheless, because she was having trouble breathing and had some chest pain Moon was asked to do a cardiac evaluation. He performed an angiogram and sent her to Realyvasquez for triple-bypass surgery and replacement of her aortic valve. She died three days later from complications related to the valve replacement. The surgery had been unnecessary. Her husband, Jack, was devastated. And then there was Ray Hicks, who, according to a well-qualified reviewer needed no surgery whatsoever, but was subjected to a quadruple-bypass operation, an aortic valve replacement, and a mitral valve annuloplasty at age sixty-four. Hicks suffered neurological complications from the surgery, deteriorated rapidly, and ended up in a nursing home requiring round-the-clock care.*

These stories burdened Mudford and later on when he repeated some of them his eyes would get moist. Among the many that touched him especially deeply were those of Zona Martin, who was seventy-four years old when he met her, and Paul Alexandre, who was just thirty-seven.

---

*Hicks died on March 13, 2006.

*   *   *

In early July of 2002, Martin, a white-haired but youthful grandmother, experienced some chest pain. Her daughter, Donna Norton, drove her from Anderson, where she lived on a neat street of tiny cottages, to see her primary care physician, Carl Wolfer, whose office was in the same building as Moon's, across the parking lot from Redding Medical Center. About five years earlier Martin had complained of chest pain and had been told by Moon that she had a minor blockage in an artery that was too small to get into with a catheter. But he told her not to worry because eventually it would close off without doing any damage to her heart. After that visit she was pain-free until this recurrence.

Like almost everyone else in far northern California, Mrs. Martin and her daughter, a registered nurse who drove trucks for a living because it paid better than nursing, were sure that Chae Moon was the best there was. He had been Mrs. Martin's cardiologist for years. He wasn't warm and fuzzy, indeed he was prickly and impatient, even arrogant, but the two women followed his orders happily because they were sure Martin could not get better care anywhere. At the same time, Norton, who was a medical professional, after all, occasionally wished Moon would clarify one or another of his more cryptic, godlike pronouncements. But she couldn't get him to do it. It was like pulling teeth to get answers from him. "He was too busy," she said, "too good to talk to you."

Wolfer arranged for them to see Moon on Monday, July 15, 2002, but not until he had established that Martin still had insurance that Moon would accept. Soon after they arrived at Moon's office a nurse performed an electrocardiogram and told them that it looked fine. Moon then came out, glanced at Martin's chart, but did not look at the EKG tracing, and within thirty seconds said without elaboration that she needed an angiogram. Norton found this snap judgment somewhat disconcerting, but thought, well, okay, maybe he didn't need to see the EKG; maybe he's going by her symptoms and his notes in the chart. Moon told Martin to go directly across to RMC. She did and was admitted to the hospital, prepped for the catheterization, and sent straight to the lab where Moon met her and performed the procedure. When he came out less than half an hour later he told Norton, "She's got to have surgery. She'll die without it." Norton didn't think her mother was that sick, but then she wasn't a cardiologist. Moon kept Martin in the hospital and scheduled the surgery with Realyvasquez for Thursday, three days later, but it was postponed until Friday, because of emergencies, they were told.

Friday morning, July 19, Martin was Realyvasquez's first case. Norton and her son, Donald, had gone home to wait after she was taken to the operating room at eight o'clock, and they did not see her when she was wheeled out around noon. A nurse called to tell them that she was on a respirator, doing fine, and they would have her sitting up by that evening. But between four and five o'clock in the afternoon Norton got another phone call, this time from Michael O'Brien, a neurologist whose name was unfamiliar to her. He said that Martin had not woken up after her operation and he was concerned that she might not survive. He said they should come to the hospital immediately. The nurses had called O'Brien and he had been at Martin's bedside more than four hours. O'Brien had ordered a CT scan, which showed no brain damage. Nonetheless, Martin was completely unresponsive, not a twitch or a grimace. "She lay there like a log," Norton said. Norton and her children were talking to her and telling her, "It's time to wake up." They kept talking to her. At one point Norton thought Martin had moved her eyebrow about a quarter of an inch, but no one else saw it. O'Brien then performed a series of tests designed to elicit a response to pain, rubbing her eye, pressing on the moon of a fingernail, and pinching the inside of her thigh. There was no reaction. It seemed to Norton that the neurologist had given up hope. He pinched her thigh one last time and, to his surprise, she grimaced. Donald said later that when he saw her expression change, even though it was minimal, he felt sure she was going to pull through. "We were all praying for her and just to have that grimace," he said, "God put a hand on her and at that point I knew."

O'Brien said he needed to find out whether Martin had suffered an ischemic stroke in which a clot or plaque debris blocks an artery depriving brain cells of oxygen, an infrequent but not rare complication of bypass surgery, or a hemorrhagic stroke, which involves bleeding into the brain. No one had prepared Norton or Donald for the possibility of a stroke and the news was devastating. Sometime afterwards Norton said with tears in her eyes that the last time she got to talk to her mother was just before she was wheeled into the operating room. "She never talked to me after that."

O'Brien ultimately determined that plaque debris had migrated to her brain, causing Martin to suffer strokes on either side of the thalamus that would leave her partly paralyzed and almost totally unable to speak. It was about a month before she opened her eyes. During this time the family held prayer meetings in the hospital. Martin had recently become a Seventh Day Adventist and her pastor came often to lead the impromptu services. Norton said, "The whole family would come in and I would call them together and we'd all kneel down and we'd pray, and we'd have the preacher come in and we'd pray some more; we'd just constantly pray. I have cousins, aunts, an uncle, niece and her husband, all of whom are involved in the church. And I have five boys. They'd come all the time."

Eventually Martin came out of her coma and was transferred to Northern California Rehabilitation Hospital in Redding. Norton said this experience "was dreadful," too, partly because Martin had fallen six times while at the rehab center. The acute care was good, but when Martin's Medicare coverage ran out she was transferred to another part of the hospital. It was there, Norton said, that she would find her mother crying, her wheelchair facing the wall. She said she signed release forms to permit her mother to be strapped into the wheelchair, but subsequently Norton learned that she had fallen and hit her head, raising a frightful bump, when she tried to go to the bathroom alone. A nurse said she had taken the restraining belt off herself, which Norton thought was impossible. Later another nurse told her discreetly that the belt had been left untied. Martin had also fallen out of bed. The nursing director said she had crawled out of bed even though she was partly paralyzed, on a respirator, and a tracheotomy tube had been inserted. "All I did was get up, go to the hospital, come home, go to sleep, get up and go to the hospital again," Norton said. "Dr. Moon avoided me like the plague. He wouldn't even come in to see my mom. He'd walk by, turn his back, he wouldn't come and talk to us. The one time we pinned him down, he said, 'Well, she would have died without it.'"

Norton, a pretty woman in her mid-fifties with a sweet smile, glasses, and light brown hair, took time off from work after her mother's surgery and eventually had to give up her job to care for her full-time. This was especially difficult because she was getting no financial support from her husband, from whom she was separated. When she first brought her mother home from the rehabilitation hospital, Mrs. Martin couldn't sit on the edge of the bed without falling over, and she fell out of her chair trying to pick up one of their two miniature schnauzers. She had almost no short-term memory although she eventually was able to remember who Norton and Donald were. Mrs. Martin had also lost much of her vision and control of her eye movement. She wore a black eye patch because light caused her serious discomfort. She needed assistance with almost everything, although with considerable effort she was able to put her pants and top on. Before her triple-bypass surgery she had been a vital woman who had enjoyed an active social life in Anderson. She had often driven her friends to bingo at the church.

After her surgery and stroke, she spent hours each day sitting in a blue recliner, her neck twisted so that she could look upward, in the cramped living room of her tiny, aqua-colored cottage. Everything was neat and clean, with bric-a-brac everywhere, including a large white china cat and a smaller white china poodle. Lots of family pictures hung on the walls and a large RCA television set had been moved opposite her chair so she could see it. She watched TV often, although it was not clear how much she understood. Martin's infrequent attempts at speaking were generally unintelligible. There was a brief stretch when her speech improved, but then it deteriorated again to the point where Norton and Donald had great difficulty understanding what she was saying. It often took five minutes or more to get an answer to a simple question. They tried to frame their questions so that she could answer yes or no, but she often persisted in trying to answer with a full sentence, which was incomprehensible. Her mobility had also deteriorated. If she tried to walk she often fell. She no longer remembered to tell Norton that she had to go to the bathroom, or she told her when it was too late, so she wore diapers. She became grossly overweight and her expression was perpetually sad.

The small house was so crowded that Donald had to sleep in the laundry room. Norton couldn't give her mother a shower because her wheelchair wouldn't go into the bathroom. For a long time, Donald and his mother could go out only to shop and to take Martin to doctors' appointments and to church. Martin began going weekdays to a state program called Golden Umbrella, where she got physical therapy and, to the extent that she was able, played games and sang songs with the other elderly people in the program. A bus picked her up at nine in the morning and brought her home at two-thirty. This gave Norton and her son some relief, and allowed Donald to complete a computer course, but they continued to suffer from constant stress and often took it out on each other.

"We're both on antidepressants," Norton said. "I have no freedom. He helps a lot, but not by taking her to the bathroom, or cleaning her up. I can't keep up with the laundry; I can't get the smell out of the house. I'm exhausted. I've been in the hospital twice; once the doctor thought I was having a heart attack." Meanwhile, Donald, who had suffered from multiple health problems for years, was overweight, had extremely high blood pressure, and might have had a small heart attack.

With neither Norton nor Donald working, the cost of caring for Martin and paying for their basic living expenses—rent, food, heat, electricity and telephone—was overwhelming. Martin's Social Security benefit was $739 a month at the time of her surgery and she was allowed 208 hours of home care a month. Norton provided the care, for which she received $1,200 a month.

Then one day about three months after Mrs. Martin's surgery, Norton's aunt, Bonnie Martin, called and told Norton, who doesn't subscribe to a newspaper, about the raid on Redding Medical Center. Neither she nor Donald had ever questioned the necessity of the bypass operation and Norton didn't question it even then. But Donald pushed her to at least look into the possibility that Martin had not needed her surgery. She agreed and requested her mother's medical records from RMC. She then called an 800 number she had seen in the *Record Searchlight* and someone at the paper gave her Dugan Barr's telephone number. When the records arrived after a couple of months, she gave them to Barr who sent them out for review. Not long afterwards he called and told Norton that Malcolm McHenry, the Sacramento cardiologist who had evaluated her mother's records, found only zero to 40 percent blockages in her coronary arteries, not the 80–90 percent lesions cited in Moon's cath report. Blockages generally must be 70 percent or greater to warrant surgery. He also said there was no threatening "tight proximal lesion" in her right coronary artery as Moon had reported. McHenry saw "no justification" for surgery.

What if anything McHenry's report meant to Martin no one can say, but for Norton and Donald, finally there was a flicker of hope, albeit mixed with anger. Money would not solve all of their problems, but it would palliate the pain and reduce the stress. The trouble was that nobody could say when, or even if, they would get any money. And if they got some, no one could tell them how much they would get. They would have to wait and see. In the meanwhile they needed to find ways to pay their rapidly mounting bills. Arguably the uncertainty, if it lasted for a long time, would increase rather than reduce their stress. Uncertainty and unmet expectations often create anxiety and dissatisfaction, especially in circumstances of illness compounded by financial need. Furthermore, the faint hope that at the end of the road there might be a pot of gold can stimulate an increased, imprudent, and ongoing willingness to incur debt. Eventually, to meet their expenses Norton and Donald fell behind by $45,000 on their credit-card payments. Two years after the raid their total debt was approaching $100,000. They were in a hole so deep that they saw no way out.

Despite their lawsuit against the doctors, as far as Norton, her mother, and her son Donald were concerned, nothing had gotten better. Norton and Donald struggled on with their lives, caring for Martin, trying to deal with their own illnesses, the financial pressure, and all of the anxiety and stress these problems created. In September 2004, Donna had bariatric surgery, which was paid for by her husband's insurer. She was going through a divorce, which contributed to the strain she was under, but out of necessity stretched out the proceedings so that she could have the surgery while still covered by her husband's policy. She lost sixty-five pounds. Her back, which had been hurting her since she had begun caring for her mother, was feeling somewhat better because she weighed less, but it was still a problem as far as working was concerned. Both nursing and driving a truck are jobs that sometimes require lifting and long stretches either sitting or standing.

Norton said she could not even go to church most Sundays because it took too long to get her mother ready. She also found it very difficult to lift her wheelchair out of the trunk of the car. This meant that she could not easily take her mother anywhere by herself. Norton took accounting courses for three semesters, but then dropped out because she was too exhausted to continue. She also considered putting her mother in a nursing home, but she felt guilty about it.

Caring for her mother had taken a toll on her physically and mentally. Her anger ran deep and while Moon and Realyvasquez were its principal targets, it was sometimes misplaced. "I'm angry with my mother," she said, "because she's a hypochondriac," by which she meant that her mother should never have gone to see Moon in the first place.

As for Donald, who looks like and is built like his mother, he too wanted to have bariatric surgery. He also needed back surgery, but he could not have it until he lost weight. He said that like his mother he didn't have a life because he always had to be available to help with his grandmother. For all practical purposes the unnecessary surgery to which Martin had been subjected had ruined not one life, but three.

The other patient Doug Mudford could not get out of his mind was Paul Alexandre, because of his youthfulness and his gentleness. There was an appealing softness in his manner, but also in his slightly moist dark-brown eyes and his lightly padded body, that Mudford found moving.

On November 11, 1996, after a three-day bout of what seemed like heartburn, Alexandre, a group-home counselor in Susanville, California, decided to visit a local emergency room to have it checked out. He was given a series of tests and waited for the results. After three hours he was told that something in his blood work indicated that he needed heart treatment. Before long a helicopter picked him up and ferried him to Redding Medical Center. On arrival at RMC he was taken straight to the cath lab. He clearly remembered someone—he was not sure who—making an incision in his groin and inserting a catheter. The next thing he remembered was Moon leaning over him and telling him, "Unless you sign this you're going to die." Moon's dire prediction having put the fear of God into him, he signed consent forms for surgery and was taken directly to the operating room. That was the last thing he remembered until waking up after double-bypass surgery. The next day his mother and his two eldest sons were in the room when he woke up. (His ex-wife was living in South Carolina with their youngest son.)

In the afternoon Moon came to see him, showed everyone still pictures from his angiogram, and said he was probably "one of the youngest people ever to have this happen." Alexandre did not remember Moon explaining exactly what had happened to him, either before he was rushed off to the operating room or after the surgery. He remembered seeing Kevin Miller, a surgeon who worked for Realyvasquez, in the cath lab, but he said Miller did not explain to him what he was going to do or why it was necessary. Miller performed the double bypass on an emergency basis, relying on Moon's diagnosis by intravascular ultrasound of a spontaneous dissection in Alexandre's left anterior descending coronary artery. To route blood flow around the alleged blockage, Miller

grafted an internal mammary artery to Alexandre's LAD and a saphenous vein to the diagonal branch of the LAD. Alexandre stayed in the
hospital for five days and then his mother brought him home to Napa,
where she took care of him for two weeks.

With the luxury of hindsight, it was obvious that every aspect of
Alexandre's case, including the diagnosis and treatment recommendation, fit Moon's MO perfectly. A patient with no previous history of
heart disease appeared in the emergency room of a small hospital in an
outlying area with symptoms of heartburn, which, while not inconsistent with coronary disease, was hardly a clear indicator of it. The hospital's ER staff, however, had been habituated by RMC's advertising and
other promotional activities to call Moon when patients presented with
even highly equivocal cardiac symptoms. Moon, as always, was available to consult and said, "We'll send a chopper to get him." The patient
arrived at RMC, was met by Moon, who did an angiogram followed by
an ultrasound, which in 1996 was a brand-new technique. He quickly
diagnosed a spontaneous dissection and sent the patient to emergency
surgery. And no one noticed anything wrong. Typically in these circumstances the patient, who was healthy, would recover well, but would
have a substantially increased chance of needing another bypass in seven
or eight years.

In Alexandre's case, however, something else happened as a result
of the surgery that did irreparable harm to him and in the process created a medical record that is almost eight hundred pages long. This
record, which includes reports written by Moon and Miller, as well as
cardiologists and surgeons who treated Alexandre subsequently, pro-
vides an invaluable opportunity to compare Moon's written reports
with those of other physicians. It turns out there are glaring differences.
Consider, for example, what James Lies, a cardiologist at St. Helena
Hospital in Deer Park, California, wrote in the history section of a cath
report dated September 28, 2001: "Mr. Alexandre is a very pleasant,
very young, 36-year-old male who a couple of years prior . . . had what
was felt to [be] a dissection of the proximal LAD. There was no note
that it was an iatrogenic etiology."

There are three things worth paying attention to here. First, Lies specified that Alexandre was young, even though he cited his age. This
emphasis on his youth seems to suggest that he was not an obvious candidate for bypass surgery. Second, Lies used the phrase "what was felt

to [be] a dissection" rather than simply accepting Moon's unequivocal diagnosis of dissection as many cardiologists would have. And finally, at the very least, he was raising a question about whether the dissection might have had "an iatrogenic etiology," which means that it was caused by the doctor. The insertion of this unusual note strongly suggests either that Lies thought the alleged dissection might have been caused by Moon or perhaps that it didn't exist at all. On the next page, in the section titled Coronary Angiography, Lies wrote: "The LAD appears to be normal throughout, I really did not see any evidence of a dissection or obstruction and flow in the entire LAD is excellent. . . ." The meaning of this is clear. In Lies's opinion Moon's diagnosis was wrong. On page 3, under "Impression," Lies wrote: "no dissection or stenosis is noted." Moreover, in contrast to Moon's report, Lies's report mentions no family history of early coronary artery disease. And in a report dated September 4, 2001, a Napa cardiologist named Daryl Dizmang wrote under "Risk Factors for Coronary Artery Disease" that Alexandre, who did not know who his father was, "has a negative history for early coronary artery disease." Moon's report, echoed by Miller's, said, "There is a family history for early coronary artery disease, both mother and maternal grandfather with premature coronary artery disease." Alexandre later denied that anyone in his immediate family had premature coronary disease.

The examinations conducted in 2001 by Lies and Dizmang were related to chest pains Alexandre had been suffering since not long after the surgery. Chest X-rays were taken a couple of times in Susanville and each time he was told that everything was okay. Alexandre moved back to Napa in 1997 and while there a doctor named Robert Klingman looked at an X-ray image and saw that the wires used to fasten his sternum together after surgery had broken. Alexandre was working at the time as an irrigation technician, which involved lifting heavy pipe, and when he did this it was possible that the broken wires were gouging him, causing the pain. Although he was not convinced the broken wires were the source of the pain, Klingman operated to remove them on August 24, 1999.

During the surgery he unexpectedly found a four-to-five millimeter gap in the upper part of Alexandre's sternum. Klingman referred the case to his partner, William Berry, who on December 3, 1999, attempted to close the gap with bone putty. But the pain persisted even after the surgery. At times it was excruciating. Alexandre could feel his sternum shifting when he moved. During this period, the company he worked for, Mexco, gave him lighter work to do and then work as a foreman.

By the fall of 2001, Alexandre could not stand the pain anymore and despite the repeated surgical failures he returned to St. Helena Hospital for another operation. A surgeon named Steven Herbers opened his chest this time. He removed the bone putty, which had turned to mush, and screwed in two titanium plates to stabilize the top of his sternum. His prognosis was "fair." But after this surgery the pain continued and the sternum did not knit back together.

In early 2003, still another attempt was made to repair Alexandre's sternum. This time Herbers removed the plates, trimmed the bone to get a clean fit, and was planning to wire the chest together again. But during the procedure Alexandre's heart adhered to the bottom of his sternum and Herbers accidentally cut his right ventricle. Alexandre had to be temporarily put on a heart-lung machine. He was discharged with a prognosis of "guarded."

On Sunday evening, February 16, 2003, Alexandre was at home in Napa recovering from this latest round of surgery. He and his wife, Janeen, were watching *60 Minutes* on television. When Ed Bradley introduced his piece on some doctors in northern California, it was the first time either of them had heard that Chae Moon, Fidel Realyvasquez, and some of their associates had been accused of having done unnecessary heart procedures. Alexandre's jaw dropped, but he felt nothing. Janeen, on the other hand, shouted, "Oh my God, Oh my God!" Alexandre's thought at the moment was "It's not me."

Nevertheless, they called *60 Minutes* and were given an email address for Dugan Barr and Doug Mudford. After an exchange of messages, the firm sent Alexandre forms to fill out, which he returned with his medical records. On July 1, Mudford sent them to Malcolm McHenry for review. On July 2, McHenry wrote back that Alexandre's angiogram showed nothing that warranted surgery or even angioplasty. Mudford called and said, "I don't know how to tell you this, but your surgery was unnecessary." Alexandre's first reaction again was to do nothing. But after a couple of days, with anger slowly simmering inside him, he decided that what he really wanted was revenge, he wanted "to put them in jail."

Alexandre continued to have considerable pain from broken wires in his chest. He used morphine patches and his spine had become crooked as a result of overcompensating for his injury. His sternum had not healed, but doctors told him that the risk of opening his chest again was too great, partly because his heart still adhered to his sternum. Nonetheless, he still thought from time to time about more surgery to correct this problem. But then he wondered whether after five surgeries he really could bear any more. When asked about working again, he said he did not think it was possible. He said he could not lift anything over ten pounds and that when he went grocery shopping with Janeen she had to carry all of the heavy packages. He filed twice for disability payments from Social Security, but was turned down both times, perhaps because he would not look for desk work, which he could do. He could not stand the idea of "pushing a pen." After five operations, one of which had been unnecessary and four of which had been unsuccessful, Paul Alexandre's life hadn't exactly ended. He had a wife who supported him and a simple but respectable home in Napa. But it was a life of intermittent pain; a life out of which much of the joy had been drained.

12

Preparing for Battle

Bob Simpson, the Redding lawyer who had narrowly avoided unnecessary bypass surgery, first mentioned the possibility of a lawsuit against Chae Moon to his partners after speaking to Mike Skeen. But they said they didn't want any part of it because "politically it was suicide." Moon and RMC were simply too powerful and too popular to take on. Friends were telling Simpson, "You ought to sue that bastard." But he for the most part still held to the view that Moon hadn't done anything wrong. "I asked for the cath," he said, "and I didn't do what he said. What would I sue the guy for? For me being stupid?" In retrospect he seemed either to have been in denial or uninterested in advertising what he viewed as his own stupidity. And he also agreed with his partners that as personal injury lawyers they were too dependent on other local doctors to sue one of their most distinguished colleagues.

Then came the raid. Simpson's gut reaction was "Holy shit!" By the next day, Thursday, October 31, three of Moon's patients had showed up at his office and told him stories similar to his own. It was not until then that it finally dawned on him that he might be dealing with a major crime. He went directly to his partners and told them "I wanna go, I want to pursue this." With some trepidation, they all got on board. Russ Reiner, a tall, elegant, soft-spoken man, said the decision to take on the RMC case was a monumental one for the firm, because if they were wrong it would destroy their practice. He meant this literally. People in Redding believed deeply in Moon, Realyvasquez, their programs, and RMC, and would likely boycott any law firm that took them on. Indeed, Reiner too had heard the rumors about the heart program at RMC, but until then hadn't believed them.

Kacie Carroll, the former RMC nurse who had joined the law firm's staff, was at home just outside of Red Bluff with her horses, dogs, and cats when she received a phone call from Reiner. "We have a situation here in Redding," he said, "and I need you to come into the office this morning. How soon can you get here?" Carroll said she would be there in an hour. Reiner told her to be prepared to stay the day, adding that there would be a briefing at ten o'clock. The paralegals and secretaries had a regular calendar meeting scheduled for that morning and Suzanne Ramsden, Simpson's paralegal, always brought donuts or scones. When she was notified that all the lawyers would be in for a special staff meeting, she increased the order to provide for the partners and staff, twenty-four in all.

Reiner and Simpson told the gathering that the FBI had raided Redding Medical Center because unnecessary heart surgeries and caths were being performed there by Realyvasquez and Moon, respectively, and this meant that they were going be inundated with clients. They told them that they would be answering a flood of phone calls and needed to get as much information as possible, which they would then try to organize and get under control. The take-home message was that the office, which was already handling some four hundred auto-accident cases, was about to be overwhelmed by a tidal wave of new clients.

The first client came in that afternoon. His name was Michael Ramos. He was about forty-seven years old and it was subsequently determined—by a process that hadn't yet been devised, let alone put in place—that he had undergone unnecessary surgery. Ronald Gibbens also came in that afternoon. An expert reviewer later said of Gibbens, who was just thirty-one years old when he had double-bypass surgery, that "Moon was so far out of bounds with this guy, I don't know where to begin." The expert found Gibbens's coronary arteries to be open with good blood flow and in no need of treatment of any kind. His surgery was called "Totally unnecessary . . . and malpractice for certain." Marlene Reed, who was sixty-six when she was interviewed at Reiner, Simpson, also had a double bypass that the expert considered grossly unnecessary.

That same afternoon, McGregor Scott, the U.S. attorney, told a reporter from Channel 12 television that he could not speak about the case, but suggested that he talk to Simpson. The local interview led to an interview on the NBC Nightly News, after which Reiner, Simpson's well-appointed suite of offices along the river on Park Marina Drive was inundated with clients. The phones were ringing nonstop with calls from people who feared they'd undergone unwarranted procedures. Every phone was in use. The seven lines in the office were clearly inadequate. By July, they would have twenty-four. Secretaries and paralegals were sitting in the kitchen, all over the office, there were so many calls coming in. There wasn't nearly enough room to handle the rapidly expanding workload. The firm ended up buying the other half of the floor in their two-story riverside building. Even then one lawyer and his secretary had to be lodged in a nearby building because there wasn't enough room for them. The firm installed shelves in all of the hallways to accommodate the explosion of files. And they added ten new employees: nurses, paralegals, file clerks, and assistants for Ramsden, Simpson's trusted paralegal, and for Bob Simpson's secretary, Kathy Bogdanovich.

Still, not everyone was convinced. Even Kacie Carroll, who had experience as a law-enforcement officer, as an emergency room nurse at RMC, and as a legal nurse, did not believe the allegations. She didn't believe them despite her involvement when Simpson had narrowly avoided unnecessary bypass surgery. She still believed Redding Medical Center was a special place to which people came from all over the country to be treated and that what was being alleged could not have happened. "These people would come in [to Redding Medical Center]," she said, "and then we were sending them upstairs and this increased their chances of survival greatly because they came to our facility."

Ted Blankenheim, another nurse who now worked for the firm, was also skeptical. He had worked in the cardiac unit at RMC and his experience was that local doctors sent their heart patients there rather than to Mercy because anyone who presented with cardiac symptoms was treated rapidly and efficiently. "It was a phenomenal thing to watch when somebody really sick came in," he said. Blankenheim had thought at the time that the number of patients being routed through the RMC emergency room to cardiac care seemed high. But then the word would come back from the cath lab that they had found a life-threatening lesion in a coronary artery, which would reassure the staff that they were a progressive and effective unit on the cutting edge of American medicine. Nobody thought for a moment that unrequired procedures were being done.

Two days after the raid, Bob Simpson took Kacie Carroll aside. He knew she believed in Moon and RMC and he was concerned that her loyalty to them would cloud her judgment. But he also knew she was smart and had the right kind of experience and he wanted her working on these cases. He asked her directly whether she thought she could be fair and impartial. She told him that she would be open-minded, but that she would need convincing and would need to see the records. Simpson told her he was happy with that. Almost immediately, Carroll began unlearning what she thought she knew. "We started screening clients," she said. "I would sit at my desk all day and I would talk to people. When they would call in they would tell you that they had had a procedure at Redding Medical Center and they wanted to know if it was unnecessary or not. And so you would basically ask them a little bit of a health history. Basic things like: Are you a diabetic? Have you had previous heart problems? Are you a smoker? Are you in good health? [Do you have] risk factors for cardiac problems? And then you would say, 'What brought you to Redding Medical Center?'

"In many cases they were referred by a physician to Dr. Moon and in many cases they came through the emergency room. But the common thread that you saw for all of them was that the same things were repeated over and over to them. They would have an angiogram and Dr. Moon would say, 'I'm going to save your life. This is your lucky day.' And you hear this once and you think, okay. When you hear it fifty times, you begin to panic because you realize that it is just like a script. Each and every one of these people heard that. And it frightened them. They felt vulnerable at the time. And to hear somebody standing there, the head of the heart program, saying 'You have a need for immediate heart surgery and I'm going to save your life.' What are you going to do? I know what I'd do. I'd get the surgery.

"What have we learned from this? Get a second opinion. And in many cases, these people wanted a second opinion, but they were stampeded into going ahead with the surgery. They were prevented from getting that second opinion. It's very difficult when you're lying there on a gurney in the cath lab and you've just been told that you can't leave the hospital because you may die and it's not like you can just physically get up and unhook yourself from everything and walk out."

Beginning less than a week after the FBI raid, Carroll and the other nurses at Reiner, Simpson were interviewing ten to fifteen people a day. By the time they were done the staff had interviewed 1,194 people. Things slowed down a bit during the Christmas holidays, but soon thereafter the *Record Searchlight* reported that Moon's malpractice insurance was going to expire on January 31, 2003. This was important because clients needed to give ninety days' notice of intention to file suit while his policy was still in force and it led to another flood of calls. The firm was also filing suits against practice associates of Moon and Realy-vasquez. And every time an article about the situation appeared in the newspaper they would get more calls. The additional staff hired included four nurses, three of whom had worked in cath labs.

Simpson was handling media calls and he and Reiner went to Texas to negotiate an association with Jim Moriarty and his partner, Kevin Leyendecker, as well as Steve Hackerman and his partner, Richard Frankel, whose previous experience with the psychiatric hospital scandal in the early 1990s would prove invaluable. They also met with the U.S. attorneys. Simpson was impressed, even somewhat taken aback, when one of them said, "Your clients have the moral and equitable upper ground and we recognize that." Simpson emphasized that this admission was really rare, "something I don't think you'll get from a U.S. attorney, ever." The government lawyers told Simpson they couldn't say much, but they were doing an analysis of Tenet's financial condition. They said that if Reiner, Simpson did their own analysis they could compare their data and conclusions. This was important because Tenet was beleaguered with other legal problems and the lawyers needed to know how much money the company would be able to pay to resolve civil and criminal lawsuits in the Redding case. Simpson agreed. Richard Frankel was put in charge of this task because he had done it before in a case involving hip replacements.

One of the things Carroll had wondered about when she became involved with the RMC case was whether Greg Gibson, the former COO, had left RMC because he knew what was going on. She tried to call him at the Tenet hospital in Phoenix, but nobody there had ever heard of him. She then asked a Sacramento-based investigator named Donald Vilfer, who sometimes worked for the firm, to track Gibson down, which he did in about twenty-four hours. Gibson, his wife, and their two children were living with his elderly parents in Huntsville, Alabama. Simpson authorized Carroll to call Gibson. She got his work number at Bob Wall's Appliance store from his father and called him. Soon thereafter Simpson, Hackerman, and Carroll traveled to Alabama to interview him and determine what kind of a witness he would make.

Gibson gave the lawyers interesting information about Realyvasquez's contract, among other things, but he said he could never be a witness for them because they "would eat me alive." This was a reference to allegations that he had abused either controlled substances or prescription drugs. He said Tenet had blackballed him. "I couldn't get a job in this industry now if I had to."

One of the early cases that helped clarify what the firm was dealing with involved a lively, intelligent seventy-six-year-old woman with a sweet smile and swept-back white hair named Shirley Wooten. She was the sister of Glen Aldridge, who had gone to the hospital for a hernia operation and ended up with a stent he didn't need. Wooten was born in May 1925, at her grandmother's house in the tiny town of Bella Vista not far from Redding and grew up on a four-thousand-acre cattle ranch near Shingletown, between Redding and Mount Lassen. She met her husband, Bob, at a schoolhouse dance in Shingletown. After they married they were never apart for more than a few days at a time. Bob drove logging trucks for a lumber mill and did other lumber-related work.

In February of 2002, Shirley, whose mother, Martha Aldridge, was alive and well at 102, experienced some pain in her shoulder. Bob suggested that she go to see their family doctor, Pat Campbell's former partner, Gary Crawford. Crawford checked her with a stethoscope and decided that he would send her to Moon. They knew about Moon by reputation, but also because he had diagnosed Bob in 1999 and had sent him for quadruple-bypass surgery. Bob didn't remember who performed the surgery, but he thought it might have been Realyvasquez or possibly Moreno-Cabral because he remembered having difficulty pronouncing the name.

Shirley and Bob went to Moon's office the next day. They thought that he had done a treadmill test, but neither of them remembered much more than that about the visit. Bob also had a vague memory that Moon had said something about Shirley having calcium floating in her blood. He also thought they might have gone to an imaging center for a calcium-scoring test. What Bob remembered more clearly, however, was that Moon had said that Shirley had plaque that would kill her if they didn't do something quickly. Their son Shannon, a beekeeper who looks and dresses like the Marlboro man and runs a few head of Hereford on the eighty acres on which his parents' neat little mobile home sits, remembered his father having an angiogram but did not remember his mother ever having had one. (Her medical records indicated she did have an angiogram and IVUS before undergoing double-bypass surgery.) Shannon said he guessed that very few people would ask for a second opinion from Moon because he was "world famous."

Shirley, Bob, and Shannon agreed that Shirley had gone directly from Moon's office to the hospital. Shannon remembered being concerned by the seriousness that this implied. But, he thought, this is the way they do it and they are going to save another life. Shannon's younger brother Kevin was also at the hospital during the operation. Shirley came home five days after the surgery. She felt pretty good until the day she walked a tenth of a mile or so to the mailbox and felt a pain in her chest. Bob said they had better call the day nurse. Although Shannon was extremely busy, something told him that he needed to go by and see his mother. His wife, Glenda, went with him. About two minutes after they arrived at the house Shirley picked up the phone. She dialed two numbers, Bob said, and "She died right there in the chair. She was dead."

Shannon said his mother dropped the phone, took a deep breath, let it out, her eyes dilated, and that was it. "I've seen two other people die," he said, "and everything is shutting down and you hear this God-awful gurgling sound. I knew what that was." "We've got to start CPR," Shannon said. "Get that chair out of the way." He moved his mother to the floor and began to give her mouth-to-mouth resuscitation. She came to and immediately began to throw up and then asked if she had passed out. Shannon told her that she had. In the meantime, Glenda called 911 and an emergency team arrived within minutes. They stabilized Shirley and took her immediately to RMC.

Shannon, who is about six feet three inches tall, said the emergency room doctor was "a little Iranian guy." He pointed at his chest and said, "The guy came up to here." He said the doctor asked them to give him a thirty-second description of what had happened to their mother. When they told him their mother had *died*, the doctor said, "No, she didn't." An argument ensued in which Shannon insisted that she had died, adding that he knew what it was like because he had previously saved someone's life. He said his brother Kevin was even angrier and was about to wipe the floor with the doctor. None of them could remember exactly what happened in the emergency room after that, but when Shirley was admitted to a regular hospital room the family was told that the surgeon would have to open her up again because there was "a breakage." The doctors did not seem to know where it was.

Then Realyvasquez's associate Kent Brusett, who had performed the original bypass operation, came in and told them that the place where he had cannulated the aorta had opened up because the "glue," or clotting material, they had used to close the wound, did not hold. He said that this had never happened to him before, but that Shirley's arteries were very friable, or crumbly, suggesting that she was diabetic, which in fact she was not. Brusett operated that evening and did not finish until about five o'clock the next morning. When he came out, he explained to them that her brain had been deprived of blood for an hour and a half as a result of which she probably would have some brain damage.

Shannon said that his mother was in a coma after the operation for about six days. A neurologist named Gary Rowe did brain scans and other doctors kept checking on her as well. Shannon rubbed his pocketknife against the sole of one of Shirley's feet and got no response at all. But when he rubbed her forehead he got considerable response on the brain scan, so they kept doing it, on her forehead and around her ears. Every time the machine was on they could see a response. At one point a doctor told them that there was very little hope. They did not accept this. They kept rubbing her head and Shannon told his father, "There's someone home in there." The next day the doctors told them that she should be unplugged because there was no longer any hope. But the family worried that she would slowly starve if they took her off the respirator and stopped feeding her intravenously. That evening, Bob and his two sons went home and discussed the options. They felt they were still getting a response when they stroked her head and they decided not to take her off life support.

The next morning they told the doctors that they wanted a few more days. The morning after that, Bob, Shannon, and Kevin were in the room with Shirley when she opened her eyes, smiled at them, and then closed her eyes again. Brusett was outside the door and they went out immediately and told him, "We're not unplugging her. She just opened her eyes and smiled at everybody." Soon thereafter, beginning on the left side, movement began to return to her body. First her leg, then her arm moved. She was full of tubes and IV lines and she was pulling at them, trying to get the oxygen out of her nose. Shannon said he thought his mother was in the hospital for about thirty days before going for rehabilitation at Northern California Rehabilitation Hospital, where she also stayed for about thirty days.

Four to six weeks after returning home Shirley went into the bathroom to brush her teeth. She bent over the sink and, Bob said, "just kept on going." She fell, hit the mirror, and needed twenty-seven stitches in her face. Two or three months later she fell in the kitchen and broke her hip. Around this time Bob had to start feeding Shirley because she was experiencing severe hand tremors. He said she would throw food all over the place, which embarrassed her. Eventually he had to help her shower and dress as well. Sometime afterwards, however, a shunt was placed in her head to drain fluid, relieving the pressure on her brain. This improved her condition considerably, although she still suffered a bit from tremors. She went into rehab again after her hip surgery.

After the raid, Shannon said, his original instinct, despite his mother's experience, was to support Moon. But when Bob Simpson's firm, which had been told of their situation by a friend of the Wootens, got in touch with them and asked if they could get their records, they agreed. And once the independent cardiologists' reviews of her records came in, Shannon changed his mind. Later he also became aware that after Redding Medical Center shut down its cardiac surgery program the cardiac surgery rates at Mercy did not significantly increase. The only explanation he could think of for Mercy's caseload remaining roughly the same after RMC stopped doing heart surgery was that some of the surgery done at RMC had been unnecessary.

Meanwhile, the nurses at Reiner, Simpson were compiling patient records, which would eventually be sent to experts for review. The record collection was a slow process because RMC took four to five months on average to provide what was requested. And topflight experts willing to work for plaintiffs had to be found. This task would fall to Kacie Carroll. Simpson asked her to assemble a "dream team" whose opinions could not be successfully challenged in court. After a number of conversations, Stanford's Peter Fitzgerald agreed to come on board and he suggested that Carroll attend some major cardiology meetings, which she did. She traveled to Washington, D.C., for a conference on revascularization, to Chicago for the annual meeting of the American College of Cardiology, to Dana Point, California, for a conference on new technology, and to San Antonio for the annual meeting of the Society of Thoracic Surgeons.

Carroll would arrive at these meetings having already identified a potential expert, find him, and begin a conversation. The cardiologist or surgeon would usually ask her what she did and she would tell them she was a nurse. Then they would typically ask, "Do you work in a cath lab?" and she would say, "No, I'm a legal nurse-consultant. I work for the lead firm against Tenet Healthcare and the unnecessary heart surgeries." When they heard that, "Boy, do you get shut down fast," Carroll said. "They want to avoid you like a skunk." But she found that if she could just get them to look at the records their attitudes would change.

As a very attractive, highly personable young woman, Carroll had a success rate with the cardiologists and cardiac surgeons, almost all of whom were middle-aged men, that was probably higher than might have been expected otherwise. One doctor she met briefly at the Dana Point conference was Randy Chitwood, a prominent cardiac surgeon from Alabama. She followed Chitwood to the STS meeting in San Antonio, reintroduced herself, and showed him some patient records. She wanted him to understand that this wasn't just a bunch of lawyers trying to persecute doctors. Carroll gave him some background on each case, and ran the film for him on her laptop, both IVUS and angiograms. As he looked at the images he kept saying, "Run me another one, run me another one. I don't believe this." After looking at about half a dozen films, he said, "If you're looking for an expert, I'll be your expert. I'm just shocked. Does anybody know about this? Have people seen these records?" Carroll said, "Very few have."

Hartzell Schaff, chairman of the division of cardiovascular surgery at the Mayo Clinic, was also at the STS meeting. Carroll had listened to Schaff's lecture at the Dana Point conference and was impressed. At one of the lectures Schaff sat down a row ahead of her. She introduced herself and told him how much she had enjoyed his lecture in Dana Point. She told him Reiner, Simpson was looking for an expert, but that even if he wasn't interested, she would still like him to see the records. Schaff, who had been told by Chitwood that he had reviewed some Redding cases and he believed surgery had been done on patients who didn't need it, agreed to look at about a half dozen records. While reviewing the cine-film and ultrasound images, Schaff kept repeating, "What did they operate on here? I don't see anything that needs operating on." Still, Schaff said he was too busy in his practice to serve as an expert. But Carroll did not give up. She kept calling him to try to change his mind and eventually succeeded. As the number of cases grew, Reiner, Simpson hired other reviewers, including David Anderson and his group in Oakland, an Oakland surgeon named Russell Stanten, and Eugene Mazzei, also a surgeon, in Dallas. Meanwhile, the defense lawyers were recruiting their own high-profile experts such as Wally Buch at Stanford and Kirk Garratt, who had recently moved from the Mayo Clinic to Lenox Hill Hospital in New York.

Not every patient of Moon and Realyvasquez was eager to sign up with a law firm, however. Don Frank, for example, had always held Chae Moon in the same high regard as the Redding citizens who joined the public demonstration in support of Moon and Realyvasquez. Frank was born in Redding in 1956, grew up in Sacramento, and returned to Redding in 1978 to work for his father in a small wholesale lumber business. The senior Frank had died at fifty-one of heart disease.

Frank, who was tall, well built, and fit looking, took care of himself. He exercised fairly regularly, but not religiously, running or walking between one and three miles, generally three to four times a week. In the summer of 2002, he was experiencing some discomfort in his chest, sometimes with exertion, but not always. The discomfort was mild and usually lasted about a minute. After roughly a month it stopped. It was a kind of tightness and he thought it might be a muscle pain. Then in early July he read that a thirty-three-year-old St. Louis Cardinals pitcher named Darryl Kile had died in June of coronary artery disease in his sleep. If it had happened to him, Frank reasoned, why couldn't it happen to me?

He mentioned this to Riaz Malik, one of his golf partners at the Riverview Country Club. Malik, the physician who had paid a surprise visit to CW1, told Frank that if he liked he would have one of his interns do a treadmill test. But before that could happen Frank received a telephone call from Moon who told him that he should have a calcium-scoring test, sometimes called a heart scan, which his office arranged at MD Imaging in downtown Redding. Frank had mixed feelings about his situation. His anxiety increased because he was now being looked after by a cardiologist, but it made him feel good to know that it wasn't just any cardiologist; he was under Moon's care. After he took the test, Moon called him and told him that it did not give him the information he needed. He said that the next step would be an angiogram.

In the interim, however, Frank had spoken to Rich Malotky, his internist. Malotky thought Frank's symptoms sounded like classic acid reflux and told him that he should take an over-the-counter antacid and stay out of Moon's mill. He warned him that there were serious risks associated with an angiogram and said that if Frank would come into his office the next morning he would give him a treadmill test. Frank then called Moon and told him that he had spoken to an internist who recommended that he take a treadmill test. "Are you going to deal with me as a cardiologist or with a general practitioner?" Moon asked. "I know what's best for you." At this point it did not occur to Frank to challenge Moon. He did ask him what his calcium score was and Moon told him that it was "one." But he did not know what this meant. He found out much later from a cousin of his who had a calcium score of 1,200 that one meant there was no indication whatsoever, based solely on that score, for additional diagnostic testing. He went ahead and made an appointment for his angiogram.

When Moon came into the cath lab, in Frank's words, it was "pedal to the metal." Moon said, "We're going to run it up, we're going to shoot some dye; you'll probably feel some heat; you might feel like you're wetting your pants. . . ." At some point during the angiogram Moon showed another catheter to Frank and told him, "I'm going to use a different tool, this will give me a different look, a three-dimensional picture. It is called an IVUS, intravascular ultrasound." After threading the IVUS catheter into Frank's coronary arteries, Moon started muttering and said: "Don, we have a serious problem here. I want you to take a look at this." He pointed to the black-and-white monitor and told Frank that he had hanging plaque in his left anterior descending coronary artery. Frank thought he could see something. Moon told him that if the plaque broke off it could kill him. Frank said that as Moon backed the catheter out he said, "Don, you have to have immediate bypass surgery," to which Frank replied, "Like hell I do." Moon said, "Yes, you do. That thing is in your left anterior descending artery, the one we call the widow-maker, and if it comes loose you can be dead before you hit the floor."

When Frank told Moon that he had to discuss the situation with his wife before making a decision, Moon said he would talk to her first. He briskly left the cath lab, found Frank's wife, Cheryl, and delivered a stern message that her husband needed immediate bypass surgery. Shortly thereafter, when Frank was able to see his wife, they talked it over briefly and decided that if Moon was convinced surgery was necessary, he would have to go ahead with it. Frank spent three or four days in the hospital waiting for Realyvasquez to return from vacation. He was convinced, based on conversations with Malik and another surgeon, and Realyvasquez's reputation, that Realyvasquez was the best cardiac surgeon around and that he was extremely fortunate to be in the hands of both Moon and Realyvasquez.

A day or two before the surgery two nurses from Realyvasquez's office came in and explained exactly what would happen. They said that Realyvasquez would stop by before the surgery and explain it again. Moon visited Frank frequently and his godparents, who knew Moon well, also visited. His godparents told him how fortunate he was to have been seen by Moon, because no other cardiologist would have diagnosed his condition as Moon did. About this they were probably right. It is unlikely that any other cardiologist would have rendered the same diagnosis.

On July 11, one day before the surgery, Realyvasquez came to visit Frank in his hospital bed. Frank found his demeanor to be arrogant, exactly the same as Moon's. Realyvasquez told him he was lucky. "You're the first [case of the day]," he said. "It's one vessel, easy, a piece of cake." Frank asked him about the possibility of doing the surgery with a small incision between the ribs rather than splitting his sternum. He said Realyvasquez's dismissive response was "Nah, that's old medicine, I wouldn't touch that." Frank then asked him about the possibility of doing the surgery with an internal mammary artery. Realyvasquez once again said, "No, you're going to be back here in seven years and we will need that then." Realyvasquez said they would use a vein graft, everything would be fine, and that was all Frank needed to know. With that, he left.

After his surgery, Frank went to see Moon, who drew all over the paper on the examining table to show him how the Lipitor he was putting him on worked. Moon spent twenty or twenty-five minutes with Frank and Cheryl. He did not have a follow-up visit with Realyvasquez, but rather met with Todd Richter, a very youthful physician's assistant. Cheryl and Don called him Doogie Howser because he looked so young. After the surgery, however, Frank was still feeling pain similar to the pain he had felt before the operation. He told Moon, who told him that everything had gone very well and he had nothing to worry about. But nonetheless Frank asked for a thallium stress test. Moon gave him the test and told Frank that the result was negative. From that point on his recovery went smoothly.

Then, on October 30, the raid took place. It did not occur to Frank when he heard about it that his surgery might have been unnecessary. A day or two later, after having a cold drink in the 19th Hole, the men's bar at the Riverview Country Club, Frank walked into the adjoining restaurant and saw Moon sitting at a table with three or four of his golfing buddies. He walked up to the table, leaned over Moon's right shoulder, and told him that he had heard about the raid and that he should know that he supported him 100 percent. Frank began to straighten up and Moon reached out and grabbed his sleeve, pulled him back down, and said, "I got to tell you, I got to apologize to you, because what they're looking at me for is exactly what I did to you."

Frank was utterly dismayed by this remark. He said nothing more to Moon and went back to his buddies in the 19th Hole. He told one of his friends what Moon had just said, and his friend said, "You've got to be kidding, he told you that?" At first Frank thought Moon was telling him only that that's what they're looking at me for, not suggesting or admitting that he might be guilty of anything. But if that was the case, he wondered later that day, why would Moon need to apologize?

Despite the raid and Moon's strange comment, Frank was not ready to go to authorities or to file a lawsuit. He and Cheryl decided that they would simply tell his story to anyone who was interested and let the chips fall where they may. He did talk to a lawyer friend named Stewart Altemus who said he would not touch the case because he used Moon and Realyvasquez in his personal injury practice as expert witnesses. He told Frank he should go see Bob Simpson. Simpson wanted Frank to sign up immediately and deliver his records so that they could be sent out for review. But Frank told him that with all due respect he was not ready to do that. He said he was going to find someone independent to review his case. He collected his records and sent them to a friend in Santa Rosa whose wife was a cardiac-care nurse. She brought them to a doctor in Santa Rosa, but he would not even look at them. The envelope was returned unopened. Frank then began looking on the Internet for cardiologists to review his records.

In the meantime, Simpson had again asked him for his records so they could be sent out for review. This time, Frank agreed. Frank also continued his own search for someone to review his records. After numerous failed attempts he called Andrew Michaels, an interventional cardiologist at the University of California at San Francisco. Michaels agreed to examine Frank, which he did on June 30, 2003, and reviewed his angiogram and intravascular ultrasound. Michaels also asked his senior colleague, Tom Ports, to look at the angiogram and IVUS, but without disclosing the patient's name. Before Michaels and Ports completed their reviews Simpson told Frank that his reviewers had said the surgery had been totally unwarranted. Soon thereafter Michaels sent a letter to Frank assuring him that he did not need the surgery and noting that Ports concurred. Michaels also wrote in his letter that Moon had not taken shots from the correct angles to see what if anything might be wrong with his arteries.

After getting word from Michaels supporting what was by then his near certainty that his surgery had been uncalled-for, he signed up with Simpson and they filed a lawsuit. But even then Frank told Simpson he could not hate Moon and could not believe that he knowingly had done unnecessary surgery. He said that the only way he could cope with this was to believe that "Chae Moon believes that he is right and that he is just outside the standard practice of medicine." Simpson then sent Frank's records to Hartzell Schaff, chief of cardiac surgery at the Mayo Clinic, who reviewed them and wrote that Frank's coronary anatomy was "normal" and that "there was no indication for coronary artery bypass for this patient." Russell Stanten, the cardiac surgeon in Oakland, also reviewed Frank's records and found no indication that coronary bypass surgery was required.

Frank said afterwards that even though he still didn't hate Moon, he had the sense of a huge violation, a huge mistrust. He remembered seeing his father after his bypass surgery with tubes coming out of him everywhere. He said it hit him right between the eyes. He thought about the effect on his wife, on his children, and other family members, of his having had this unrequired bypass surgery. He also thought about a friend who lost his job because the cardiac program was closed at RMC. He said it was a direct hit on the whole community. Frank also blamed Realyvasquez for operating on him. "He's a medical doctor who did surgery on people that wasn't necessary," he said. "It continues to haunt you."

13

The Company

Despite the serious allegations against Moon and Realyvasquez, which were repeated frequently in the local and national news media, a substantial percentage of Redding's population—very likely more than half—continued to stand behind the doctors. But in the touchy postraid environment there turned out to be considerable skepticism in town about Redding Medical Center's corporate parent, Tenet Healthcare, by then the second-largest for-profit hospital company in the country after HCA, the healthcare behemoth founded by Senator Bill Frist's father. Ron and Carolyn Reynolds, both of whom were established members of the Redding business community, strongly supported the hospital and the doctors, but had no difficulty believing that Tenet's charges might have been excessive. The retired general practitioner Jim Charles, although he wholeheartedly vouched for the integrity of Moon and Realyvasquez, allowed for the possibility that Tenet might be run by crooks. And even Sheryl Hallstrom, the RMC cardiac nurse who defended the doctors and the hospital passionately, criticized the company for overcharging patients.

It is not absolutely clear why this suspicion of Tenet took hold in Redding months after the raid except that over the years the company had gotten its fair share of bad publicity. The worst case in human terms was the one involving the incarceration on false premises of children, adolescents, and adults until their insurance ran out. But these events had taken place a decade or more before the Redding raid when the company was still known as National Medical Enterprises. Few if any of Redding's residents had ever heard of it, and if they had they didn't remember it. On the other hand, while most were not able to cite specific examples of predatory pricing or other wrongdoing, many local people had a gut feeling that Tenet's charges were much higher than those at most other hospitals, which they were.

Some of the townspeople might have read in the newspapers that Tenet marked up drug prices more than seven times at their hospitals nationwide, whereas the national average for all hospital systems was under three and a half times. Front-page stories about this appeared in the *San Francisco Chronicle* soon after the raid on November 24 and November 28, 2002. In California, where Tenet maintained its corporate headquarters and forty of its 115 hospitals, it charged more than ten times the average of what the drugs cost the hospitals. And Tenet's combined inpatient and outpatient nationwide median gross charge was $34,079, just short of twice the national average.[17] Moreover, RMC was first in California for net income per adjusted patient day at $1,125.39.[18] People in Redding might also have read that in fiscal years 1999 and 2000 five of the ten most expensive operating rooms in the country were in Tenet hospitals. Use of RMC's OR for a four-hour bypass procedure was billed at upwards of $47,000. The total bill for bypass surgery was often more than $150,000 and sometimes more than $300,000.

What none of them knew, however, was that Jeffrey Barbakow, Tenet's CEO, true to his Wall Street background, was almost exclusively interested in driving up the price of Tenet stock and his top lieutenants knew how to do it. By the mid-1990s, Tenet had a system in place developed by chief operating officer Thomas Mackey that assured regular increases in share value. Every quarter Tenet's numbers crunchers would look at the revenues securities analysts were predicting the company would generate and calculate how much of an increase in gross charges it would take to meet or beat those expectations. The word was then passed on to the regional vice presidents, whose job it was to make sure that hospital executives would meet the goals. By 2000, David Dennis, an investment banker, joined the company as chief financial officer and together with Mackey put ever-increasing pressure on the regional executives and hospital CEOs to meet higher and higher earnings targets.

Under this system, from fiscal years 1997 to 2002, Redding Medical Center's pretax income surged spectacularly, aided by an equally spectacular surge in cardiac procedures. For the year ending May 31, 1998, RMC's pretax net income was $39,646, 804. The next year it was $43,567,374 and the year after that it reached $55,904,603. For the

year ending June 30, 2001, it jumped to $71,658,322. And the follow-
ing year it hit $93,619,706, a year in which Mercy, the slightly larger
nonprofit hospital across town, earned about $5 million. For the quar-
ter before the raid the 238-bed Redding Medical Center's pretax net
income was $32,975,407, which on an annual basis works out to a
stratospheric $131,901,628. By way of comparison, the Washington
Hospital Center, a 900-bed nonprofit hospital in the nation's capital with
a nationally renowned heart program earned $14.2 million in FY 2004.

Not all of RMC's unusually high earnings were generated by doing
unnecessary procedures and overbilling for the use of operating rooms.
Double billing and billing for supplies and devices that were not used,
or for which there was no documentation of their use, was rampant.
Darla Wilson, a nurse auditor, did a study of billing fraud at the hospital for Bob Simpson's law firm and found dozens of examples, not to
mention examples of plain old overcharging. In 2002, the hospital was
charging $282.50 a day for a bit of salt water used to flush out IV lines.
An electrocardiogram that Mercy Hospital billed at $76.05 was billed
at $397 by Redding Medical Center. An hour of oxygen at RMC cost
$50 compared with $11.05 at Mercy. And so on. Interestingly, California, the state in which Tenet was based and in which it had by far its
largest concentration of hospitals, had the second-highest cost-to-
charges ratio in the country, topped only by lightly populated Nevada.
On average in California, hospital charges were more than triple the
costs in 2002. In Maryland, the state with the lowest ratio, charges were
less than a third higher than costs.

While concerns about overcharging were present, they were not
sharply etched in people's minds. Chances are the raid brought them to
the surface. But if not for the series of aftershocks set off by the raid they
almost certainly would have sunk back into the town's collective uncon-
scious. What most people in Redding did not know, however, was that
at the time of the raid Tenet was facing twenty-six lawsuits relating to
corrupt business practices and unsanitary conditions at its hospitals in
various states. Between 1994 and 2003, Tenet was the subject of fifty-
three federal investigations and paid more than a billion dollars in fines.
Charges against the company ranged from upcoding, a fraudulent means
of overcharging Medicare and Medicaid, to billing insurance companies
for medications and treatment that were not provided and bribing doctors for referrals. All of this was going on while Tenet was operating

under the corporate integrity agreement entered into with the federal government as part of the settlement reached in the NME psychiatric-hospital cases in 1994.

At the time of the FBI raid, Christi Sulzbach, the same person who had signed the agreement for NME, was serving as Tenet's chief corporate officer, executive vice president, general counsel, and compliance officer. What this meant was that she had the responsibilities of insuring that Tenet was abiding by its corporate integrity agreement and defending the corporation against legal challenges resulting from allegations of violations of the same agreement. Sulzbach, remember, was the officer who took the phone call from Hal Chilton, CEO of Redding Medical Center, reporting that the FBI was about to search the hospital, its record storage facilities, and the offices of Chae Moon and Fidel Realyvasquez. After telling Chilton to cooperate with the investigation, she reported to her boss, Jeffrey Barbakow, who was in New York for a lunch with stock analysts. Barbakow had been named chief executive officer of NME in July 1993, one month before six hundred federal agents raided the company's psychiatric hospitals in seventeen states and a year before the corporate integrity agreement was signed. These two holdovers, with several other executives and board members, were still running the company.

Tenet's multitude of legal problems did not seem to worry investors. They just followed the upbeat forecasts of Wall Street analysts who were oblivious to how the company was generating such phenomenal profits. Tenet stock kept rising, allowing Barbakow to realize $115 million in 2001 from exercising options. Mackey realized $14 million and Sulzbach realized $7.25 million. Tenet's shares were trading in the low fifties in 2002, a year in which Barbakow was the country's highest paid chief executive of a publicly traded company. Things seemed to be going swimmingly for Tenet, its officers, and directors. Between January 9 and October 16, nine of them sold shares whose total value was more than $140 million, $111 million of which went to Barbakow. During this period Tenet was rated a "buy" by most of the analysts who covered the healthcare industry, even though they were aware that the company pushed the envelope on pricing, was awash in lawsuits, and had been or was the subject of dozens of federal investigations.

It's worth noting here that Tenet is not the only big for-profit hospital chain with a history of corruption. In 2000, HCA, the largest such concern and Tenet's chief competitor, paid $1.7 billion in criminal fines and penalties for overcharging Medicare and paying kickbacks to doctors for referrals. During the investigation leading to the criminal charges, HCA stock dropped below $20 a share. But HCA seemed to have cleaned up its act. In the first half of 2005 the stock price, which had already recovered substantially, shot up from $40 to over $58. In that six-month period top executives cashed in on $165 million worth of stock and options. But Tenet was the poster child for corporate profiteering in the healthcare industry. It is now startlingly clear that the company's market value had been driven sky-high by wildly inflated profits resulting from illegal schemes and overly aggressive pricing policies. In retrospect, this was clear then too, or should have been, but no one seemed to be paying attention.

On October 28, 2002, Tenet, already immersed in lawsuits from Florida to California, had suffered what would turn out to be a devastating blow from an unexpected direction—Wall Street, previously the company's best friend. A stock analyst at UBS Warburg named Kenneth Weakley released a research report disclosing that Tenet was benefiting excessively from a provision buried deep in the dense verbiage of the thousand-plus pages of Medicare legislation. This provision triggers an extra payment from the U.S. government to hospitals meant to cover costs, known in the healthcare industry as outliers, that are incurred in treating the most expensive patients such as those who have coronary bypass and heart valve surgery. Redding Medical Center, with its booming heart business, was near the top of the list of individual hospital abusers of this provision. These payments were the nucleus of the RMC scheme, which was designed to generate extraordinarily high profits by doing an inordinate volume of cardiac procedures, most of which would generate excessive and undeserved outlier income.

Tenet headed the list of corporate abusers of the outlier-payment provision. Because of its regular quarterly increases in base charges and the ever-increasing number of high-priced procedures, Tenet hospitals—led by RMC—also benefited from a secondary trigger mechanism that added a bonus payment. In May 2002, Congress was about to instruct the Centers for Medicare and Medicaid Services that outlier payments overall should not exceed 5 to 6 percent of its annual payments for basic medical services. The CMS was also on the verge of raising the threshold charge that would trigger the payments. Tenet told the SEC that these changes would not affect its business, but did not disclose the extent to which it had become dependent on income from outlier payments. Redding Medical Center earned 118.6 percent on outliers in fiscal year 2002; that is, it earned $55.7 million in outlier income compared with $47 million in ordinary Medicare income. In other words, outlier payments accounted for 59 percent of RMC's pretax net income in 2002, which was just under $94 million. Tenet overall earned more than three-quarters of a billion dollars, or 23.5 percent of its Medicare income, from outlier payments, and Medicare income accounted for 31.8 percent of Tenet's net patient revenue in 2002. The same fiscal year, HCA received outlier payments that were right around 5 percent of its ordinary Medicare income. Meanwhile, between 1997 and 2002, Tenet also received $1 billion in stop-loss payments, the functional equivalent of outliers, from private insurance companies.

On Wednesday, October 30, two days after UBS Warburg issued Weakley's report and just as Mike Skeen and his agents were fanning out through Redding Medical Center looking for evidence of fraud, stock analysts met with Tenet executives over lunch at the St. Regis Hotel in New York. Sheryl Skolnick, a managing director of Fulcrum Global Partners, who had followed the company for years and knew many of its top executives, did not mince words when she asked Jeffrey Barbakow, "Did you or didn't you commit Medicare fraud?" She was asking him about the outlier scheme identified by Weakley, not the raid on the hospital. Skolnick and the other analysts had no idea the raid was underway and Barbakow didn't tell them. Indeed, Barbakow did not let investors know about the raid until the following day. It is not clear precisely when he found out about it, but the luncheon meeting began at 12:30 p.m., which would have been 9:30 a.m. in Redding. Hal Chilton, the hospital CEO, called Sulzbach at about 9:05 a.m., which would have given her plenty of time before the meeting began to alert her boss. On Friday, November 1, Barbakow tried to reassure investors during a two-and-a-half hour conference call that the FBI raid involved only a couple of doctors and a single hospital and would not threaten the company's financial performance. Over the next week, however, the value of the company's shares declined by roughly $11 billion.

Meanwhile, Skolnick wanted to know whether Tenet was jacking up its list prices with the sole purpose of triggering outlier payments, thereby raising revenues and the price of Tenet stock. "Why was it good that you were getting all these outliers?" Skolnick asked. "Aren't you supposed to lose money on outlier patients?" The second question was overstated, but Barbakow would get the point. Skolnick was asking how Tenet could justify turning outlier patients into a profit center. When she asked these questions she thought Barbakow had a look on his face that could only mean "Holy shit, she's figured it out" or "What's this all about?" To this day Skolnick believes it could have been either, but she also wonders whether Tenet's strategic emphasis on high-priced specialties like cardiology and orthopedics was designed to generate outlier payments, if not by Barbakow then by his subordinates.

Barbakow had issued a statement the morning of his meeting with the analysts saying, "Let me state categorically that we are confident that our hospitals are fully compliant with Medicare rules and regulations, including those governing outlier payments, and that Tenet hospitals are entitled to all payments they receive." His position was that the Medicare regulations allowed Tenet to charge whatever it wanted for services irrespective of what they cost. And Barbakow was not alone in this belief. Paul Gallese, a former Tenet executive, acknowledged that by the mid-1990s the company's mantra was to make the numbers at any cost. But he added that executives like Tom Mackey and David Dennis might have been "just better at playing the game" than the government. His point was that they might have taken advantage of a poorly written regulation rather than breaking the law. Nonetheless, a little over two months after the release of Weakley's report, anticipating action by federal regulators, Tenet reduced its monthly outlier reimbursements from $65 million to $8 million.

When the Redding raid and the outlier scandal blew up in Tenet's face, the company was struggling to manage a number of other crises, including over a hundred civil suits linked to extremely high infection rates at Palm Beach Gardens Medical Center in Florida. Among the unsanitary conditions believed to be responsible were dried blood on IV pumps and operating rooms infested with ants, fruit flies, beetles, and gnats. And just six weeks after the raid on Redding Medical Center, federal agents with a search warrant showed up at Tenet's Alvarado Hospital in San Diego. Criminal bribery charges were subsequently filed against Alvarado and its chief executive, Barry Weinbaum. Alvarado and Weinbaum were accused of paying doctors for referrals, a violation of federal antikickback laws.* But Redding Medical Center, which had been the brightest star in Tenet's firmament, quickly morphed into its preeminent crisis, along with the closely related abuse of Medicare's outlier-payment provision. Federal investigators understood from the outset that the high number of cardiac procedures at RMC triggered—in their view almost certainly intentionally—a substantial windfall in outlier payments for Tenet. But because the outliers would add a significant additional workload to an already overburdened U.S. Attorney's office in Sacramento a decision was made almost immediately to exclude them from McGregor Scott's responsibility and include them in a separate investigation of possible outlier fraud in Tenet hospitals nationwide.

It was for Tenet and a number of its executives, including Christi Sulzbach and Jeffrey Barbakow, in the immortal words of Yogi Berra, "déjà vu all over again." The Redding cases at the end of 2002 were in many ways remarkably similar to the psychiatric hospital cases a decade earlier. But this time around there was a critical difference; one that would make it significantly more difficult to link the company to the crime. There was no high-level Tenet executive who would tell government investigators, or a grand jury, how to connect the dots. And Tenet's management appears to have learned from its earlier experience. Directions about how to maximize profits irrespective of legal niceties, or within the letter but outside the spirit of the law, were much more elliptical, done more with a wink and a nod than with an explicit instruction. This did not mean there was no evidence, or even that the argument that Tenet masterminded the Redding scheme could not be made persuasively. It meant that the evidence was more circumstantial, at times more equivocal, and might not be strong enough to stand up to a legal standard as rigorous as beyond a reasonable doubt. Moreover, government lawyers were notorious for their unwillingness to bring actions they thought they might lose, partly to protect their own reputations, but also to avoid wasting the public's money and out of fairness to defendants.

From the beginning of Mike Skeen's investigation there were strong hints of corporate involvement in the Redding scheme. John Corapi and Joe Zerga had told Skeen about CEO Hal Chilton's apparent lack of

---

*On May 17, 2006, Tenet and the U.S. Attorney in San Diego announced that they had settled the Alvarado case for $21 million. The settlement required Tenet to sell the hospital.

interest in investigating their allegations about Moon, even though they had three opinions from board certified cardiologists and one from a board certified cardiac surgeon sharply disagreeing with Moon's diagnosis. Doctors like Pat Campbell, Bob Pick, and Roy Ditchey had told Skeen that they had reported their concerns about Moon and Realyvasquez doing unnecessary procedures to various hospital CEOs and other executives and were consistently ignored or told pointedly to mind their own business. The doctors did not view these threats as idle. Campbell had been warned by Jerrald Pickering, the lawyer he hired to look into the possibility of alerting state or federal officials to what was going on at RMC, not to risk getting involved because it was too dangerous. This suggested to Campbell that the scheme was being directed not by the doctors, but by the leaders of a powerful corporation. Rich Malotky, Bob Simpson's primary care doctor, thought the same, believed his life could be in danger, and began carrying a gun. CW1 also felt threatened. But these facts were mostly unknown around town. The FBI investigators and the U.S. attorneys held this information closely and there were no leaks.

Tenet's scores of other problems made it imperative to find some way to minimize the harm caused by the complicated situation in Redding, which involved possible criminal charges against the company, civil damage awards that could run into the hundreds of millions of dollars, and whistle-blower lawsuits. The national media were all over the story and the company's stock was in free fall. Tenet needed to negotiate a global settlement with the federal government of all of its outstanding legal problems, including the RMC cases, or its survival would be threatened. To do this, Tenet management had concluded that they needed new lawyers who would be more conciliatory, less confrontational, and would help them avoid the potentially fatal criminal and civil fines the company was facing. One of the firms they hired, Stevens & O'Connell in Sacramento, seemed to be an especially good choice. Both name partners, Charles Stevens, a Democrat, and George O'Connell, a Republican, were former U.S. attorneys for the Eastern District of California, the office that had jurisdiction over the Redding case.

Before being appointed U.S. attorney by President Clinton in 1994, Stevens had been in charge of the Sacramento office of Gibson, Dunn & Crutcher, the big Los Angeles firm that had represented Tenet since it was called National Medical Enterprises. That he was well known to the Gibson, Dunn lawyers, that he was a former U.S. attorney, and that he had the right temperament, all made him a perfect fit for the assignment. His job was to negotiate a settlement with the government that would involve no admission of guilt by Tenet. The government wanted a lot of information and it wanted it quickly. Stevens's instructions were to give the government what it wanted.

Stevens and the lawyers working with him believed there was an urgent need to establish as fast as possible that members of the hospital staff, from the most recently hired orderly to Hal Chilton, the CEO, were not complicit in anything illegal. This task was made easier because the company had made a hard-nosed decision almost immediately to separate itself from the doctors and take no position on their guilt or innocence. The company, demonstrating no loyalty toward its two rainmakers, would contend that if the doctors had done anything wrong they had done so as private practitioners, not as hospital employees. And this contention would be technically correct because although Moon and Realyvasquez held directorships in cardiology and cardiac surgery, respectively, at the hospital, they were contractors, not employees. Tenet hoped that this argument would insulate the company and the hospital from blame and, it was hoped, from prosecution. Tenet executives also were deeply concerned because RMC, one of their most profitable hospitals, had become almost dysfunctional. For weeks, even months after the raid, RMC was in a kind of institutional state of shock. Staff members came to work and did their best, but they were thoroughly demoralized. Things only got worse as the hospital's occupancy rate dropped sharply, and not long afterwards 150 employees were laid off.

Just five days after the raid Tenet had commissioned an independent study of RMC's heart program that the company hoped would give the hospital a clean bill of health irrespective of its findings about Moon and Realyvasquez, both of whom, the company emphasized publicly, were independent contractors, not hospital employees. A major goal of the study was to reassure stockholders, whose assets were evaporating in front of their eyes, that the company was blameless. And if the report arrived at the conclusions Tenet was hoping for, it would also serve as a morale booster for the hospital staff. Although Tenet never said so explicitly, it was widely assumed that when completed the report would be made public, for how else would stockholders be reassured and the staff's morale boosted? If the study, carried out by Mercer Consulting, a division of Marsh & McLennan and known as the Mercer Report, found that the doctors had acted on their own and were not aided or encouraged by hospital or corporate officials, that conclusion would not only comfort investors and hospital staff, but Tenet would be in a much improved legal position. Of course, if Mercer did find complicity with the doctors at the hospital or corporate level Tenet could be in big trouble, but only if the findings were disclosed.

Around the time of the layoffs at RMC, when the U.S. government was on the verge of beginning serious settlement negotiations with Tenet, there still had been no word from the company about what the Mercer investigators were finding. Talks, however, were going on between Stevens and Michael Hirst, an assistant U.S. attorney from New York. Hirst had been assigned to handle civil aspects of the Redding cases while Laura Schwartz and Dan Linhardt, both assistant U.S. attorneys, ran the criminal investigation. Stevens took it as an encouraging sign when Hirst told him that no one in the hospital's management was a target of the criminal investigation. Hirst also told him that the government was not interested in putting the hospital out of business, but rather that it wanted to identify individuals who had committed crimes and prosecute them, which Stevens took to mean the doctors. But neither of these comments necessarily meant that hospital executives were in the clear, only that none of them had yet been implicated. Nevertheless Stevens chose to draw the most optimistic conclusion from Hirst's characterizations— that the government did not view the RMC matter as a conspiracy case and that while the prosecutors would likely pursue the doctors, they would not prosecute Tenet or its subsidiaries criminally.

The defense then began to focus on what to do if the federal government took civil as well as criminal action against Tenet and RMC, which was also an option. There were obvious civil issues such as malpractice that could have been pursued, but Stevens and his colleagues knew that as a tactical matter criminal prosecutors were wary of related civil proceedings and sometimes tried to discourage them. The most common reason for doing this flowed from the Brady rule, a 1963 court ruling that requires prosecutors to turn over to defendants any evidence that might help prove them innocent. The relevant implication of this rule was that exculpatory evidence might be developed in the civil case that would then have to be given to the defense in the criminal case.

At the same time at least one defense lawyer was beginning to believe that the U.S. attorneys had come to understand that they were facing a far greater challenge than they originally had realized if they sought to prosecute the doctors criminally, a perception that could benefit Tenet. Proving criminal intent, which was necessary to win a fraud conviction, was not going to be easy. Government lawyers, who had been concerned from the outset that their case could turn into a battle of experts, had even told Tenet's lawyers at one point that they were not sure they had a fraud case. If they couldn't make a criminal case against the doctors, the defense lawyers recognized, they could hardly hope to make one against Tenet or the hospital. Moreover, the defense lawyers believed the government would be less likely to risk compromising the criminal case against the doctors by bringing a civil case against Tenet because one or more potential expert witnesses for the prosecution might say something beneficial to the defense, thereby triggering the Brady rule. On the whole things were looking reasonably bright for Tenet and RMC.

The U.S. attorneys were now faced with some difficult decisions. Criminal convictions of Moon and Realyvasquez were their clear priority. They had a great deal of time and money invested in the investigation, but more important, with the help of the FBI and HHS, they had gathered an impressive body of evidence. They believed the doctors were guilty and deserved to go to prison. The investigative team was still working hard to establish a conspiratorial chain between the doctors and RMC administrators and Tenet executives, but they had not succeeded and it was by no means evident that they would. It was beginning to look like the best way to advance their most important goal—getting a criminal conviction—was to reach a settlement with Tenet. If Tenet settled, this would create an appearance that would help the government's criminal case against the doctors. It would tend to validate the idea that there had been wrongdoing. The settlement might also include a cooperation agreement with Tenet that would give the government access to evidence it might not otherwise be able to get. And finally, quite simply, something was better than nothing.

Given these circumstances, the U.S. attorneys decided to seek a civil settlement with Tenet. Hirst was asked to propose it to Stevens, which he did. Stevens liked the idea because he thought it would be a good way to advance Tenet's strategic goal of improving relations with the government. The same was not true of all of his colleagues, however. Some of them thought that Tenet should tough it out because the government simply did not have a good enough case against the hospital or the company. But Tenet was in so much trouble in so many places with the federal government that those in favor of settling argued effectively that the company should do whatever it took to make the problems go away, even if it cost many millions of dollars. What Tenet really wanted was to settle all of its problems with the U.S. government so that they would disappear at once. But this was not in the cards. In the end, at least in the Redding case, the conciliators prevailed over the warriors and settlement talks got underway.

Tenet took the position that the company had not committed fraud, so Stevens asked Hirst how they would settle if there was no liability. After thinking about it, Hirst came up with the idea that Tenet could offer to reimburse the government for the procedures. Neither Tenet nor the hospital had to admit to anything, but since neither disputed that the doctors might have done unnecessary procedures they could simply act as good corporate citizens and cover the government's costs. Tenet accepted this premise, but the company wanted two things out of the agreement—language that made clear that while the doctors might have performed unwarranted procedures, the hospital did not cooperate in fraud, and credit for cooperating with the government. In return the government would recover its losses and get Tenet's cooperation in its investigation of the doctors. The elements of a deal were now in place.

By early summer of 2004, however, what had seemed like a mutually beneficial arrangement began to unravel. From the defendants' perspective Hirst was asking for too much. For one thing, Tenet wanted the time frame for computing the settlement amount to be two years shorter than what the government had proposed, thereby substantially reducing the number of procedures on which the settlement would be based. Hirst was also seeking double damages for each unnecessary interventional procedure such as an angiogram and double damages and penalties for each uncalled-for surgery. Not only would this result in a much higher settlement amount than the defense expected, but it would look exactly like a settlement based on the provisions of the False Claims Act, which would undermine the defense claim that the hospital was not complicit in fraud.

Jerry Hurst, the healthcare fraud auditor in the Sacramento U.S. attorney's office, came up with the formula for calculating the amount. Procedures at RMC were compared with a norm arrived at by using

Medicare data and the *Dartmouth Atlas of Health Care*. The excess procedures above the norm were deemed unnecessary. The number of procedures in each category—bypass surgery, valve surgery, angiogram, single-vessel angioplasty, etc.—was then multiplied by an average price arrived at using similar data. Penalties of $10,000 were then added to each unwarranted heart surgery. No penalties were added for angiograms because it is much more difficult to prove that a diagnostic procedure was unnecessary. This method yielded a total amount of about $58 million, which was far more than Tenet had anticipated. Stevens and the rest of the defense team were not at all happy. The government, however, refused to back down. By midsummer 2004, the deal looked like it was on the verge of collapsing.

14

The Civil Cases

In the days following the raid, Stephen Boreman, California's deputy attorney general, asked the Shasta County Superior Court to issue a restraining order prohibiting Moon and Realyvasquez from practicing medicine in California. But on November 13, the doctors won what looked like a significant victory when the chief judge of Shasta County Superior Court, Monica Marlow, denied the state's motion, which drew heavily on the FBI affidavit, on the grounds that the allegations in the affidavit were based largely on hearsay. In the end, however, Judge Marlow's failure to enjoin the doctors from practicing medicine had no practical effect. On November 22, Medi-Cal, the state insurance program for the poor, canceled Moon's and Realyvasquez's rights to receive reimbursement for their medical services and in mid-December Blue Cross and Blue Shield followed by canceling their contracts. By February 2003, therefore, Moon and Realyvasquez were forced to suspend their medical practices. Moon really had no choice. His malpractice insurance had expired on February 1 and he could not get a new policy.

Judge Marlow was also asked by the Judicial Council to pick a judge to preside over the RMC civil cases. No one yet knew how many there were going to be, but estimates ran as high as 1,500. She selected Superior Court Senior Judge Jack Halpin, who had already reviewed the situation at the request of the council to determine how the cases might best be managed. Halpin, who had never presided over anything remotely like this huge, complex mess of litigation, was an interesting choice. He was a tall, straight and fit-looking seventy-six-year-old with little gray in his hair and bags under his eyes. His manner was laconic, confident, but not arrogant. His infrequent smiles were subdued, but seemed genuine.

Halpin was graduated from Stanford Law School in 1951 in the same class as former Chief Justice William Rehnquist and former Associate Justice Sandra Day O'Connor, both of whom appeared as references on his resume. Those days being what they were, none of the five women in the class, including O'Connor and Halpin's wife, Sydney, could get jobs, except as secretaries. Halpin accepted a job at a law firm in San Francisco and he and Sydney spent many of their weekends traveling around California looking for a place to open a practice together. The population of Redding was 12,500 when they arrived there in 1953 and decided to stay. When one of the two local judges retired in 1962, Governor Pat Brown appointed Halpin to replace him. He was thirty-six years old. But two years later he was appointed deputy director of finance for the state of California and did not return to Redding until 1991. While he was practicing law with Dugan Barr's brother Duncan in San Francisco he was offered a chance to return to the bench in Redding and he jumped at it.

Almost from the outset—that is to say after the bulk of the civil tort suits were filed against Tenet and the doctors—there were on-and-off negotiations to settle them, which Halpin facilitated. Because both Moon and Realyvasquez had lost their rights to reimbursement from Medi-Cal and Blue Cross and Blue Shield, which effectively eliminated their ability to practice medicine, they had a strong incentive to reach a quick settlement. Meanwhile, Moon was out regularly playing golf at the Riverview Country Club and Realyvasquez, the subject of only infrequent sightings, was spending a lot of time working on his ranch and overseeing the building of a new house on the northern California coast. But both men wanted to get out from under the threat that hung over them, which included the grim prospect of spending time in a federal prison.

Several things were clear from the start, the most important of which was that Tenet, although beleaguered—its cash reserves were draining away and it was facing bankruptcy—still had the closest thing to deep pockets. No matter what the doctors did, if the company did not settle there would not be enough money to compensate a large cohort of civil plaintiffs, which eventually totaled 769, not to mention their lawyers. The lawyers would be handsomely rewarded if they won, but they knew that it would cost them millions of dollars to litigate these cases and they could lose. The plaintiffs' lawyers also knew from experience that it was generally fruitless to go after the personal assets of defendants, in this case the well-heeled surgeons and cardiologists. This meant that they very likely would get at most $24 million from each practice group, the full amount of their insurance. For the plaintiffs and their lawyers to be well compensated therefore would require Tenet to add hundreds of millions of dollars to the pot, which given the financial condition of the corporation was a prospect fraught with uncertainty.

Bob Simpson, Russ Reiner, Dugan Barr, Doug Mudford, Luke Ellis, and their Texas colleagues, Jim Moriarty, Steve Hackerman, and Richard Frankel, believed they could wring the money out of the company—an absolutely essential task—otherwise they would not have taken the cases. But as time passed Tenet was getting rid of hospitals, some at fire-sale prices, and the possibility of a bankruptcy loomed larger, which frayed their nerves. Tenet's executives, led by Jeffrey Barbakow up to May 2003 when he resigned as CEO, and Trevor Fetter after that, and their lawyers, were aware that the company had some leverage in its negotiations with the civil plaintiffs because of its relatively deep pockets. Tenet was also aware that the possibility of bankruptcy was real, especially if the Justice Department, the SEC, and an influential senator, Charles Grassley, a tough pig farmer from Iowa who was chairman of the Senate Finance Committee, decided to push the company over the cliff. In this environment and under pressure from Grassley, Christi Sulzbach and several other Tenet executives resigned.

Throughout 2004, Judge Halpin, whom lawyers on both sides found quirky, but intelligent, had been exercising his considerable skills as a mediator trying to get the doctors to participate in sustained settlement negotiations. He had invited both the cardiologists and the surgeons to settlement conferences with their insurers. But after a while it became plain that the surgeons were not interested in settling. The cardiologists were not pressing for a settlement either, but they seemed more inclined to talk. It was only when an executive of MIEC, the malpractice insurance company representing the cardiologists, whom Halpin had known from previous cases, said to him privately, "You know, I think we ought to settle these cases," that the judge understood that conditions were really ripe for a settlement. Halpin invited Moon, his associates, and their insurers to a settlement conference once again. They accepted the invitation, and serious talks got underway.

It seemed likely to Halpin that the insurance company wanted to settle because the amount for which the cardiologists were insured would not have been nearly enough to cover any jury award at trial. Also,

MIEC would have had to pay a substantial amount in legal costs to defend the case. But the insurance company could not settle without the consent of their clients. In California the insured party has an absolute right to veto a settlement. There were, however, incentives for the doctors to settle, too, including the possibility that otherwise they could lose their licenses to practice medicine in California. It was not unusual for physicians to settle cases they thought they might win to eliminate any risk of losing their licenses. Halpin thought Moon was worried that he might lose his license and that all of the cardiologists might have given up hope of ever again getting malpractice insurance. He did not think this was true of the surgeons, however.

While Halpin was trying to nurse along the talks between the plaintiffs and the cardiologists, settlement negotiations were also going on outside the court's purview between Tenet's lawyers and the plaintiffs' lawyers. At one point Tenet gave consideration to trying to consolidate their settlement talks with the doctors, but the idea was rejected, probably because the doctors brought neither a significant amount of money nor anything else the company needed to the bargaining table. Tenet had two main reasons for wanting to settle. First, the company believed it was important to get the hospital out from under the black cloud that since the raid had been hovering over it, scaring away patients and depressing staff. Second, Tenet was desperate to improve its relations with the federal government. Although Tenet still was not willing to admit to participating in fraud, the company was willing to consider a negotiated settlement with the plaintiffs based on the theory that the doctors had been guilty of negligence. Tenet and RMC would take the position that even though there had been no fraud, "what happened had happened on our watch, so we'll pay." The plaintiffs' lawyers, who were becoming progressively more concerned that Tenet would run out of money, accepted this basis for settlement.

Over the next several months the parties met periodically with Eric Green, a nationally known mediator from Boston who had served as the court-appointed mediator in the Microsoft and Enron/Arthur Andersen cases. Green taught law at Boston University and was busy with other cases around the country, so it often took weeks to schedule a half-day session with him. But Green's approach involved more contact with the parties separately than together and he did much of this by phone. He understood that a case as complex as this one could not be settled in a day and that it was critically important to establish his credibility with both sides, and this took time. One way he made Tenet feel comfortable with his mediation was to praise them frequently for their willingness to pay the lion's share of the settlement. Normally in situations of this kind settlement payments are shared based on an apportionment of fault. But since the doctors' insurance did not come close to being enough to compensate 769 plaintiffs, if there was going to be a settlement the bulk of the money would have to come from Tenet, irrespective of fault.

At one point Tenet, which understandably was not happy about having to pay hundreds of millions of dollars, sought to reduce the amount by asking that an impartial panel of experts be appointed to decide which cases were truly unnecessary. But Green was able to convince the company that the panel's decisions would inevitably be disputed, efforts to resolve these disputes would go on forever, and no one would get closure. This argument, and indeed Green's choice of the right word, resonated with Tenet because from the beginning it was seeking closure for the hospital. The company dropped the idea and from then on the discussions revolved around money.

By July, Moon and his associates, Russ, Fletscher, and Chandramouli, also had decided to avoid the costs and risks of going to trial and were engaged in serious settlement negotiations with the plaintiffs. Halpin had long believed that settlements were almost always better for the state and the parties than costly, emotionally draining trials. He was also acutely aware that malpractice cases, if they went to a jury trial, were all but impossible for plaintiffs to win in Shasta County. In the thirteen years he had been back on the bench in Redding he could recall only one verdict for the plaintiffs. But this statistic, while striking, was misleading. The really strong malpractice cases from the plaintiffs' point of view never got to a jury. They were always settled. This time, with Judge Halpin playing an active role, the plaintiffs and cardiologists reached an agreement in October 2004 to settle for $24 million, the limit of the cardiologists' malpractice insurance. This must have been a painful decision for these doctors because it would substantially curtail their ability to get malpractice insurance, without which they would not, for all practical purposes, be able to practice medicine again.

It was not until December 21, however, five months after Tenet Healthcare sold Redding Medical Center to Hospital Partners of America for about $60 million, that Tenet and the 769 plaintiffs reached an agreement to settle all outstanding litigation between them for $395 million. This sum was a hundred million or so short of what Simpson, Barr, and their colleagues had hoped for based on their perception of Tenet's early negotiating position, but they decided to take it rather than shoot for the moon and risk losing everything. In retrospect, they seem to have made the right choice because six months later Tenet's financial position had deteriorated still further. But this did not put an end to the civil litigation.

Realyvasquez and the other surgeons were still holding out. Their decision was to take on in court the 642 plaintiffs who had filed suit against them. The plaintiffs' lawyers were puzzled because they thought that in some ways they had a stronger case against the surgeons than against the cardiologists. In their view it would be easier to convince a jury of the guilt of physicians who had actually cut open chests and bypassed wide open arteries than those who had simply seen blockages where there were none. Dugan Barr was fantasizing about projecting angiograms on a large screen in the courtroom and asking Realyvasquez, "Exactly what is it that you were bypassing, doctor?" But coincidentally, on the day the Tenet settlement was announced, Stephen Boreman, California's deputy attorney general, provided a kind of framework for answering Barr's question. He was quoted in the *San Francisco Chronicle* as saying, "Surgeons get to rely on the cardiologists' referral." Boreman's surprising contention was that the standard of care in northern California did not require a surgeon to independently evaluate a cardiologist's treatment recommendation before operating.

Standard of care is a somewhat slippery concept, but there is a generally accepted legal definition. Legally, the standard of care is the level at which an average prudent provider in a given community would practice, or how similarly qualified practitioners would have managed a patient's care under the same or similar circumstances. This definition, of course, tells one nothing at all about how "an average prudent provider in a given community" actually practices, which means that determining the standard of care can be highly subjective. But conversations with surgeons around the country strongly suggest a consensus view that prudent and ethical practice for a surgeon, or any other physician, always begins with careful consideration of what is best for the patient. Tom Fogarty, a respected Stanford cardiac surgeon said this was so and Paul Corso, an internationally known cardiac surgeon at the

Washington Hospital Center, said that if Boreman were right "you might as well train a bunch of monkeys" to be cardiac surgeons. In other words, Corso and Fogarty agreed that a surgeon could not meet the standard of care for performing surgery without reaching an independent judgment as to whether surgery was the optimal treatment, which, it appeared, Realyvasquez on many occasions had failed to do. Although the medical board had filed an extensive accusation against Moon, it had failed to move against Realyvasquez, apparently because of the position Boreman had taken on the standard of care issue.

Even though the surgeons were not prepared to settle, the Tenet settlement was a major development that provided some satisfaction and in many cases badly needed financial support for the plaintiffs. CEO Trevor Fetter said in a statement accompanying the announcement that "We believe this settlement is the fair and honorable way to conclude this very sad chapter. It would likely have taken multiple trials and many years to assess liability in these cases. By settling all the cases at once, we put this matter behind both the plaintiffs and us, and we bring closure to this unfortunate event. We are building a new Tenet on a solid foundation of quality, transparency, compliance and integrity, so that the safety and efficacy of the patient care our hospitals deliver is always above reproach."

Fetter's statement was really quite remarkable. It came within a hair of an admission of guilt, which was highly unusual in a civil settlement that required no such admission. And it doesn't take a linguistics scholar like Noam Chomsky to parse the last sentence in the quotation above. If the new Tenet was going to be built on quality, transparency, compliance, and integrity, one could hardly help concluding Fetter was implying that the old Tenet had been built on something like shoddiness, opacity, noncompliance, and unscrupulousness. Still, only time would tell whether there would be any Tenet at all when the smoke cleared and if there was, whether it would be substantially different from the old Tenet. But with respect to at least one criterion specified by Fetter, transparency, a signal had been sent that the future might well look a lot like the past. The settlement agreement itself was shrouded in secrecy. Moreover, as in the psychiatric-hospital scandal, the company had refused to release or even acknowledge the existence of either a report or informal findings based on the investigation that Mercer Consulting had been commissioned to carry out.

The money from the cardiologists was distributed to the plaintiffs in mid-February 2005, and the Tenet checks were handed out on March 1, almost exactly two years and four months after the raid. The payoff was not fast enough for some of the plaintiffs, who were desperately in need of the money to stave off personal bankruptcy resulting from medical expenses and inability to work, but by the standards of mass-tort litigation, it was relatively quick. The money was divided according to a formula devised by the plaintiffs' lawyers based on the procedure performed—surgery was worth more than catheterization and three-vessel bypass more than two—complications or death arising from the procedure, and the patient's age. If two patients underwent the same procedure, had no complications, and both survived, the younger patient would get more money. The lawyers' fees were negotiated separately by each law firm with its clients. Most were in the 40 percent range. None of the 769 plaintiffs rejected the settlement money, but in both a bodily and financial sense, many were not made whole by it either.

The settlement was a vindication of sorts, but what many of the victims wanted most of all was to see the doctors, who they believed had inflicted their injuries, pain, and suffering, go to prison, preferably for a long time. But the federal government was pursuing its investigation deliberately and they would have to wait, first for indictments, if there were to be any, and then convictions and sentencing.

In December of 2004, when the settlement with Tenet was reached, Zona Martin's daughter, Donna Norton, was one of those on the verge of declaring bankruptcy. Donna did not want to disclose the exact amount of her mother's settlement share, but it was enough to pay their debts and buy a new Toyota Sienna minivan in which she could carry her mother's wheelchair and potty chair easily and leave a small cash cushion for the future. She said she had cut up and thrown away all of her credit cards. She no longer planned to put her mother in a nursing home, but she had found a facility nearby that would take her for short stays so that she and her son, Donald, could get away once in a while.

Paul Alexandre, whose sternum would never knit back together after it was sawn open and ratcheted apart during unnecessary bypass surgery, said that the money would help some. His settlement was one of the largest because he was so young when the unnecessary surgery was done and he had suffered such serious complications. Even after the lawyers' 40 percent cut his payment was likely to have been in the mid-six figures. But it didn't change the fact that he couldn't fish for salmon again, which is what he really loved. He said the salmon whipped him, he couldn't reel them in. He tried to go trout fishing even though it was painful and if he fell he could be hurt very badly. He knew he was going to be in pain and taking pills for the rest of his life, but he accepted this. He said he had never realized that "everything goes through your chest." If he turned his head or moved his foot, he felt a pain in his chest. He was unable to sleep flat on his back and found it very hard to get into a comfortable position to sleep at all. Sometimes it hurt so much that he couldn't get out of bed. It hurt even more when the weather was cold. But he still dreamed of going salmon fishing in Alaska.

Shirley Wooten's son Shannon thought the settlement was better than nothing, but what he really wanted was for the doctors to get theirs. "These guys cut on people and they died," he said. "They didn't care. They didn't give a damn." He also said he didn't care if Tenet were put out of business. He knew the company had a bad history. Shannon did not think that the $300,000 his mother eventually received in compensation came close to making up for her pain and suffering. But he had nothing but praise for their lawyers and did not begrudge them their $200,000 share of the half-million dollar settlement.

As for Shirley, in mid-September 2005, she lost her balance while getting into bed, fell, and hit her head on a stool. At first it didn't seem as if she had hurt herself. There was no break in her skin and she said she felt all right. But that evening Bob found her covered in vomit, her head on her chest in a coma. Blood vessels had ruptured causing a severe cerebral hemorrhage that was crushing her brain. She was rushed to the hospital, where she died on September 21, 2005. Shannon was certain that like her fall in the bathroom and the fall that caused her broken hip the accident that killed her had resulted from the surgery that she should never have had. Shirley Wooten came from a long-lived family and had been in good health for a woman her age before her surgery. It is likely that she had many good years remaining. Four months after Shirley's death, on January 23, 2006, her mother, Martha Aldridge, died. She was 106. Her family believed she was the oldest person in Shasta County.

15

The Intensivist

While the various legal teams meticulously built their cases and simultaneously looked for ways to settle them advantageously, FBI agent Mike Skeen pressed ahead with his investigation. He had worked hard for months to produce an affidavit that was compelling enough to get a federal court to issue a search warrant. But he knew that to construct a fraud case strong enough to stand up in court would take much more work. In fact his investigation was really just getting underway. Many other sources and a lot of additional evidence were going to be needed. But on the whole Skeen was optimistic. His hard work was paying off. Slowly but surely more knowledgeable sources of information were turning up at his door. One disaffected RMC physician who found his way to Skeen not long after the raid was Frank Sebat, a cantankerous twenty-year veteran of RMC and the chief of intensive care at the hospital who had once been close to Moon and had hosted his fiftieth birthday party. Over several meetings during 2003, Sebat, who still had a hard time believing Moon had intentionally overtreated and misdiagnosed patients, told Skeen a story that supported the FBI agent's strongly held hypothesis that Tenet had not only created the conditions that made unnecessary surgery possible, but had encouraged it.

In 2000, Hal Chilton, who had worked at RMC from 1986 to 1989 as chief operating officer, returned to Redding to become RMC's fourth CEO in a little over four years. By Tenet's standards, he was a great success. In 2002, RMC's pretax net income was just under $94 million, the highest among the company's forty California hospitals. But here and there within the hospital, if not at corporate headquarters in Santa Barbara, concerns were being expressed about another measure of success, the quality of patient care generally and at the California Heart Institute in particular.

Not long after Chilton arrived, Sebat, who was a member of the hospital's board of directors, was named to a task force formed to identify and recommend ways to improve peer review, the in-house oversight process designed to monitor quality of care. Chilton and Realyvasquez were also members of this task force. The group had met three times, but had not begun to grapple seriously with the issues when it was summarily disbanded on orders of Dennis Brown, Tenet's regional vice president. Sebat was upset by Brown's decision, which was conveyed to him by Chilton. He subsequently told Brown that the task force's work was not done; indeed, that it had barely begun. Brown's response to Sebat was brief and to the point—their work was done and he should let it go.

But early in 2001, shortly after his conversation with Brown, Sebat, whose tenacity and abrasiveness at times strained relations even with his close friends, felt he had to express his concerns about patient care directly to Chilton. In a carefully worded letter dated February 21, he suggested that for various reasons "malfeasance" at the hospital was going either unidentified or undocumented because the peer review process had "fallen below reasonable expectations." Although Sebat's letter was somewhat vague and didn't name names or specify the malfeasance he had in mind, it was a conspicuous act of courage in an institution, and within a corporation, ruthlessly committed to bottom-line results. In a clear indication that he understood the corporate ethos he wrote this shrewd final sentence: "Although this feedback may initially be viewed with skepticism, over time it will result in benefit to the individual, to the patient as well as to the hospital and ultimately *positively impacting the bottom line.*" (Italics added.)

In fact, Sebat was troubled by something much deeper than just a lack of effective peer review, which had concerned other RMC doctors* and was the ostensible issue his letter addressed. He had come to believe that bottom-line considerations were driving patient-care decisions, especially

---

*Marshall Hall, chief of surgery at RMC during 1997–98, said in a sworn deposition on September 12, 2005, that he complained to Steve Schmidt, the hospital's CEO at the time, about the lack of peer review of the cardiac surgery program. He was told it was outsourced to Sacramento and he should forget about it. This troubled Hall because as chief of surgery it was his responsibility to see that peer review was performed, but he did not believe it was his job to tell the CEO how to run the hospital, so he dropped the matter.

in high-revenue departments such as cardiology and cardiac surgery, and that as a result quality was suffering. Bill Browning, the pharmacy chief, shared this view. "Physician peer review was suppressed," he said, "because the heart program was a golden goose." Although he didn't say so in his letter, Sebat also knew of cases involving Moon and Realy-vasquez in which the hospital administration had overridden medical staff decisions on the grounds that carrying them out would have reduced revenues. One such case pertained to a medical staff effort to suspend Realy-vasquez for falling too far behind on his dictating. The administration overruled the staff and assigned hospital support staff to assist Realy-vasquez in catching up. It was Sebat's belief that Hal Chilton was actively subverting quality of care in these two areas. Sebat said he also knew of cases in which patients' charts had been falsified, but did not specify them.

Sebat understood enough about the way Tenet ran its business to know that for any meaningful change to take place, the word would have to come down from the top. The hospital's board of directors, which operated in an advisory more than a governing capacity, could not override Tenet policies and exercised special care in areas that might affect revenue. Moreover, the board, which had about twenty carefully selected administrative, medical staff, and lay members, lacked the power to hire or fire administrators. It was in effect a mouthpiece for Tenet with little independence or autonomy.

With this reality in mind, Sebat made three general recommendations, nominally to the board, but he was fully aware that whether or not they would be implemented would be decided by Dennis Brown at regional headquarters or Tom Mackey and other top executives at corporate headquarters. He recommended, first, that the board of directors, which has formal responsibility for patient care, should notify the medical staff that its most important charge is to assure quality through peer review and it should provide the medical staff with the means to carry out this charge. Second, the medical staff should review and restructure the peer review process to eliminate its defects. Finally, everyone—the medical staff, directors, and administrators—should treat peer review as a mandatory mechanism essential to the running of the hospital as a successful business.

None of these recommendations was ever put into practice.

Around the time Sebat sent his letter, another peer review task force was in the process of being formed. Sebat, who had been the prime force pressing the administration to improve peer review at the hospital, expected to be named to the new group, but he wasn't. The members were Daniel Alcala, Sebat's bike-riding partner and friend of more than twenty years, Gill Fitz, the chief of staff, Maja Sandberg, a vascular surgeon who shared office space with Realyvasquez, and Charles Springfield, the director of emergency medicine. Fitz was the nominal chairman of the task force, but Springfield, who was close to the administration, set the agenda. Sebat came to believe that the only reason for setting up the second task force was to allow the administration through Springfield to gain control of the process. Alcala, who had trained with Sebat at the University of Southern California in the late 1970s, told him that he supported his membership, but that the others said they thought he would be disruptive and influence their deliberations negatively. This group too was eventually disbanded without accomplishing anything.

Over the next year, Sebat concentrated on his ICU duties and an office he had set up—and for which he had raised $200,000—to improve the quality of intensive-care medicine. Then, on a sunny spring day in 2002, he was approached in the hall outside the ICU by Sandberg, a very tall, elegant-looking woman from Iowa who considered herself to be Realyvasquez's friend and who frequently assisted when he did bypass surgery, especially on difficult cases. In the early years of the heart program Sandberg harvested saphenous veins from patients' legs. Later, however, this task was performed by physicians' assistants, which left her free to assist Realyvasquez with the bypass itself.

She said, "Frank, I want to talk to you for a second." He said, "Okay," and without superfluous pleasantries, she told him that Realyvasquez, who was not trained to interpret intravascular ultrasound images, had become quite concerned about doing heart surgery on patients sent to him by Moon when the diagnosis was based solely on IVUS. Sebat was puzzled and asked her why she had come to him with this particular problem. She said that she and Realyvasquez didn't know what to do about it and wanted his advice. Sebat's initial response was "Well, I'm not in a position to do anything." But he thought about it for a minute and made a suggestion. He said, "Okay, here's what we'll do. We'll go ahead and set up an educational conference that will take place in the Liberty Room. We'll present the case in question. We'll have Dr. Realyvasquez there, Dr. Brusett there, you, Dr. Moon, myself, a lot of the nurses and other physicians. And just like you do in any other educational conference, you present the case, you discuss the pros and cons, and maybe in that process we can tease out the issue and raise the questions and figure out what, if anything, is appropriate."

Sandberg agreed to Sebat's suggestion and he set up the conference. But when it took place about a month later neither Realyvasquez nor Sandberg showed up. Brusett might have been there briefly, but if he was he said nothing and left early. As far as Sebat can recall only one other physician attended, Moon, who dominated the session. Moon presented the case, which had been selected by Sandberg, in detail. He explained the specific nature of the disease (types and number of lesions, in what vessels, etc.), what he identified when he used IVUS that was not obvious on the angiogram, and why he recommended bypass surgery instead of medical treatment, angioplasty, or angioplasty with one or more stents. Sebat listened carefully and was not satisfied by Moon's explanation. He pressed him on why he recommended surgery rather than stenting, but he found Moon's response no more convincing than his original explanation and left frustrated by the entire exercise. He subsequently told Sandberg that she should have been there, but said nothing about it to Realyvasquez.

Around that time, Sebat went to see Hal Chilton in his office to discuss a number of matters. In the course of this conversation the subject came up of the behavior of Tom Russ, Moon's associate. Sebat disapproved of what he considered Russ's dismissive treatment of both patients and staff and in his typically outspoken fashion had been trying to do something about it. Chilton, clearly exasperated and implying that Sebat had a bad habit of involving himself in matters that were none of his business, said, "Frank, why do you do this?" to which Sebat answered, "Because it's the right thing to do." Chilton became agitated. He stood up behind his desk and said caustically, "You cost me two million dollars. That money should come out of your directorship." Sebat was dumbfounded. He understood Chilton to mean that the money was lost because Russ had been taking his patients to another hospital, but it seemed absurd to him that even if this were true a loss of that magnitude could have resulted. He was also amazed that Chilton was entirely focused on the lost revenue and seemed to have no interest at all in what was to him Russ's totally unacceptable behavior. Sebat tried to calm Chilton down and asked him to sit so that they could discuss the matter in a civilized fashion. But Chilton remained on his feet and directed Sebat to leave his office. Sebat tried again to get Chilton to sit down so that they could talk about the Russ situation. This time Chilton, now furious, told him that if he didn't get out of his office he would call security to throw him out. Sebat left.

Shortly thereafter Sebat received a registered letter from Chilton notifying him that his contract as director of intensive care was going to be terminated. Not long afterwards Sebat was approached by Springfield, the director of emergency medicine and his fellow board member. Springfield told Sebat that he might be able to salvage his contract if he resigned from the board, the medical staff executive committee, and the medicine committee. It was clear to Sebat that Springfield was acting as a delivery boy for Chilton, although he did not say so explicitly. Springfield also made it clear to Sebat that unless he did what was asked of him no one in the administration would talk to him. And indeed this was what happened. Chilton did not return his phone calls; neither did Linda Leavell, the director of nursing, who later became the hospital's chief clinical officer. When he passed these people in the halls they would look the other way or scowl at him. Over the next few weeks Sebat had a number of similar conversations with Springfield, each of which centered on the premise that if he resigned from his medical staff positions things would get better for him at the hospital. Springfield warned him that he had no chance of winning this battle with Tenet. But Sebat did not resign from the board or from these committees and his contract, which had two years to run, was not immediately terminated.

While he was dealing with these problems, and with his patients and other hospital duties, as part of his medical staff responsibilities Sebat interviewed two cardiologists who were being recruited for the California Heart Institute. He met with them separately in a small room in the administration area used for this purpose. Satyendra Giri, a Harvard-trained cardiologist who was director of interventional cardiology at the University of Texas Medical School in Houston, was extremely well qualified for the job in Redding, perhaps overqualified. Sebat talked to him first. Remembering his conversation with Maja Sandberg and Moon's failure to satisfactorily answer his questions at the case conference they had ginned up, he asked Giri what he thought of Moon's use of IVUS and his management of patients he diagnosed with soft plaque and dissections in their coronary arteries. Giri and Sam Ward, the other recruit, rather surprisingly had been shown a number of IVUS cases by Moon as part of the recruiting process. Giri said, "Frank, I think that they're not dissections." "What do you mean?" Sebat asked, and Giri answered, "Well, I think he's overreading, and I don't think they're dissections and I don't think they should have any kind of intervention."

Sebat found Giri's assessment troubling. Until his conversation with Sandberg had put some doubt in his mind, Sebat had been deeply impressed with Moon's ability to identify and treat potentially deadly lesions. Moreover, he liked Moon. Sandberg's comments had planted a seed, but until his meeting with Giri he hadn't really thought much about it. Now Giri's reaction to Moon's IVUS images convinced him that Moon was treating patients inappropriately. He said to Giri, "You have to come. We have to fix this. You have to come here."

Sebat then talked to Ward in the same room, asked him the same questions, and got the same answers. Sebat passed on what the two cardiologists told him to the RMC administration, but he never found out what if anything they did with the information. A few weeks later, Sebat ran into Realyvasquez in the hallway and invited him into his office. He felt certain that Realyvasquez would be happy to hear that Giri and Ward had in effect confirmed his instinct that Moon's diagnoses with IVUS were suspect. He told Realyvasquez about his conversation with Sandberg in which she had mentioned his concerns about Moon's use of IVUS, and about his interviews with Giri and Ward in which they disagreed with Moon's diagnoses based on IVUS. But to his dismay, Realyvasquez told him he no longer had any concerns about Moon's IVUS-based diagnoses. He was happy with things the way they were, and he wasn't sure he wanted Ward to come to RMC. By way of elaboration about why his concerns had dissipated, Realyvasquez said, "You know, Frank, I've measured flows intraoperatively and they have good flow, therefore the lesion that I'm bypassing must be significant." Realyvasquez's point was that even though he couldn't see the blockages angiographically he could be sure he was bypassing flow-limiting lesions because his intraoperative measurements showed there was good flow through the graft.*

---

*The government's experts, the plaintiffs' experts, Paul Corso, and Tom Fogarty all agreed he was wrong. Even if there is no flow-limiting lesion in the native artery, they concurred, there will generally be adequate flow in the graft immediately after it has been sewn into place. The blood pumped by the heart will simply divide at the point where the graft has been sewn on with roughly half continuing to flow through the native artery and the other half flowing through the graft. Later on, however, if there continues to be substantial flow through the native artery, the graft, whether it is a vein or an artery, could fill up with clot material or even collapse.

Unlike most other cardiac surgeons, Realyvasquez frequently used saphenous veins for his grafts even when internal mammary arteries, which last longer, were available. Saphenous veins are larger in diameter than internal mammary arteries and have no muscular tone, so they are less likely to spasm and collapse or form clots as a result of low blood flow, which might eventually result if blood were still flowing freely through the bypassed artery. By using veins instead of longer-lasting arteries Realyvasquez was trying to do what he could to improve the odds that people on whom he did unnecessary bypasses wouldn't have heart attacks from clots in their grafts or have the grafts shut down soon after surgery. But using veins instead of arteries increases the chances that the patient will be back for another bypass, sooner rather than later.

Although Sebat did not fully understand Realyvasquez's explanation, it left him feeling dissatisfied. He was still worried that at the very least Moon was overaggressive, possibly dangerously so, and that despite the personal risks involved, he had to do something about it. He was gun-shy after his experience complaining to Chilton about Russ, who had nowhere near the clout Moon did, but he felt he had to go to Chilton again. Sebat never mentioned Moon's name during their meeting, but he framed his comments so that there was no doubt about whom he was talking. He said he thought there was a big problem with a very powerful doctor who brought a lot of money to the hospital. But to avoid being subjected to Chilton's anger he also told him that if he didn't want to hear about it he, Sebat, would take his concerns to the medical staff. Chilton told him curtly that he should go to the medical staff, and that was the end of their conversation. But going to the medical staff was problematical too because Moon was a member of the medical committee, the appropriate body to deal with the complaint. In the end, all Sebat thought he could do was discuss it informally with other committee members. No action was ever taken.

Shortly thereafter, Sebat called five or six other cardiologists around the country to see if they agreed with Giri and Ward about the appropriate uses of IVUS. They did—unanimously. They all said that recommending surgery on the basis of IVUS alone was a major deviation from the standard of care. It was important to confirm the IVUS finding with other tests such as nuclear stress tests and echocardiograms to determine that the patient had cardiac ischemia, or deprivation of blood to the heart muscle, and that the lesion identified on IVUS was the culprit.

Sabat also stayed in touch with Giri and Ward after their conversations at RMC, hoping he could persuade them to come to Redding and help deal with the Moon problem. But neither came. The hospital appears to have stopped courting Ward. Giri apparently felt that under Moon it would be difficult if not impossible to institute the changes he thought were necessary. Moreover, it was unclear when if ever he would be able to succeed Moon as director of cardiology, which would have been a prime inducement for him to come to RMC.

For the same kinds of reasons that initially influenced Pat Campbell's thinking, Sebat was having great difficulty accepting that Moon was doing anything other than what he genuinely thought was best for his patients. Even after his interviews with Giri and Ward and his conversations with the other cardiologists, Sebat still found a great deal to admire and respect about Moon. He continued to be impressed by Moon's knowledge and skills and his availability at any hour of the day or night. He also thought that Moon was on the cutting edge of cardiology practice and that he was generally right about the new technologies he elected to introduce. He believed that Moon thought first and foremost about the welfare of his patients and paid no attention to whether or not they had insurance. What it boiled down to was this: Although Frank Sebat was not especially naïve, there were certain possibilities he either couldn't or wouldn't believe about a very hard-working and therefore apparently very dedicated colleague. And there were things he simply did not know.

But after the raid, whatever was left of Frank Sebat's confidence in Moon collapsed and his relationship with RMC management deteriorated even further. While attending a conference on thoracic medicine in San Diego in early November 2002, he had a tart telephone conversation with Springfield. He told the ER director bluntly, even crudely, that he thought he was bright and could be a great chief of staff at RMC, but only "if he could put aside drugs, sex, and money. . . ." Sebat was referring to Springfield's well-known history of using cocaine and other controlled substances, his reputation as a womanizer, and the widespread belief that he was rewarded handsomely by Tenet for serving as one of their agents in the hospital. As far as Springfield's drug use was concerned, Bill Browning said he had seen him come to meetings "so stoned it was just terrible." Sebat also told Springfield that they had to find out the truth about what had been going on in the heart program. Springfield's response was that he was going to give serious consideration to doing everything in his power to keep Sebat, Alcala, and another doctor named Dave Johnson out of the medical staff hierarchy.

A couple of weeks later, Sebat asked Michelle Hammer, secretary of the medical staff, to get him a copy of his February 21, 2001, letter to Chilton. He wanted the letter to prepare for any follow-up on the threat by Springfield. Hammer called Chilton's office to get a copy, which led to a phone call from Springfield who said to Sebat, "Frank, you need to come to my house." Sebat said, "I'm working. I'm seeing patients. I can't come to your house." A short time later, Springfield showed up at Sebat's office wearing sunglasses and jeans. Sebat thought he looked and behaved like he was on drugs. The first thing Springfield said to Sebat was "This conversation never took place." Sebat looked at him sideways and laughed, but he wanted to hear what Springfield had to say, and said, "Okay, this conversation never took place." They sat down and Springfield, who had a folded-up copy of the letter, told Sebat that Chilton and Tenet's lawyers were furious that he had asked for it. As Sebat started to respond, Springfield took a piece of paper from Sebat's desk and began taking notes. Sebat grabbed the paper out of his hand and said, "I thought this conversation never took place." Springfield then began writing on his jeans. Before he left Sebat's office, Springfield somewhat discordantly complimented him on how well his letter was written although he said he disagreed with his use of the word "malfeasance."

After that Sebat had a number of other conversations with Springfield, on the telephone, in the corridors of the hospital, and sometimes outside where they could talk privately. Sebat would say things like "We've got to get to the bottom of this"; "The medical staff has a responsibility"; "You're going to be chief of staff—you've got an opportunity to fix the problem here." Springfield in response said to him more than once, "You don't want Hal to go to jail, do you?" Sebat's standard reply to that was "I want justice done. I don't necessarily want anybody to go to jail, but that's not my decision."

Tenet was not sharing any information about the Mercer investigation with the medical staff and was discouraging the doctors from mounting their own investigation. According to Alcala, the only physician at RMC who supported the administration's approach was Springfield. Alcala, as chief of staff, wrote a letter to Jeffrey Barbakow expressing his strong belief that the medical staff should not only be fully informed about, but should be involved in any review of the heart program. He appears not to have gotten a response. The medical staff couldn't even get information about patients who were in the pipeline for surgery, so they had no way to investigate who needed it and who didn't.

As time went by and Sebat kept pressing relentlessly for the administration to come clean, Springfield became increasingly threatening. He reiterated the threat in Chilton's letter that Tenet would terminate Sebat's contract. But Sebat, who by then was convinced that a unilateral termination of the contract without cause would be illegal, said that would be fine because it would make him a rich man. Springfield eventually figured out that Sebat was probably right about this and toned down the threat. The new approach was "If you continue pursuing this line, your contract's not going to be renewed and your research office is going to be eliminated." He also told Sebat he would continue to be frozen out by the administration. All three of these things happened. First Brown forbade him to continue raising money for the critical care office and withdrew the hospital's support, which, as a practical matter, made it impossible for him to get grants. Then, when Sebat was away on a trip, the office was shut down and the staff was fired. And when Sebat's contract expired in 2004, it was not renewed. Sebat sent numerous emails to administrators including Jerry Stocks, the COO, and Linda Leavell, the nursing director, none of which were returned. It was not until he sent them registered letters that he got responses.

None of this stopped Sebat, however. At one point he called Chilton and Brown from a cell phone in his car in the Mercy Hospital parking lot. Chilton called Sebat a loose canon and said he wouldn't talk to him unless someone else was in the room. Chilton then hung up midway through the conversation and Brown had to call his secretary to get him back on the line. During this conversation Sebat recounted the episode in which Chilton told him that he had cost him two million dollars and threw him out of his office. He was almost certain that Brown knew about this and even suspected that he had been frozen out by the administration on Brown's orders. But he wanted to be 100 percent sure that Brown was aware of what Chilton had said to him. He also alluded to Springfield's activities, at which point Chilton asked him whether he was threatening Springfield. Sebat said he wasn't threatening anybody. Brown then said it was important to keep the dialogue going because it was obvious that there was a lot of misunderstanding.

                                      *   *   *

In the aftermath of the raid, the hospital was in a semichaotic state and
many, perhaps most, of the doctors did not know what to make of it.
While some of them had been suspicious of Moon and Realyvasquez for
a long time, others continued to believe they were first-rate ethical physicians. They thought it was unthinkable that the two doctors would have
done unnecessary procedures, and considered Sebat's demands for an
independent investigation at best disloyal and more likely treasonous. It
was in this atmosphere that Sebat addressed a letter to the entire medical staff saying that his sole objective was to ascertain the truth about
the cardiac program and that he hoped it would vindicate Moon and
Realyvasquez. He said in the letter that he had never done anything "to
the detriment of the program or these physicians."

    One thing Sebat might or might not have known was that the Califor-
nia Department of Health Services, a body involved in the licensing and
accreditation process for hospitals, did investigate RMC's cardiac program in July 1999. The investigators found that at least from 1997 on
there had been virtually no peer review and, with respect to the appropriateness of diagnosis and treatment, none whatsoever. After the Department of Health Services survey, RMC filed a plan of correction, but
within a couple of months whatever little peer review had been instituted
ceased. Moon and Realyvasquez said dismissively that they were too busy
to participate and no serious effort was made to make them do so. A second survey was conducted by the Department of Health Services in
December 2002, after the FBI raid. This time state investigators found
that for the first eleven months of 2002, peer review in the cardiac program was for all practical purposes nonexistent. More than three thousand angiograms were done—an astonishing number for a hospital the
size of RMC—and only six cases were reviewed. All of these were for
complications; none were for appropriateness of diagnosis and treatment.

    Oversight, it seemed, was failing at every level. Neither the medical
staff nor the administration of RMC saw to it that a system of peer
review was in place to protect patients against negligence, sloppy or otherwise inadequate performance by physicians, systemic errors that
should have been correctable, and abuses such as intentionally misleading diagnoses and unwarranted surgery. But this failure did not keep the
hospital from being regularly accredited by the Joint Commission on
Accreditation of Healthcare Organizations, the private body that under

Medicare regulations inspects hospitals. Why this poor performance did not result in a loss of accreditation is not clear, but it is worth noting that JCAHO had a conflict of interest. The organization also taught hospitals how to pass its inspection, for a fee.

In December 2002, a survey for the federal Centers for Medicare and Medicaid Services carried out by state investigators had found violations, but the minimal action that had been taken had no practical significance. And despite the fact that for years the rate of cardiac procedures at Redding Medical Center had been far higher than state and national averages—in some cases several times higher—Medicare and Medicaid had shown no interest and neither had private insurers. The latter had simply raised premiums when they found they were paying out too much to settle claims. The California State Medical Board and the California State Medical Society, the doctors' own professional organization, also had seemed blissfully ignorant of or uninterested in what was going on in Redding.

16

"Qui Tam"

After the raid, for the first time in a long time, John Corapi had felt a sense of satisfaction. Finally someone had paid attention; someone had done something. Corapi and Zerga had taken their story to the state medical board, to Blue Shield, and to any number of lawyers. No one, they believed, had taken them seriously. The best they got in response were form letters. But Mike Skeen, despite Corapi's initial skepticism, had turned out to be different. In the end, through his investigative efforts, he had brought down the full weight of the federal government on Chae Hyun Moon, Fidel Realyvasquez, their practice associates, Redding Medical Center, and the Tenet Healthcare Corporation. All of these were now subjects of a large-scale investigation—although not yet formally targets—specifically for "conspiracy to commit health care fraud, false statements relating to health care matters and health care fraud in violation of 18 U.S.C. Sections 371, 1035, and 1347."

The satisfaction he felt, however, did not leave Corapi free of anxiety. People kept telling him, "You're in for it; they'll come after you. You don't go after a large corporation like that without personal costs." Corapi was also anxious about the Schirmers' lawsuit, which had bubbled up again soon after the raid. It was a difficult time for him and he had to force himself not to give in to anxiety and depression. Among other things he was concerned about his future and uncertain that the church, the institution to which he had committed his heart and soul, would look after his material well-being. After all, until then it never had. He had been sent out to make his way in the world on his own as a preacher and that was what he had done. The church had given him no financial support. He worried that he was almost sixty years old and he had no pension. The church did not even provide him with medical insurance. The church had helped him by buying his tapes and DVDs, but he believed they got good value for what they paid. At one point he said wryly if not bitterly, "I wasn't doing unnecessary heart surgery." At the same time, he did have a certain amount of ambivalence about the way he supported himself. Turning the Gospels into a commodity sometimes made him feel a bit queasy. But, he rationalized, "Even the pope does it." He was referring to the sale of books written by the pope, and copyright infringement suits filed by the Vatican on the pope's behalf.

By 2002, Corapi's business was generating $1 million a year in revenues, some undisclosed percentage of which he donated to his religious society and other Catholic causes. He said his assets consisted solely of his house and about $100,000 in cash. He owned no other real estate and no stocks or bonds. He acknowledged that he lived better than a lot of people. But he was quick to point out that he did not own anything frivolous like, for example, "a yacht in the Caribbean," nor did he aspire to such luxuries. All he wanted, he said, was a quiet place to live. But what if he ended up with a couple of million dollars as a result of filing a successful whistle-blower lawsuit? Then his future would be secure. He might continue to live as he did. He said he probably would use the money for what he considered the highest and best use of it—to further the Gospel. And very likely he would do this by increasing and expanding his speaking activities and the sale of his products, perhaps to Europe.

As far as his financial security was concerned, Corapi said with an almost inaudible laugh, "Yes, here is the way I've discussed it with God. I hate to say this, I don't trust the people in the church, I don't trust the bishops. They don't care about me, they'd probably be happier if I'd die, or go away, or disappear. They will do nothing to support me. They won't even pay for medical insurance for me. So, what [a financial windfall from a whistle-blower suit] could be is an antidote for anxiety. Because if at some point in time they say, 'Go away, shut up, we don't want you around anymore,' I will just recede and become a quasi-monk. I'll live here and I'll pray, but I won't have to worry where my next meal is coming from."

Therefore, one of the first things Corapi had Barr and Mudford do after the raid—together with Danny Marks, the Las Vegas lawyer Corapi and Zerga first retained to represent them—was to file a qui tam suit. They had held off until after the raid at the federal government's request, but they knew that any further delay could be fatal. The False

Claims Act requires an informant to speak up before the government acts against a potential defendant and the legislation has a strict rule that appears to absolutely bar anyone but the first filer from claiming a whistle-blower award. Corapi and Zerga believed they were safe on the first point because they had delayed filing at the government's request. As far as the second was concerned, they did not know whether Pat Campbell or anyone else would also file a qui tam suit, but they weren't taking any chances.

Zerga pulled together the information Corapi had provided to Skeen, including Corapi's medical records from RMC and the reviews done by the three cardiologists and one cardiac surgeon in Las Vegas, and gave it to Marks, who organized it into a draft brief. Barr was astonished to see Zerga listed as a co-relator on the draft, which would entitle him to half the award minus legal fees, so he checked with Corapi to make sure that this was not a mistake. The priest assured Barr it was not. Barr thought Corapi was a pretty damn generous friend, maybe too generous, but it was his call. He then quickly whipped the material into final shape and filed the suit on November 5, just six days after the raid.

At the same time, Barr and Mudford had begun meeting with the first wave of potential clients, all of whom thought they might be entitled to compensation, although in some cases they hadn't had any surgery at all at RMC, let alone unnecessary cardiac surgery. The office was in such a state of confusion that someone placed the qui tam suit, which was meant to be filed with the federal district court under seal, in an out box. Copies of it were mistakenly delivered to all the lawyers on the service list for the civil plaintiffs and defendants, including those for Tenet. The error was discovered within twenty-four hours, but the process server had already delivered the errant copies. It did not defeat the purpose of the seal, however, which was to protect the whistle-blower if he was an employee of the defendant and to give the government time to complete its preliminary investigation. Since Corapi and Zerga did not work for Tenet and the government had already completed its initial investigation leading to the issuance of a search warrant, neither consideration was relevant. But the law firm's mistake did give the defense in the state civil cases access to the filing, which made Corapi a bit anxious.

Then, on November 8, three days after Barr filed Corapi and Zerga's suit, David Rude, a bright, combative, somewhat temperamental lawyer in San Jose, filed a qui tam suit on behalf of Patrick Campbell. Campbell had known about qui tam suits since October 1999, when he read an article in a magazine called *Medical Economics* about a dermatologist in North Carolina who had filed one. The magazine provided a toll-free number for anyone who wanted advice from this physician on filing a similar suit. Campbell called the physician who urged him to get in touch with a law firm in New York called Getnick & Getnick, which had represented him. Campbell sent them the same four cases he had given to Jerrald Pickering, the lawyer who, after making inquiries for him about how to proceed against Moon and Realyvasquez in March 1999, advised him to keep his mouth shut. They told him the evidence he had gathered was too thin and that he should try to collect additional data.

Campbell asked four local cardiologists for help: Steve Mendelsohn, Michael Stewart, Bob Pick, and Roy Ditchey. Mendelsohn and Stewart elected not to get involved, but Pick and Ditchey said they would help. They supplied data on about twenty additional patients they believed had been subjected to unnecessary cardiac treatment at RMC. Campbell sent this information to a lawyer at Getnick & Getnick in June 2001. Shortly thereafter this lawyer referred Campbell to Mark Kleiman, a lawyer in Los Angeles who, like Getnick & Getnick, specialized in qui tam suits. Kleiman told Campbell that his case seemed problematic. He said that the Department of Justice had limited resources and "only went after low-hanging fruit," but that he would discuss it with the U.S. attorney in Sacramento before making a decision about whether to pursue it. Campbell said he never heard from Kleiman again.

When Campbell finally filed his qui tam suit, he was still unaware of the suit filed by Corapi and Zerga. He read about it afterwards in the *Sacramento Bee*. Campbell filed his suit in the belief that without the information he had provided to Mike Skeen and the sources he referred to Skeen, in particular Pick, Ditchey, and CW1, the government would not have had sufficient evidence to mount a full-scale investigation into the activities of Moon and Realyvasquez. To a substantial degree, his contention was supported by the sixty-seven-page affidavit Skeen had already filed with the federal district court in Sacramento that resulted in the granting of the search warrant that led to the raid.

Apart from Corapi's story, which involved only his own experience with Moon and some library and Internet research he and Zerga had done, the bulk of the material in the affidavit came from Campbell, Pick, Ditchey, and other medical professionals, some of whom were referred to Skeen by Campbell. Moreover, Corapi was insured by Blue Shield. His singular case did not involve a payment by any federal agency; therefore, the government did not suffer a loss and the False Claims Act did not apply. Also, there was a history of complaints being rejected because there were too few cases to demonstrate a pattern of fraudulent activity. All of these facts encouraged Campbell. But he had two problems.

First, there was a dispute as to whether he had sought out the FBI or whether the FBI had sought him out, which raised questions about the legitimacy of his status as a whistle-blower. Marge Beck, the well-connected Redding insurance agent, had called Campbell at the end of July 2002 and asked him if he would be willing to tell Skeen what he knew. After much cajoling by Beck and considerable agonizing, he had said he would. On this much everyone agreed, but on the rest of the story each participant's memory varied slightly but significantly from the others. Campbell said he then called Skeen. Campbell also remembered Skeen telling him explicitly that if anyone asked he should say that Skeen contacted him, not vice versa. Such a request would have carried with it the implication that Skeen was subtly supporting Corapi and Zerga's qui tam claim because it would have implied that the government went to Campbell, not vice versa. Skeen disputed Campbell's claim. He said he got Campbell's number from Beck and called him and that he did not recall telling Campbell that he should say anything about who called whom, or anything else for that matter. Beck said she did not remember giving Skeen Campbell's number, but she couldn't say with certainty that she hadn't.

In the end, though, did it really matter who called whom if Marge Beck referred Campbell to Skeen in response to Skeen's request for the names of doctors who might be helpful? This did not seem to be in dispute. The question then becomes, did it disqualify Campbell as a whistle-blower under the False Claims Act if he didn't come forward entirely on his own, but rather in response to an initiative made by Skeen and mediated by Beck? To a layman the language of the statute seems quite clear on this point. It says that the relator must have "voluntarily provided the information to the government before filing an action under this section which is based on the information." Campbell appeared to have met these conditions since he acted without compulsion or obligation before filing his qui tam suit.

Campbell's other problem was that he was not the first to file suit.

Buried in the fine print of the False Claims Act was a brief paragraph barring anyone but the government from becoming party to a whistle-blower lawsuit. In the past the courts had viewed this provision as exception free. There could be no doubt that John Corapi and Joe Zerga had filed suit before Campbell. But what if under some other provision of the act the priest and the accountant did not qualify to file a qui tam suit because the information they provided was either publicly available or not directly relevant to the alleged fraud? Would the fact that they were first to file then lose its relevance and open the way for a suit by Campbell? On the court's interpretation of such arcana hung the distribution of millions of dollars. A major battle was brewing.

17

The Townspeople and
the Fisher Case

Pat Campbell, John Corapi, and Joe Zerga were now more focused on their qui tam suits than on any wrong that might have been done, but they felt sure that Moon and Realyvasquez had fraudulently diagnosed and operated on hundreds of Redding citizens. So did Mike Skeen, Bob Simpson, Dugan Barr, and Doug Mudford. But there were plenty of people in Redding who simply didn't believe it.

Take for example Ron Reynolds, a labor-relations consultant and member of Redding's leading Rotary club. Reynolds was outraged when he learned about the raid. Soon afterwards he called Moon at home and talked to him for over half an hour. Moon told him that the federal government had accomplished its goal, which was to shut down RMC's heart program because it was costing Medicare too much money, which Reynolds had no trouble believing. Like a great many people in the vast area served by RMC, Reynolds had good reason to believe that Chae Moon had saved his life. He was angry and frustrated because he felt certain that the federal government had destroyed "one of the very best cardiac-care units in the world." And he held vaguely conspiratorial suspicions about how and why it happened. He wanted to know more, for example, "about the alleged Catholic priest." He wanted to know if it was true that when Corapi went to a deposition one of the lawyers asked him to open his shirt and he refused because he not only needed, but actually had undergone bypass surgery and it had left a scar, a rumor for which there was no evidence.

Reynolds's perspective was consistent with his experience, which belied the notion that Moon and Realyvasquez were running a surgery mill. He was first referred to Moon's practice when he was in his mid-fifties for a checkup. One of Moon's associates told him he had a strong heart and should not come back until he was sixty. He did not go back until about eight years later, in January of 1998, when, while shopping for a camper shell, he felt a brief tightness in the middle of his chest of a kind that he had never experienced before. He's sure about the time because it was just when he and his wife, Carolyn, president of a small foundation, bought their comfortable new house in a pretty cul-de-sac on the outskirts of Redding. He wasn't sure what was causing the odd feeling, but he was concerned enough to tell the salesman where his wife could be reached. Soon the sensation went away, however, and Reynolds felt fine until a week or so later during a phone conversation with a woman on whose mortgage he was about to foreclose. She was begging for more time and Reynolds was rejecting her plea when he felt the tightness again. It lasted five to eight minutes this time and he told his wife, who insisted that he see Moon.

Moon gave him an EKG and asked about his family history, behavior at odds with other accounts of patients who arrived in Moon's office and were rushed straight to the cath lab with no workup at all. Reynolds told Moon that his father and both grandfathers had all died of heart attacks by the time they had reached his age, sixty-one, and described his symptoms to Moon, who said they were not symptoms of a heart attack, but the symptoms that presage a heart attack. Moon told him, "That was a warning. You are trying to have a heart attack." Moon then said that the only way he could determine whether Reynolds had blockages or not was to do a cardiac catheterization. During the procedure at RMC, Reynolds asked Moon how his arteries looked. Moon, who had been uncommunicative up until then, said, "Significant." When Reynolds asked him what he meant by "significant," Moon said something like "Significant blockage" and told Reynolds that he needed bypass surgery. Moon then left and a nurse handed Reynolds X-ray pictures and explained to him that he had three arteries that were each about 90 percent blocked. But even with this dire-sounding diagnosis Reynolds was not kept in the hospital. He was sent home without a date for the operation.

Reynolds tried for a week or two to get his surgery scheduled, but couldn't. Then somebody in the cardiac unit, probably a nurse, told Carolyn surreptitiously that she couldn't really give her advice, but if she took her husband to the emergency room and said he was feeling a little pain they would admit him. Since they had been unable to get a date for several weeks and were worried that Ron could have a heart attack, they did as they were told and he was admitted for surgery. The operation, performed on Thursday, March 17, 1998, was a MIDCAB—a minimally invasive direct coronary artery bypass. Ricardo Moreno-Cabral, the only cardiac surgeon Realyvasquez ever made a partner in his practice, performed the surgery. Instead of splitting Reynolds's chest open, Moreno-Cabral made a small incision between his ribs and used special instruments to perform the surgery. Based on a thallium stress test after the operation, Moon told Reynolds that one artery was not functioning, but the problem soon resolved itself and Reynolds recovered and returned to an active life.

Reynolds's wife, Carolyn, who had been an administrator of convalescent hospitals owned by NME, had some doubts about Redding Medical Center's accounting practices, but none whatsoever about Moon's honesty. Several years ago a doctor in Red Bluff had told her that she needed heart surgery. She said no way and returned to Redding to see her primary care doctor, Dinesh Mantri, who sent her to Moon, as he did almost all of his cardiac patients. Moon performed an angiogram and told Carolyn that she did not need heart surgery and was perhaps suffering from stress. By chance, when she was undergoing her angiogram she saw a pack of cigarettes in Moon's pocket. She said, "Dr. Moon, you smoke," to which he replied, "You never mind, young lady, you're the one lying on this table, not me."

Like many others in Redding, Carolyn Reynolds was prepared to agree that Moon did not have the world's most agreeable bedside manner, but she never questioned his integrity. She said it would have been the easiest thing in the world for Moon to send her to surgery, but he didn't. When asked how she thought he and Realyvasquez could have been accused of doing unnecessary procedures on healthy patients, she said, "You know, with the two hospitals here it has been politics and religion from day one. Half the town loves Redding Medical Center and the other half loves Mercy." She was essentially right about that. The rivalry between the two facilities had been long and at times fierce.

Jim Charles's feeling about the raid was pretty much identical to that of Ron and Carolyn Reynolds. Perhaps the oldest living physician in

town, Charles was a co-owner of Memorial Hospital, which eventually became Redding Medical Center. He was a cheerful, trusting man,
but not when it came to John Corapi. Because of his faith in Moon,
he was absolutely convinced that John Corapi secretly had bypass
surgery elsewhere after Moon diagnosed him. When asked how he felt
about what had happened, Charles said, "I'm a little bit prejudiced
because Moon diagnosed me as having coronary artery disease and
RV operated on me." Charles had a double bypass around 1994. He
said that there were some small changes on his EKG, Moon did an
angiogram, and based on his findings Realyvasquez performed the
surgery. Consistent with his trusting nature and his personal experience with Moon and Realyvasquez, it never occurred to him to look
at his own films.

Charles said that over the years he had worked a great deal with both
Moon and Realyvasquez. He was certain that they were both great doctors, and that both were as honest as the day was long. He said he
thought the whole problem with Moon was that he was so much faster
than any other cardiologist in town. He said Moon could do coronary
artery studies in fifteen or twenty minutes at most that could take the
other cardiologists in town an hour or more to do. He also said that
Moon could see lesions with IVUS that required treatment and could
not be seen on angiograms. He strongly implied that Moon's less competent colleagues were simply envious, and refused to believe Moon
could be doing what, by all appearances, he was doing only by fraudulent means. As for Tenet, Charles was more circumspect. He said he did
not know whether or not the company was crooked.

Another prominent Redding citizen, Harry Barker, a crusty retired
radio executive who served on the RMC board from 1984 to 1990 and
was chairman from 1987 to 1989, didn't believe the allegations against
the doctors and the hospital either. He placed the blame for what happened squarely on the man he called "that pseudo-priest Corapi" (which
he pronounced Core-Aah-Pie instead of Co-rah-pee, the correct pronun-
ciation) and his lawyer, "that goddamn Dugan Barr." Barker, who had
once owned the radio station Barr held forth on daily, was conservative
even by Redding's standards, and he found Barr's pungently expressed
and by his standards extreme liberal views infuriating. He also found it
hard to believe that a Catholic priest would go to RMC rather than to
Mercy, a Catholic hospital, for treatment.

Rudy Balma, a thoughtful, even-tempered mortician turned banker, learned about the raid the morning after when he picked up the *Record Searchlight*. He said his first reaction was shock "to think that they would come with fifty people." But, he said, "The more I rationalized it, I had to come to the conclusion that they really had to have had an awful lot of evidence. You know, to not just come and quietly say, 'We want to talk to you guys, and we want to get a little information. They did not take that approach at all. It went through the town and left everybody in total shock." But then, seeming to sense that some elaboration was necessary, Balma went on to say, "You can find a lot of people in Redding and the surrounding areas who attribute the fact they're alive to Dr. Moon's expertise."

Balma said, "Doctors are all human, and they are all subject to errors and mistakes, and it could happen with anyone. But with the magnitude of this thing," he continued, "it's terribly unfortunate that it's happened to the community because the damage that it has done to an otherwise excellent facility is tragic. And the people who have been hurt are the people who are working every day in the hospital and in a lot of cases they are single-parent families that are dependent on the livelihood from their employment and it's been a tragic thing. With a community that has about 30 percent of its population basically on some form of public assistance, probably some of those people in dietary and housekeeping [at RMC] would be included in that, so the impact to those folks would be great."

If the city of Redding was hit hard by the raid, perhaps the people who were hit hardest were those who thought they knew the doctors best, the nurses and technicians who worked with them every day in the cath lab and in the operating room. These healthcare professionals had every reason to believe that they were working in a nationally recognized program of very high quality. The hospital administration stressed it regularly, citing rankings by HealthGrades, which not only rated hospitals, but for a fee marketed them as well. Many employees, like Sheryl Hallstrom, the clinical supervisor for cardiac nurse liaison, had been trained locally at Shasta College and had worked in other hospitals with far fewer resources than the well-equipped and well-staffed RMC. Redding Medical Center's physical plant was impressive and well maintained and there was a helicopter to airlift patients from outlying areas to the hospital. Although it had only 238 beds, RMC had something of the look and feel of a university medical center. Hallstrom said she had worked in poor hospitals, and rich was better.

Like Rudy Balma, Hallstrom, who grew up in Redding, believed the raid had been devastating to the hospital and to the community. She said it had engendered an "environment of immense suspicion. Nobody trusts anybody." She too said the biggest losers were the little people who had lost their jobs. And like several other people in town she was convinced that Tenet shared in the blame and that the federal government had used the situation to get at Tenet because of its high billings. Hallstrom was very disappointed that Tenet did not support Moon and Realyvasquez and thought that somehow the cardiologists who practiced at Mercy had found a way to get at Moon and Realyvasquez. She believed that other doctors, including Campbell and Pick, were envious of Moon and that if they really believed something was wrong they should have dealt with it in the medical community rather than complaining to the RMC administrators. Then, in an almost self-contradictory fashion and without elaboration, Hallstrom volunteered that she thought Campbell's and Pick's concerns about how the two doctors practiced were not entirely without foundation. She said that the allegations against Moon and Realyvasquez were not "totally without a basis in fact."

Hallstrom, who had begun working at RMC in 1983, four years after Moon arrived and four years before Realyvasquez got there, knew the two doctors as well as anyone else at the hospital. She had worked in cardiac care since the beginning of her nursing career, and she was involved in the start-up of the cardiac surgery program at RMC. Around 1989, she began teaching patients about their procedures, including angioplasty, bypass surgery, and valve surgery. Hallstrom said Moon was a powerhouse, with loads of energy, and he was extremely intelligent. She said he never asked patients about their insurance and his basic attitude was that "Thou shalt not have a heart attack around us if there is anything we can do about it." She also pointed out that Moon had brought new medicines and devices to Redding Medical Center, including streptokinase, a clot-busting drug, and the intra-aortic balloon pump, a device to assist the output of failing hearts. And she said that he had invited Marcus DeWood, who had proved James Herrick's seminal hypothesis that clots caused most heart attacks,* to RMC's first or second annual cardiac conference.

According to Hallstrom, there was always a feeling at RMC that you were doing the absolute best for the patients and that Moon deserved most of the credit for that. "It was just awesome to be with these people who were at the forefront of [treating] cardiac disease." Hallstrom did not have the impression that Moon was ahead of the country, but simply that he was ahead of the curve in Redding and was pulling the other cardiologists along. She said Moon was always looking for technology to help his patients, citing as an example transmyocardial revascularization, an experimental technique for getting more blood to the heart muscle by drilling tiny holes in it with a laser. TMR, as it is widely known, had a brief and not notably successful vogue and is now rarely used. Hallstrom clearly thought Moon was innovative, but she did not think he was "working outside the box at all."

Hallstrom allowed that Moon might have had a bigger ego than most physicians, but she found this unsurprising because she had observed that interventional cardiologists in particular had "a God complex." But, by way of mitigation, she said, "I don't think that Moon had it any worse than any other interventional cardiologist." Even though Moon sometimes yelled at her, she believed he respected her and he respected the nursing profession. Although he sometimes "behaved like a jerk toward her," she understood that it was about a situation, not her personally. She thought in general the people toward whom he behaved badly were people he didn't believe were professionally competent, and she attributed some of this behavior to his having grown up in a hierarchical society in Korea. She said Moon had a very human side too, but conceded that he did not show it to many people. The only example she cited was that Moon had invited the cath lab staff to his house for a barbecue and did all the barbecuing himself. He sometimes talked to Hallstrom about his golf game, and, she said, he showed interest in other people's families.

---

*In 1912, Herrick published an article in the *Journal of the American Medical Association* (*JAMA*) in which he provided compelling although not conclusive evidence that most heart attacks were caused by blood clots in the coronary arteries and that some were survivable. In 1918, he published another article in *JAMA* including electrocardiographic evidence that supported his 1912 hypothesis. It was not until 1980, however, that DeWood, using a tool unavailable to Herrick—selective coronary angiography—proved the hypothesis.

Moon once talked to her about people who criticized him for sending too many patients to surgery instead of doing procedures like angioplasty. He told her, "You know what, I don't think I have anything to prove and I don't have to keep having patients coming back to me time and time again." Hallstrom said she knew with 100 percent certainty that "if Moon ever overdiagnosed he never did it with a malicious thought. There is no doubt about it," she said. "His patients are his life." When asked about Moon's phenomenal speed with a catheter, she smiled and said, "He cathed smoother than anybody," adding that his angiographic pictures were always beautiful. For comparison, she mentioned another cardiologist who, she said, took an hour and a half to do a procedure that Moon could do in fifteen minutes.

While strongly supportive of Moon in just about every way, somewhat surprisingly Hallstrom volunteered that Moon might not have always known the noncardiac health status of his patients. This is not a trivial criticism. That information is important in deciding whether a particular patient is a suitable candidate for surgery. She emphasized, however, that he could tell you in detail about their coronary situation. Then, realizing that she hadn't said quite all she'd meant, or possibly that she had said more than she meant, she obliquely addressed Moon's reputation for overaggressive diagnoses by explaining that the interpretation of angiographic films was subjective. In sum, Hallstrom seemed to believe that much of the opposition to Moon and the criticism of his work was ego driven. She said she believed that at least one cardiologist in town told patients they didn't need surgery without even looking at the film simply because Moon had been the referring cardiologist.

Hallstrom had also worked with Realyvasquez and knew him well. She called him an artist as a surgeon and said he once told her, "When I'm in the operating room I am the conductor of an orchestra and everybody had better watch how my hands are moving, and they had better know what each of those hand movements means." He said surgeons had to do more than four hundred cases a year to keep their skills up. Although this was an unusually high volume for the population served by RMC, she said she did not believe Realyvasquez performed unnecessary operations to keep his numbers up. She believed his claim that he took all comers and never cherry-picked cases to keep his mortality rate low. And contrary to what many patients eventually disclosed, Hallstrom was confident that Realyvasquez talked to every one of his patients before surgery, except perhaps in dire emergencies. She also emphasized Realyvasquez's humanity and community spirit and said she had pictures of him ringing a Salvation Army bell. She said he had a heart of gold for little old ladies and that he would sit on the edge of the bed, hold their hands, and talk to them.

Even Lou Gerard, chairman of the board of Mercy Foundation North, which is associated with RMC's crosstown rival, was skeptical that Moon and Realyvasquez had done what they were accused of doing. He had heard about problems in the RMC heart program for years, but he said his knowledge was scant and limited to inferences from doctor friends and acquaintances, some of whom suspected that unnecessary procedures might have been done at RMC. Gerard read about the raid in the *Record Searchlight* the morning of October 31. At first he wasn't sure what to think. That morning, though, it was the hot topic at his 9:30 coffee group. "I don't know that any of us really knew an awful lot about it," he said, "except that it was somewhat of a surprise and I guess we also said, 'Well, you know, this links into some of the rumors we'd heard.' I was surprised that there would be such an impact on a medical facility by federal agencies. It seemed a little startling that such a thing could actually occur here in Redding."

As more time passed, though, Gerard felt less certain about whether what he was reading in the paper and hearing around town had actually happened. He was struck by how subjective the allegations were. He was especially concerned that people didn't seem to be taking adequate account of the fact that medical diagnoses were matters of judgment; that honest doctors could differ about what constituted appropriate treatment. "I think that until today," he said. "If a wrong has been committed, and particularly something of this nature, then I would suspect that arrests would have been made; that there would have been some broader determination of guilt."

The fact that so much time had passed since the raid and no one had been indicted reminded Gerard of a drug case in 1999 involving a physician named Frank Fisher and a married couple named Stephen and Madeleine Miller who ran a pharmacy in Redding. The case centered on Fisher's alleged excessive and inappropriate prescription of OxyContin and other powerful opioid painkillers from his office in Anderson just south of Redding and the Millers' dispensing of these drugs. With the RMC situation in mind, the *Record Searchlight* resurrected the case in

August 2004. The paper published a series of articles on how Fisher and the Millers were forced to cope for years with charges of murder, resulting from deaths attributed to patients' drug overdoses, and other felonies, and losing their reputations and livelihoods before all charges were finally dropped. They each spent five miserable months in the Redding jail and they suffered crippling financial damages. "That kind of behavior on the part of government really bothers me," Gerard said. "I don't think that's fair game."

It's easy to see, especially in a place like Redding, why Gerard was not alone in thinking that the Fisher/Miller case provided a relevant backdrop against which to consider the charges against Moon, Realyvasquez, and some of their associates. And twenty-two months after the raid, when the *Record Searchlight* articles appeared and there still had been no criminal indictments, the old case seemed more relevant than ever.

At the same time, the federal government did not win any friends in Redding when it disgraced the hospital, forced its sale, and, as many locals saw it, caused hundreds of their friends and neighbors to lose their jobs. For many of them, quite simply, it boiled down to this: Drs. Moon and Realyvasquez were more credible than the faceless bureaucrats with who knows what agenda in Washington, D.C. It was widely believed in Redding that no local jury would convict these two doctors. Of course, many people in Redding did not yet know—perhaps because local news media had never told them—that well-qualified independent cardiologists had certified that unnecessary heart procedures had been done on 769 patients at Redding Medical Center, most by Moon and Realyvasquez. Nor did they know that a statistical sampling done by the federal government had produced almost identical results.

But in the main, a couple of years after the raid, with the exception of those who were directly affected, most people in Redding had put the events at RMC behind them. Very few spent time reflecting on exactly what had happened and why it had happened. They all knew a scattering of the elements, but only a few knew more than that, and fewer still were sufficiently interested to figure out how the pieces fit together.

Had they known enough, their reasoning would very likely have gone something like this: At the end of the 1980s and the beginning of the 1990s, when RMC began building its heart program seriously, Redding was a town in need of a lift. Its economy was at best flat and there were no bright prospects on the horizon. As a result, local citizens were unusually receptive to the saturation advertising campaign Tenet launched to promote the California Heart Institute and the man recruited to run it, Chae Moon. The program's volume rose rapidly, driven by advertising and word of mouth, and before long it was the city's greatest source of pride. Inside the hospital a parallel campaign sold the heart program and its leaders just as effectively to the nurses and technicians, many of whom were relatively unsophisticated graduates of two-year associate-degree programs with little or no experience outside of Redding. These employees were every bit as vulnerable to the high-powered promotional efforts of Tenet as the average citizen in the community and they became some of the heart program's most effective proselytizers.

Moreover, the healthcare environment in Redding was unusually conducive to reckless medical practice. Redding was not welcoming to managed care, so a level of oversight was missing from the two hospitals and from medical practice in the city generally. And there was little or no peer review at Redding Medical Center, most notably in the heart program. To the contrary, Tenet and RMC actively opposed such reviews as a drag on revenue. The discouragement of quality control at RMC was also abetted by the fact that Moon and to a lesser degree Realyvasquez were believed to be so powerful that no physician in Redding or the surrounding rural counties had the courage to openly challenge them.

Moon, for example, had regularly diagnosed and claimed to have successfully treated a rare condition (spontaneously dissecting coronary arteries) that was almost always fatal. He also had done three to five times more interventional procedures than would be expected in a hospital the size of RMC. And Realyvasquez had performed excessive numbers of cardiac operations despite seeing no indication for them on Moon's angiographic images. For the most part, the federal government had paid the bills. But the real price in fear, pain, severely reduced quality of life, and shortened lives had been paid by Zona Martin, Paul Alexandre, Shirley Wooten, and hundreds of other innocent patients at Redding Medical Center for whom justice and compensation remained tantalizingly uncertain.

18

The Doctor, the Priest, and
the Accountant

While the FBI and U.S. attorneys were continuing to develop evidence and present it to the grand jury, and the plaintiffs' lawyers were seeking a settlement with the surgeons, a nasty legal battle was underway. This competition for millions of dollars between Pat Campbell and John Corapi and Joe Zerga was destined to survive only in the minds and bank accounts of the participants and in a few yellow newspaper clippings. But it raised vexing questions about why these three middle-aged men of substance, all respected members of their learned professions, who started out with the same disinterested goals of stopping unnecessary surgery, ended up at each other's throats. Their fight over money was playing out as a tawdry sideshow while hundreds of RMC patients, with scars down the middle of their chests serving as constant reminders of the uncalled-for surgery they had undergone, were waiting for justice to be rendered.

To this day there is nothing to suggest that when Corapi, Campbell, and Zerga went to the FBI their motives were anything but pure. None of them even knew what the False Claims Act—let alone a qui tam suit— was when they first tried to stop Moon and Realyvasquez. There was no valid reason for anyone to think they did what they did except to end the harm, the suffering, and false hopes they believed were being inflicted on innocent patients. But when the prospect of large sums of money entered the picture some observers' perceptions began to change. People in and around Redding, especially the considerable number who believed in the doctors, began to raise questions even though there was no real reason to doubt that Campbell, Corapi, and Zerga were genuinely outraged.

Campbell had witnessed what he became convinced was a long, cold-blooded history of fraud at Redding Medical Center and had tried sporadically and unsuccessfully to stop it. And Corapi came to believe that his personal experience with Moon was not unique. It also seems fair to say that Zerga shared his friend's outrage, but was quicker to recognize an opportunity associated with what initially seemed to Corapi like an altogether negative situation. In any event, in the three months between the time they provided information to the FBI and the raid on the hospital they all had learned about the millions of dollars in reward money available under the False Claims Act and all were in hot pursuit of it.

But then, wasn't the whole purpose of the False Claims Act to reward good citizens just like them? Why shouldn't they take the necessary steps to get what they deserved? There is of course something in all of us that responds positively to altruism, pure acts uncontaminated by less noble motives no matter how understandable or justified; actions driven solely by concerns such as justice, relief of suffering, and protecting the innocent and vulnerable. But in fact the False Claims Act was never intended to inspire altruism. Its original intent when it was enacted in 1863 was to short-circuit fraud by military contractors during the Civil War by providing an incentive for betrayal in the form of a cash reward to tempt whistle-blowers to rat on their confederates. The language of the law is quite clear about this:

> The effect of the [qui tam provision of the act] is simply to hold out to a confederate a strong temptation to betray his coconspirator, and bring him to justice. The bill offers, in short, a reward to the informer who comes into court and betrays his coconspirator . . . based . . . upon the old-fashioned idea of holding out a temptation, and "setting a rogue to catch a rogue. . . ."

The original drafters understood then as we do today that even for well-meaning people in risky or threatening circumstances it might take more than good intentions to inspire action that, whatever the motivation, serves the public interest. The Senate report that accompanied the 1986 amendments to the act said explicitly that the monetary reward in its qui tam section was meant to encourage more citizens to file whistle-blower suits.

The law was designed to expose the defrauding of government programs and to recover the stolen federal funds. Under its provisions the first informant who furnished information that enabled the government to get back its money was to be awarded between 15 and 25 percent of the amount recovered if the government joined the case and up to 30 percent if the government didn't join. Congress intentionally provided this often spectacular financial incentive to motivate government or corporate insiders with detailed knowledge, but no statutory obligation to disclose what they knew, to overcome their reticence and fear and speak out despite the risks involved. It was also Congress's clear intention that the amount of the award be directly linked to the amount of the recovery.

In the Redding situation, however, a more fundamental question arose that was unrelated either to the amount of the recovery or the amount of the reward. The Justice Department had doubts about whether the government should make any award at all. As it happened, none of these men, not Campbell, not Corapi, and not Zerga, were precisely the kind of citizen the authors and amenders of the False Claims Act had in mind. Campbell came closest to fitting the act's legislative intent, at least with respect to being an at-risk insider. He worked at the hospital and his income was closely linked to his access to the hospital. But he did not work for the hospital, or for Tenet, or for the government. Therefore he was not a perfect fit. And Corapi and Zerga did not seem to fit at all. They were neither at-risk insiders nor did they have detailed information of possible fraud.

The Justice Department initially concluded that each of their claims was fatally flawed and was not disposed to waste the government's money by paying a reward to persons it considered to be valuable but unqualified informants. However, Senator Grassley, a media-wise sponsor of the 1986 amendments, who was loathe to see no money at all awarded in this high-profile case, intervened. Members of his staff met with both Corapi and Zerga and Campbell.

Possibly because of pressure from Grassley, the Department of Justice decided to award 15 percent of the recovery from Tenet to Corapi and Zerga because they had filed the first claim, beating Campbell by three days. At least three knowledgeable insiders were convinced that without the senator's intervention no award at all would have been granted. In a memorandum opposing Campbell's suit on July 11, 2003, the government had argued in federal district court that even if Corapi and Zerga had not been qualified to receive the award, the simple fact that Campbell was not the first to file a suit eliminated him from contention. And consistent with its view that Corapi and Zerga might not be qualified either the government included a footnote in the memorandum saying that "jurisdictional problems may warrant dismissal of the Corapi complaint, as well."

But Campbell had not exhausted his legal options and was not ready to quit. Three years after the raid on Redding Medical Center the doctor, the priest, and the accountant were still locked in legal combat over the contested qui tam money. No doubt they all knew from the start that their whistle-blowing would entail some personal risks and inconvenience. But very likely none of them understood just how expensive, frustrating, and unpleasant it would become once they were enmeshed in the web of legal and financial consequences they had woven. On the other hand, the stakes were not inconsequential.

Pat Campbell had been struggling with the moral and emotional implications of the RMC debacle for the longest time. He had suspected wrongdoing by Moon and Realyvasquez for seven years by the middle of 2002, had been warned not to get involved, and knew his decision to go public involved significant risks, including loss of income, social and professional ostracism, and costly, time-consuming litigation. But he underestimated the personal costs of his involvement. It was perhaps unsurprising that he had been shunned by some of his colleagues and frightened by the lurking threat of retaliation by Moon, Realyvasquez, RMC, and Tenet. But he was also excoriated for being greedy by the U.S. attorney's office, which he didn't see coming. And most difficult of all, the pressures were shredding the fabric of his family, already worn threadbare by the strains of a difficult adoption in 2002. Six months before the raid, Campbell and his wife, Carolyn, who is also a physician, had brought home a thirteen-year-old boy named Peter from Russia. From the beginning the adjustment was stressful. This compounded the already considerable stress of practicing medicine, living in a tense, divided medical community in which some treated him as a pariah, and dealing with an expensive lawsuit in which millions of dollars were on the line.

The risks John Corapi was taking were considerably smaller because he was a complete outsider. His life and living were not linked to Redding. He had left just months after the raid for Whitefish, Montana, in the Flathead Valley, twenty-five miles west of Glacier National Park, where Joe Zerga had a vacation house on a lake. He bought a solid, two-story cedar house a few miles outside of town on eleven acres of land with a view from his back porch straight out to the Rockies. It was comfortably furnished in a slightly rusticated style, but there were amenities, including a forty-five-inch Toshiba television set in an upstairs sitting room. Off the sitting room Corapi had set up a small chapel. Photographs on the wall showed Corapi at his ordination in the Vatican and with Pope John Paul II. The house had enough space for his office, and a storage room for the tapes and DVDs of his homilies that he sold to earn a living. Outside in a garage and a barn he kept two small boats, one for duck hunting on a nearby lake and the other for fishing on any of several rivers in the area. The airport was just a few miles away, there were good restaurants in town, and the hunting and fishing in Montana were every bit as good if not better than what he had given up in the mountains near Redding.

What Corapi had not anticipated was the prospect of being tied up in litigation—as it turned out, for years—with the deep-pocketed Moon, Realyvasquez, and especially Tenet. The experience of going through his lawsuit with the Schirmers, the couple that at one time managed his business, had been unpleasant. Although he believed he had a strong defense, he ended up settling the suit for around $250,000, which left a bad taste in his mouth and a hole in his bank account. He did not want to repeat this debilitating experience, and he had other fish to fry. If Zerga, a long-time Las Vegas insider who liked both the stakes and the odds, had not relentlessly pressed Corapi to tell his story to the FBI and file the qui tam, personal injury, and California Insurance Code lawsuits, he almost certainly would have dropped the matter.

Pat Campbell's qui tam suit had been dismissed on July 31, 2003, not simply because he had filed three days after Corapi and Zerga, but also because the court deemed the underlying facts to be the same. But Campbell appealed. The formal grounds for the appeal was that Corapi and Zerga were not "original sources" of information and therefore lacked standing to file a qui tam suit, which, Campbell argued, meant that the previously inviolable first-to-file bar did not apply. After much consideration, however, the Justice Department decided that the courts would probably conclude that Corapi and

Zerga were original sources because they had direct and independent knowledge of fraud resulting from their meeting with Chilton, Caudle, and Chicoine at the hospital.

But Corapi and Zerga faced another obstacle. Federal law required relators to provide information with a high degree of specificity. The only firsthand information they turned over to the government pertained to Corapi's single procedure. Of course it could be argued that because both Corapi and Zerga had investigative backgrounds in Nevada they might have been more likely than the average person to understand that what had happened to Corapi was fraudulent and was not likely to have been a unique incident. Moreover, Zerga had once audited a medical center and might have understood among other things that RMC was doing a very high number of cardiac procedures. The court could also decide that none of this was relevant and the only thing that mattered was that Zerga and Corapi had provided information that led to the opening of an investigation that in turn led to the recovery of funds by the U.S. government.

Meanwhile, Corapi and Zerga's lawyers, Danny Marks and Dugan Barr, were fighting a running battle of their own over everything from strategy to fees. It would be hard to find two men less likely to work well together than Marks and Barr. Marks, who worked out of a gloomy office in downtown Las Vegas faintly evocative of Sam Spade's or Philip Marlowe's, was thin, prickly, and taciturn. His infrequent smiles, like those of babies, seemed more attributable to gas than pleasure. Barr on the other hand was massive, ruddy, and ebullient, often expressing himself in a colorful northern California vernacular that substituted expressions like "it went sideways" or "it went upside down" for "it went wrong." He smiled easily and had a taste for life that included bluegrass music, cooking, small-batch bourbon, and fine wine. The two men did have at least two things in common—a short fuse and an acid tongue. Their correspondence, mostly by email and fax, was corrosive. Over time, the contentious relationship between the two lawyers only got worse, to the point where they wouldn't even return each other's phone calls. This made negotiations with the government over the award much more difficult than they needed to be and might even have come close to scuttling their chances of getting any money altogether.

Over the next few months, as they continued to snipe at each other,

Marks and Barr waited anxiously for the government to act, which it finally did on August 4, 2003, imposing a $54 million fine on Tenet, the largest ever involving unnecessary medical procedures. While this was the amount on which the qui tam award would be based, much more important, it settled the government's civil action against Tenet and removed the threat of criminal charges against the corporation. Individual Tenet executives, however, remained vulnerable to prosecution. The settlement agreement between Tenet and the federal government, reached nine months after the raid, was the first signal that Tenet wanted to dispose of the whole matter and that the hundreds of civil plaintiffs might eventually be adequately compensated. The agreement also required Tenet and RMC to cooperate with the government's criminal and civil investigations of these individuals and the doctors and to take specific actions to ensure that no further unwarranted procedures would be performed. It did not require the corporation to admit guilt. The $54 million payment was solely to compensate the United States and the state of California for reimbursements to RMC and Tenet to which they were not entitled. Tenet and RMC also agreed to a number of conditions, one of which was an external audit of the hospital's heart program twice a year.

The agreement also specified that the government could impose administrative sanctions on RMC and Tenet, including removing the hospital from federal programs such as Medicare and Medicaid, penalties that if applied would put the hospital out of business. Soon afterwards the Department of Health and Human Services actually began a process designed to exclude the hospital from these programs based on unnecessary or substandard treatment. This had never happened before. So, finally and inevitably, on December 11, 2003, Tenet sold Redding Medical Center.

In the end Tenet had agreed to settle because its lawyers had been able to negotiate a reduction in the total amount from about $58 million to $54 million and an agreement that both parties could characterize the settlement as they wished. This permitted Tenet to deny any implication of fraud. There were also side letters to the agreement, one of which required the hospital to comply with standards of care and another that specified that if additional uncalled-for procedures were identified Tenet would be liable for payment based on the formula used in the agreement.

*   *   *

Because Judge David F. Levi had dismissed Campbell's qui tam suit five days before Tenet settled with the government, it looked as if the big payday was finally in the offing for Corapi and Zerga. They were looking forward to sharing $8.1 million, which represented 15 percent of the $54 million total, minus a 20 percent cut for each of the lawyers. Barr began negotiations on behalf of Corapi and Zerga with Michael Hirst of the U.S. attorney's office, who was continuing to handle all civil matters relating to the Tenet/RMC cases. But Hirst immediately expressed concerns to Barr that his clients might not be qualified relators because they had not filed suit until after details of the events at Redding Medical Center had become public. Barr told Hirst over the phone that they would have filed sooner had the federal government not asked them to hold off until after the raid. Hirst, a quiet but tough negotiator, told Barr that he thought the Justice Department would approve an award if Corapi and Zerga would accept less than the statutory minimum of 15 percent. His big bargaining chip was his contention that despite Barr's arguments, the department still had concerns about the legitimacy of their status as relators. He might also have thought that Corapi and Zerga knew nothing of Senator Grassley's interest and therefore might decide to take less because there was a real possibility that they might end up with nothing. He would have been right about that; while the priest and the accountant had met with Grassley's staff, they did not know about Grassley's involvement in pressing for an award. But they flatly rejected this offer anyway insisting that they were entitled by statute to at least $8.1 million.

Meanwhile, Pat Campbell was feeling bruised and battered, but not ready to give up. He thought he had a good lawyer in David Rude and they had decided not only to appeal the district court's ruling rejecting his qui tam suit, which seemed like a long shot, but also to challenge the government's action against Tenet. The grounds for this challenge was that the recovery didn't include outlier payments and treble damages and therefore was far too small. In a motion filed on August 13, 2003, they argued that the U.S. government should have collected something closer to $450 million than the $54 million it actually collected from Tenet. They also asked the government to disclose the methodology and precise numbers used to arrive at the $54 million figure. In other words, this aspiring classical violist turned primary care doctor in rural northern California was not satisfied with taking on the giant Tenet Health-care Corporation, a Roman Catholic priest, and a tough, savvy Las Vegas accountant. He was now directing his fire at the United States of America.

This was chutzpah on a grand scale, and Campbell, who because of the time and pressure involved gave up his private practice and became a hospitalist, a nine-to-five physician who takes over the primary care of patients while they are in the hospital, would pay a price for it. Not only would his challenge to the amount of the settlement with Tenet be rejected, but he would be publicly accused by Hirst in an article in the *Sacramento Bee* of showing more interest in personal gain than in the public welfare.[19]

The government also accused Campbell of continuing to refer patients to Moon long after he felt certain that the cardiologist was doing unnecessary angiograms, and of sending patients who didn't need it to surgery. Hirst wrote that Campbell's "failure to speak out allowed the surgeries to continue unabated for years."

Was Campbell greedy? Did he try to jack up the Tenet fine so that if he won all or part of the qui tam award it would be worth $67.5 million, not $8.1 million? There is no way to be sure how much money influenced his behavior after the raid, but a persuasive case can be made that at least at the outset he was a genuinely aggrieved, concerned physician whose sole motive was to do the right thing. At some point, however, the smell of money seems to have provided additional motivation. Campbell's efforts were not heroic, but in the main they seemed to have been those of a well-intentioned physician with just a bit more moral courage than his colleagues and with his full share of human frailties. At times he made mistakes, at other times he was naïve or didn't know how to go about exposing Moon and Realyvasquez, and at still other times, as he freely admitted, he was simply afraid to do more. But he tried when the others didn't. Still, Hirst was right in observing that Campbell's courage failed him grievously when he continued to send his patients to Moon long after he was convinced that Moon was referring patients for surgery who didn't need it.

Campbell was locked into a profession whose members, like those in other professions, but possibly to an even greater degree, were hesitant to blow the whistle on colleagues, no matter how egregious their conduct. Medical societies around the country were notorious for failing to discipline their members who violated standards of practice. Mike Skeen among others also had noted that cardiac nurses must have seen that something was wrong, as CW1 did, when they looked at charts of patients who had been scheduled for bypass surgery or who had undergone bypass surgery without indications of coronary disease. But no nurse turned in Moon or Realyvasquez either.

After the raid the medical community's failure to stop Moon and Realyvasquez became an uncomfortable subject for Redding doctors. A few physicians in town expressed their deep regrets that they had done nothing to put an end to what in their guts they knew was at the least very bad medicine. Roy Ditchey said: "I view it to my discredit that I didn't figure out something to do sooner. This was a very unusual, very complex situation in which the people involved had tremendous power in the medical community. I had heard from other physicians that people had attempted to raise issues and had gotten nowhere with it. Maybe I should have made another attempt as well and in some respects I wish that I had [although it] probably would have just caused ill feeling and day-to-day trouble without accomplishing anything."

Lang Dayton, an intensive-care doctor at Mercy Hospital who had worked at RMC, expressed almost mournfully what must have been on the minds of many of his colleagues, but on which they never acted. "We really are culpable," he said, "because this happened right under our noses and we didn't do anything about it."

Gary Crawford, Pat Campbell's former partner, spoke almost inaudibly, his voice cracking and tears in his eyes, when he said: "You have a responsibility to the community and this should be done right. I beat myself up. How could I just go on and keep getting uneasy feelings? But then I'd go, 'Well gosh, who am I? You know, I'm just a general internist, not the brightest one either.' And surely the other cardiologists in town, they would say something if things aren't on the up-and-up. Why were there no checks and balances? Where did it fall apart? It's really hard on me at the sunset of my career to realize that I'd missed an opportunity to protect the community."

As the months passed, Campbell pressed on with his qui tam appeal and his effort to get the Department of Justice to renegotiate its civil settlement with Tenet upward by almost $400 million. In a move that especially angered Hirst, who believed he had negotiated an excellent settlement, the Redding doctor filed an extensive amended declaration under seal that laid out what he knew in considerably more detail than his original filing. The embittered Campbell also continued to believe that the U.S. attorney's office in Sacramento, and especially Michael Hirst, was pursuing a vendetta against him and would do anything it could to prevent him from succeeding, a contention that Hirst vigorously denied.

19

A Normal Life

Unlike Campbell, who at times seemed obsessed by his qui tam suit, John Corapi was weary of the whole business. It's not that he was indifferent to the money, but lawsuits had dominated his life for years and he wanted them over with. He was irritated both by the backbiting and what he considered to be the incompetence of his lawyers, as well as the pressure he felt from Zerga to focus on the cases, and the media attention they were getting. But he also understood that Campbell's challenge was serious and he could well end up with nothing. And this, despite his frustration with lawyers and lawsuits, at some level he was not prepared to do without a fight. At the same time, all he really wanted was to live quietly in his simple but comfortable house in Whitefish, continue delivering sermons around the country, run his business, and find time to hunt and fish.

The speaking engagements, which usually required air travel, were beginning to wear on him, though, and he wanted to cut back to something less than the twenty-five to thirty weekends a year he had been spending on the road. But cutting back had professional and financial consequences. The sermons he delivered to live audiences and their televised versions made it possible for him to reach a far larger audience than would otherwise have been possible, which significantly increased his income. Apart from the money, these appearances were his ministry. They were what he did as a priest and they often drew on his tumultuous life story. They were all meaningful to him, but in August 2004, he made what should have been an unusually poignant appearance in Oxnard, California, the place where some twenty years earlier he had descended to the low point of his life. Yet if being there moved him in some way it was not evident.

Corapi was in Oxnard to speak and serve at a special mass in the gymnasium of Santa Clara High School, home of the Santa Clara Saints, perennial basketball champions of the California Interscholastic Federation. It was hot and sunny when he arrived in the late afternoon. White banquet tables were set up forming a large square outside of the gym, and a large banner announced the Second Annual Marian Eucharistic Conference. A sales force made up mainly of several middle-aged women tended to customers from inside the square. One woman's black T-shirt declared in easy-to-read white letters, "Truth in its essence is not a something, it is a somebody. His name is Jesus Christ (John 14:6)."

The mood was festive and business was brisk, especially for DVD versions of Corapi's fifty-hour catechism of the Roman Catholic Church, "The Teachings of Jesus Christ," which was selling for $299, a discount from the TV price of $325. The VHS version was available for $195, down from $245. A sign on one of the tables for Santa Cruz Media, Inc., Corapi's company, specified MasterCard and Visa only. Jars of free candy were set out on the tables for the customers, who were handing over not only credit cards, but in many cases cash.

The crowd was large and cheerful. It included a smattering of nuns, some of whom were speaking Spanish and turned out to be from Spain. The nuns were clearly thrilled to meet Corapi, who had studied in Spain, but whose Spanish was rusty from lack of use. He was gracious with everyone, shaking hands and proffering blessings, but he seemed diffident, perhaps shy, for someone whose presence in front of a large audience was totally commanding. He seemed happy to get away when a young man came up and said, "Father, it's time to vest." First he would deliver a homily, which, after a break, would be followed by a mass.

Corapi next appeared inside the gym in elegant vestments of emerald and gold, in procession with several other similarly attired priests, followed by altar boys and girls. As they moved down the center aisle, the congregation of 1,200 or so casually dressed men, women, and children—many if not most of them Hispanic—followed them with their eyes as they approached the altar behind which hung a large crucifix banner. Corapi began by intoning the Hail Mary in his unusually deep and resonant voice. The converted to whom he was about to preach were raptly attentive. His all-embracing subject was "Fatima Today: What is God trying to say to us?" Sitting among the faithful, one was hard put not to wonder what God had been saying all along to Corapi about his qui tam suit and how it compared with the advice he was getting from his tough-minded, tightly focused friend Joe Zerga.

"There will always be an evil that has to be fought," he began, speaking without text or notes. "Good and evil, truth and lies, life and death will go on until Jesus comes again. Anything I can say worth saying is not going to be new; it's going to be ancient. God is the absolute and pure reality. God is the creator. Everything else is created. If you are out of touch with God you are out of touch with reality. You are insane in a certain sense."

He told the audience in a relaxed and conversational tone that he preached on "basic stuff, God, grace, heaven and hell." Then, to drive home his message on penance, he switched to secular and religious clichés and aphorisms, repetition and beatific rhythm, oddly enough like some clerical Kerouac or Ginsberg. "Look at a crucifix," he said. "No pain, no gain. No cross, no crown." He was getting up a head of steam. "We're in crisis today. Families are in crisis, government is in crisis—greatness, leadership, heroes—we're crying out for heroes. No pain, no gain! Every athlete knows that. Discipline! Discipline! Humanity tends toward mediocrity. The army stole God's saying: Be all you can be. I like it. I like it. Be all you can be. Be all you can be. Mediocrity drains the life out of a human being. If you're doing it for Jesus it should be as perfect as you can make it." Corapi's left hand reached for heaven, his index finger twisted in the air for emphasis. Then, softening his voice and dropping it another half octave, he intoned, "The enemy's favorite color is gray. Why?" he asked rhetorically, and answered, "No black and white." He was in his element. The diffidence was gone. Any thought of lawsuits or whistle-blower awards had vanished.

In a more personal vein and conversational in tone again, Corapi said, "I could never be a politician because I don't care what anybody thinks of me. A woman once said to me, 'Your greatest gift is you don't give a fat rat's —— about what anybody thinks.' I said, 'Right on!' Jesus never said that eternal truth should be determined by a democratic vote. I was on a plane once and my seatmate was looking at a poll in a newspaper. He asked what I thought about the fact that 74 percent of Catholics thought abortion was okay in certain circumstances and 68 percent thought priests should be allowed to marry. 'What do you think of that, Father?' he asked. 'Doesn't that tell you something?' Yes, it tells me that 68 percent have lost their faith for this reason and 74 percent have lost their faith for that reason. That's all it tells me."

The smiling audience broke into applause. Corapi raised his hand, spreading his fingers wide and then clenching them into a victorious fist. He shifted tone and style again, this time from storyteller to moralist. "We have been desensitized," he said, "a degree at a time. Fifties television was wholesome. Today's TV is porn. And we call it freedom. Freedom, no, license! I must tolerate the full spectrum of the good, but I do not have to tolerate evil. There are certain things that are good and evil in themselves. There are moral absolutes. Do you know what they are? I will come back to that on your deathbed! You have an obligation to learn your faith up one side and down the other." Corapi then threatened to come into the audience with the microphone "and find a guilty face who won't know the Ten Commandments. And," he said, "I'll torture you with that." Moments later he finished to a standing ovation that lasted several minutes.

The congregation streamed out into the sun, many hoping to have a word with Corapi, or perhaps even to be blessed, but he quickly disappeared into a kind of green room. The women were back behind the tables, though, and business was booming again. For twenty minutes credit cards and twenty-dollar bills were everywhere. Then the word spread that mass was about to begin and the faithful, including many families with well-behaved young children in their Sunday-best, filed back in and took their seats. The priests returned in procession to conduct the mass, and almost everyone responded with a vibrant sense of joy in their faith. This was especially true of the handful of charismatic Catholics among them. One large woman in a gray dress with pink flowers stood through the entire mass. Most of the time her arms were outstretched, her palms facing upward at enough of an angle to display long, pink, square-cut fingernails and two glittering rings. Her fingers wriggled rhythmically.

In his sermon toward the end of the mass, Corapi returned to some of the themes he had treated earlier. He said human sexuality was meant to be between a man and a woman, adding, "I could give a long lecture on that at this juncture in history. It's Adam and Eve, not Adam and Steve. Same-sex marriage is another nail in the coffin of a dying society." He went on to lament the fact that "the average Catholic was no different from the average denizen of the neo-pagan culture. The fifty percent divorce rate includes Catholics, too." He said he even knew of a priest who sanctioned abortion. "When I entered the priesthood," he continued, "it was a respectable thing to do. But I was spat on in the St. Louis airport because of the [sex] scandals in the church." He spent a few minutes damning television sets and computers, calling them "black boxes of sin," so there was a certain irony toward the conclusion of his remarks when he told the audience about his website, which, although he didn't mention it, was bringing in about $100,000 a month.

20

The Endgame

Judge Jack Halpin's small office was on the third floor of the old courthouse. Next door a brand-new stone-and-glass administrative center for the courts was under construction, one of a number of major projects being built in Redding that included a big library across town on Cypress Avenue. It was hot outside, which was normal for early fall. Halpin could deal with the heat and the construction noise, though. He was used to both. He felt good about the fact that a settlement had been worked out with the cardiologists, but 642 cases involving the surgeons remained and no settlement of those cases seemed to be in the offing. He was also frustrated with the federal government. The U.S. attorney's sluggishness in deciding whether to ask the grand jury to indict the doctors in the criminal case was causing a problem for him. Two years had passed since he had been assigned to preside over the RMC tort cases in Shasta County Superior Court, but because of linkages to the federal criminal case he had been unable to bring any of his cases to trial. One of Halpin's most important goals from day one had been to move his cases along as swiftly as possible.

Bob Zimmerman, Steve Enochian, and the other defense lawyers had argued from the start that it would be unfair to force the doctors to defend themselves in civil trials while they were still in negotiations with government lawyers to either drop or settle the criminal matter. These negotiations might turn out to be unsuccessful after all, which meant that if the doctors were criminally indicted testimony they gave in Judge Halpin's court would be admissible in federal court. Even if they took the Fifth and didn't testify, that too would likely prejudice their criminal case. At one point Sonja Dahl, who was one of Moon's civil lawyers, had bolstered her argument for delay by emphasizing what was at stake for her client. She said Moon was at risk of going to prison for the rest of his life and of losing everything he'd ever had or would ever own. Despite his desire to get the cases moving, Halpin was sympathetic to this argument and went along with the defense for about a year and a half. By February 2004, however, in the interests of orderliness and efficiency, he had set January 10, 2005, as the date for the first of twenty civil trials to begin. Halpin had been determined, within the constraints of fairness to the plaintiffs and the defense, to do everything possible to stick to this schedule.

Meanwhile, despite repeated hints, the U.S. attorney in Sacramento, McGregor Scott, still had not disclosed when, or even if, the government was going to ask the grand jury to indict the doctors. Scott had told Halpin almost a year before, without being specific, that "something was imminent" in the federal case. And on February 10, 2004, the *Record Searchlight* had reported that lawyers in the case had said in court that the grand jury was expected to be asked to hand down indictments within two months, which did not happen.

Even though more than two years had passed since the raid, almost everyone involved in the case who was willing to talk about it still seemed to believe that Moon and Realyvasquez would face criminal trials. But when many more months passed and nothing happened, skepticism and concern began to mount among the plaintiffs, many of whom cared more about seeing the doctors sent to prison than about financial compensation for themselves. There was also growing skepticism in the wider Redding community about the government's case. If the government didn't have sufficient evidence yet to indict the doctors, people wondered, would they ever? Judge Halpin, whose seventy-ninth birthday was coming up, suspended judgment about what Scott might eventually do, but he was certainly not inclined to permit his cases to be held hostage to proceedings in another jurisdiction, even if that jurisdiction was the United States of America.

Judge Halpin was not alone in his frustration, nor were the people of Redding alone in in their skepticism. Mike Skeen, who was patient and methodical—surely not the kind of man who rushed to judgment—was distressed about the amount of time that had passed. It was hard for him to imagine why it was taking Scott so long to seek indictments. Skeen was familiar with the evidence, having collected much of it, and he was impressed with its depth and quality. He had interviewed dozens of sources, reviewed angiograms in the presence of experts, studied the medical records, and read the medical experts' reports. If the prosecution had grade B experts and the defense had grade A experts, if the percentage of unnecessary procedures had been 15 instead of 40 or more, the case would have been a wobbler, Skeen thought. But that wasn't the situation at all. He understood that proving criminal intent was the biggest challenge facing the prosecution. Until then the investigators had not been able to find corroborating evidence such as double billing directly associated with unnecessary surgery, for example. Without this kind of supporting evidence it would be harder to persuade a jury that what had happened was not just simple malpractice, albeit on a grand scale. But he was convinced that the government could make its case.

Skeen had never stopped working on the RMC matter. Among other things, he had interviewed Fidel Realyvasquez twice during the fall and winter of 2004–2005. During one of those interviews, Skeen remembered, Realyvasquez had dissolved into tears under questioning about his directorship fee and on-call pay. The scene was reminiscent of his similar breakdown when CW1 told him she had not turned him in. Skeen, however, unlike CW1, was not moved. He had seen other interview subjects cry during FBI interviews and believed that more often than not it was a technique they used to win the agent's sympathy. He thought Realyvasquez was a particularly gifted manipulator of other people's feelings and was able to will himself to cry convincingly, so convincingly perhaps that he himself might have believed the tears were real.

But Skeen also had a heavy load of other matters occupying him that winter. There were several child pornography cases, a money laundering case, a couple of fugitives to track down, several terrorism leads, and the regular assistance he and his new partner, Mark Montgomery, were providing to local police in their antigang activities. While he was not opposed to collecting additional evidence to make the RMC case as airtight as possible, by the end of 2004, Skeen felt certain that the government already had enough evidence to convict Moon and Realyvasquez. He also knew, however, that to persuade a jury that Tenet executives had conspired with the doctors to defraud Medicare and other federal programs, better evidence was needed. Perhaps, he thought, Scott's desire to construct a conspiracy case was what was holding things up in Sacramento.

Skeen was always mindful of the psychiatric-hospital cases a decade earlier as a result of which Tenet, then known as National Medical Enterprises, was successfully prosecuted for criminal fraud and for unlawfully detaining and abusing patients. He hadn't forgotten that executives and doctors had been convicted and had gone to prison that time. He also understood the differences between the NME situation and the cases he was investigating. Back then NME executives, hospital administrators, and individual psychiatrists had been sloppy and arrogant, speaking too freely about the illegal activities they were engaged in and even putting incriminating policy directives in writing. These corporate-level character flaws, plus the federal government's ability to convert a complicit executive into a federal witness, had made a successful prosecution relatively easy.

In the RMC cases, however, dozens of interviews and computer searches yielded no incriminating memos and there were no witnesses to conversations in which executives displayed complicity with the doctors. There were suspicious circumstances such as the numerous occasions on which hospital administrators had ignored medical staff complaints about Moon and Realyvasquez or had explicitly told the complaining physicians to mind their own business. There also was clear evidence of an excessively high number of cardiac procedures at the hospital, which any alert administrator should have noticed. Moreover, monthly reports on the revenue generated by the heart program were sent to corporate headquarters and carefully reviewed. When the numbers slipped hospital administrators were admonished for it. And, just as in the NME psychiatric hospital scandal, Moon and Realyvasquez were being paid fat stipends for directorships and on-call agreements that involved little or no additional work, which could easily be interpreted as indicators of collusion.

But none of these examples rose to the level of the smoking-gun evidence needed to prove a conspiracy. Without the smoking gun—the memo that said "Ratchet up the numbers, we don't care how you do it, and we're all going to be rich"—it was easy for an administrator to argue that he would have had no way of knowing whether a given treatment was appropriate. The CEO or COO could say, "Never in my wildest dreams would I have imagined that those doctors would do something to somebody who didn't need it." Skeen believed that by then the top Tenet executives, many of whom were NME holdovers, had learned the lessons of the psychiatric-hospital scandal all too well.

In his own mind, Skeen had drawn a clear distinction between the doctors and the administrators. He believed that when you rose above the level of the physicians you were dealing with bureaucrats and administrators and businessmen. To them these weren't patients, these weren't people; they were revenue generators. And so there was always a strong emphasis on building the programs, building revenues, and building patient base. At some point, Skeen was convinced, a transition was made from human beings to numbers. Management was constantly pushing for numbers. As a result Skeen believed that the doctors, who had an unambiguous moral responsibility to treat patients appropriately, were under steady pressure to generate ever-higher revenues that could not be achieved without treating some patients inappropriately. He did not believe this mitigated the guilt of Moon and Realyvasquez one bit, but he did believe hospital administrators and Tenet executives were guilty, too. And it was eating him up that they might get away with it.

The investigative team had tried more than once to persuade executives and administrators to turn on their colleagues and testify against them, but they had been unsuccessful. Having failed in this effort, Skeen believed that the best strategy would be to indict Moon and Realyvasquez sooner rather than later. In his experience there was nothing like an indictment to bring fence-sitters over onto your side. He believed that with an indictment the case against the doctors, which was already strong, could only get stronger. But the more time that passed without an indictment, the more often the investigators were hearing from potential witnesses that they didn't believe there would ever be a trial, so they didn't see any point in getting involved. While Skeen was confident that an indictment would strengthen the case against the doctors by attracting witnesses who could testify to billing fraud, for example, he also hoped it would bring through the door someone, anyone, who could confirm his strong conviction that there had been a conspiracy involving higher-ups. But for reasons of his own, McGregor Scott wasn't buying Skeen's argument. The investigation went on, but no indictment was forthcoming.

With the January 2005 civil trial date fast approaching, because of issues raised by the complex, interlocking federal and state litigation, as expected the surgeons' lawyers asked for a continuance. Naturally the plaintiffs' lawyers opposed another delay on the same grounds they had opposed delaying the cases previously, that many of their clients were poor and some were so old that they could easily die before the cases came to trial. Halpin was not at all eager to grant a continuance, but he didn't think he had an option. He recognized that the issues the defense lawyers were raising were still legitimate. If nothing else he felt he had to grant a continuance because nothing material had changed. Sworn testimony given in the civil cases could be used against the defendants in a federal criminal trial, which, despite the amount of time that had passed, still seemed likely to him. Halpin rescheduled the first trial for July 25, 2005, but as the July trial date approached there were signs that the situation was finally beginning to change in a way that militated in favor of another continuance. Halpin put the first trial off again, this time until November 8.

Sometime during the summer of 2005, there appeared to have been a leak from the U.S. attorney's office. A plaintiff's lawyer had learned that a momentous decision had been made, or at the very least was being seriously considered, not to seek an indictment of the doctors. Apart from that one leak, this information had been very closely held. Not even Mike Skeen knew about it. Indeed Skeen was confident that the investigation was moving slowly but inexorably toward a prosecution. He was busy with a host of other matters, but even though the pace had slowed to a crawl in the RMC case he had never stopped gathering evidence. He continued to be concerned that it was taking the prosecutors too long to go to the grand jury for an indictment, but he continued to believe, perhaps because it would have been too hard not to, that it was just a matter of time.

What Skeen did not know was that the Justice Department had suffered what it viewed as a potentially fatal blow to its case. The prosecutors had asked one of their expert witnesses to recommend several other well-credentialed cardiologists, one of whom they could select to serve as a rebuttal witness. This was an attempt to shore up their case in response to the malpractice defense they had concluded the doctors would use. The government asked its own expert to recommend three cardiologists, and Linhardt and the other assistant U.S. attorney working the criminal side of the case, Laura Ferris (formerly Schwartz) essentially picked one of them at random. They did not investigate this physician's background, which they would soon regret. The reason they didn't check further was that they believed strongly in their case and were convinced that any well-trained cardiologist from a leading institution would uphold the opinions they already had received from their other experts. To Ferris's and Linhardt's chagrin, however, in each case that the new expert reviewed, he rendered an opinion that the treatment the other experts had considered unnecessary was actually appropriate. The two assistant U.S. attorneys knew that under the rules of evidence this information would have to be turned over to the defense, which they believed would be devastating to their case.

Skeen, on the other hand, thought the testimony of the physician who had offered these opinions was vulnerable because he had learned that the doctor had been overheard expressing an opinion that was highly skeptical of government oversight of medical doctors. However, this was not a point of view among physicians that would place him outside the mainstream. A bit more encouraging for the prosecutors perhaps was the fact that this expert's opinions about the treatment were outside of American College of Cardiology guidelines. But here too there was a problem for the government. There is a well-known saying in medicine that guidelines follow practice, not vice versa, meaning that it takes time before new guidelines are written to reflect actual practice patterns in the community. Reaching a judgment that a particular treatment was appropriate based on criteria yet to be ensconced in ACC guidelines or consensus statements would not necessarily be perceived by the medical community as putting the expert outside the mainstream either.

Faced with these realities and the daunting prospect of trying to convince a jury that Moon and Realyvasquez had done unwarranted procedures with the intent of defrauding the government, the unexpected opinion had to be disheartening. But it turned out to be even worse than that. Linhardt and Ferris, who were already worried that their case was precarious, concluded that this expert's testimony would sink it. With real regrets, because they believed the doctors were guilty, they recommended to Scott that he drop the criminal case. This was a painful choice for the government, which had spent three years and millions of dollars on this highly publicized investigation. Pulling the plug on the prosecution after spending so much time and money on it was going to make a lot of people wonder exactly what the government thought it was doing. At best it would make the U.S. attorneys look inept. At worst there was likely to be speculation—by Pat Campbell, among others—

that politics had played an improper role in the decision not to prose-cute. Campbell, who right around that time had told his family that he had accepted an offer to join a practice in Eugene, Oregon, believed for example that Scott, when he was district attorney, might have heard sto-ries about unnecessary medical procedures being done at Redding Med-ical Center.

21

The Settlement

Despite the high political price of dropping the criminal case, U.S. Attorney McGregor Scott accepted the reasoning and judgment of Linhardt and Ferris that the odds of winning were no longer acceptable and elected to pursue a civil settlement. Their argument went something like this: The doctors probably would have used a malpractice defense in which they would concede that they had been overly aggressive or had made mistakes in their treatment, but they would deny criminal intent. Malpractice was not the sort of thing physicians generally liked to admit having committed, the prosecutors acknowledged, but the prospect of a long prison sentence sometimes helped them to get past their reluctance. The two assistant U.S. attorneys knew their chances of overcoming a malpractice defense were not good. But even if the doctors took the position that they were practicing good medicine the case would have turned into a battle of experts, which would have been at best a crapshoot in court. Based on these conclusions they decided that going to trial would not only involve throwing good money after bad, but would be unfair to the defendants. As a general rule, when prosecutors decide they are unlikely to win, from both a public interest perspective and a perspective of fairness to the defendants, they look for another option.

Once again Scott turned to Michael Hirst, who was planning to leave the U.S. attorney's office for private practice at the beginning of the new year. If Hirst was hoping for a relatively leisurely couple of months at the end of his tenure to finish up his affairs, he had another thought coming. His last months as an assistant U.S. attorney were going to be hectic and demanding. He was about to face a challenge that would probably be as difficult as negotiating the Tenet settlement had been, if not more so. This was true for many reasons.

Like the government lawyers, the defense lawyers were smart and experienced. They knew from the beginning that proving fraud would be very difficult. Indeed some of them wondered why it took the government lawyers so long to reach that same conclusion that it would be too hard to prove. In any event, knowing that the government finally had given up gave them the leverage they needed to demand that Hirst orchestrate not just an end to the criminal case, but a comprehensive settlement that would include the 642 tort cases against the surgeons. They would also try to use this leverage to minimize the amount the doctors would have to pay out of pocket to settle their cases. And they would demand blanket immunity for their clients from federal and state prosecution for the crimes the federal government had been investigating.

As if this were not enough of a challenge for Hirst, the defense demanded that the qui tam dispute involving Corapi, Zerga, and Campbell, who had by now moved to Oregon but whose family had declined to move with him, should be included in the global settlement. They wanted the whistle-blower suits included because the doctors still had legal exposure in those lawsuits as a result of not having settled with the federal government as Tenet had. Hirst would also be asked to settle Corapi and Zerga's California Insurance Code case. The outward appearance of what was going on was that Scott or someone else wanted the entire RMC matter to disappear all at once, possibly for political reasons. But the facts belied the appearance.

One thing that did seem clear was that once a decision was made to seek a civil settlement, everyone wanted it to happen as quickly as possible. Hirst was leaving for private practice and Linhardt was retiring. The doctors might have been playing golf—Moon—and driving a tractor around his ranch and overseeing the building of his new house on the coast—Realyvasquez—but for three years both men had been living under the dismal threat of long prison terms, up to life. And the longer the negotiations stretched out the more they would have to pay in legal fees, which had already cost them millions of dollars. But many of the issues to be worked out were difficult and there were inevitably going to be conflicts. Some of those could take months to resolve or, in a worst-case scenario, could derail the negotiations altogether.

There were four negotiating tracks, each of which was mired in multiple complexities. The first and most important involved the four doctors in the criminal case, Moon, Realyvasquez, and Realyvasquez's former associates, Kent Brusett and Ricardo Moreno-Cabral. The principal matters to be settled were the amounts of money each would be required to pay the government, whether they would surrender their medical licenses for life, and whether they would receive guarantees that no future legal actions relating to the procedures at issue would be taken against them. Each of these three matters presented problems. With respect to the money, Hirst had to devise a formula for calculating an amount that both sides could live with and that each doctor could afford to pay. While Moon and Realyvasquez had substantial resources, Brusett did not. Although he was formally under investigation it seemed unlikely that Moreno-Cabral would be required to pay anything because of a lack of sufficient evidence.

The licensing question was much more straightforward. Either each doctor would agree to give up his license or he wouldn't. If any one of them refused to do so, the U.S. attorneys would have to decide whether they were willing to settle on that basis or not. As far as immunity against future prosecution was concerned, the federal government was prepared to grant it as a matter of course. Settlements of this kind would be largely unachievable without such a guarantee. But the federal government could not commit the state of California to a grant of immunity, or as it is known in legalese, the release of a claim. Only Jerry Benito, the Shasta County district attorney could do that.

The second track encompassed the surgeons' tort cases, the first of which Judge Halpin had scheduled for trial in November. Settlement of these cases, which involved Realyvasquez, Brusett, Moreno-Cabral, and two other surgeons, Kevin Miller and Louis Elkins, was, as far as the defense was concerned, an absolute condition of settling the federal case. Elkins and Moreno-Cabral were being sued in only a handful of cases and arguably neither should have been included in the tort lawsuits. This track was further complicated because of a dispute between Realyvasquez and his insurance company and because Miller was represented by a different insurance company from the others. Also, a settlement would require the agreement of the plaintiffs. A mitigating factor was that Halpin, who favored settlements over trials, and who had reviewed none of the evidence and had formed no opinion as to the guilt or innocence of the surgeons, could be counted on to support the government's efforts.

The task on track number three was to get Pat Campbell and John

Corapi and Joe Zerga, who had been at war with each other for three years, to reach a compromise settlement. They had submitted their dispute to mediation many months before, but the effort had failed. It had been self-evident all along that each of them would walk away with millions of dollars if they settled. But neither side seemed ready to compromise enough to end their dispute. After such bitter competition for the whole $8.1 million for almost three years, resolving this matter alone looked like a full-time job for Hirst for the next several months. But there was a small opening.

On August 22, 2005, a three-judge panel of the Ninth Circuit Court of Appeals in San Francisco had ruled in Campbell's favor and remanded the case back to the district court to decide whether Corapi and Zerga were original sources. If the court decided they were, they would get the money. If it decided they were not, Campbell's suit would be reinstated and he might get the money. The court was not empowered to split it between them. However, the plaintiffs could agree among themselves to divide the money. The appeals court's decision meant they all had to confront the possibility that a roll of the dice could leave them empty-handed, which created an incentive for both sides to consider the option of splitting the proceeds. Campbell, the loser in the first round, had been willing to consider a split for some time. Corapi and Zerga on the other hand had not. But the Ninth Circuit's decision had shaken the confidence of the priest and the accountant. Until the case was remanded they thought they had a lock on the money. Now a compromise at least seemed possible.

The fourth track was the narrowest and to some eyes at least the oddest of the four. The little noticed whistle-blower provision in the California Insurance Code that Dugan Barr had vaguely remembered, but Joe Zerga thought might make him and his old friend John Corapi really rich, could conceivably end up either securing or scuttling the overall settlement. Everyone, everyone that is but the U.S. government, had an interest in seeing the insurance code case settled. If Corapi and Zerga were to prevail in that case, it could end up costing Tenet and the doctors millions of dollars. But because the California case had the potential to be a deal breaker, the government was left with no choice but to include it in the overall settlement package.

Michael Hirst was under an unusual amount of stress while all of this was going on. Apart from the responsibility of managing a very complex, very high profile case for the government, he was deeply engaged in negotiating a partnership agreement with a lawyer in Connecticut that among other things would involve setting up law offices in Sacramento and Berkeley. He had to be as organized as possible—otherwise, he risked losing control of both situations and there was too much at stake to let that happen. He thought through carefully what he had to accomplish on each track to get to the bottom line, which was resolution of all outstanding RMC-related issues. He also knew that he was under pressure to do it quickly, not only because he was planning to leave within months, but also because the third anniversary of the raid was only weeks away. The amount of time that had passed without action was becoming increasingly embarrassing for the government.

Hirst, who had been involved in the qui tam dispute from the very beginning, thought both sides were crazily stubborn for not having split the money long ago. His job was obvious: to ascertain how much each side needed to settle and find a way to bridge the gap between them, if necessary by sweetening the pot. He brought the parties together in a sterile conference room in the U.S. attorney's office in Sacramento to get a sense of their opening positions. The first thing he did, however, was to tell them that the government was not going to prosecute the doctors, which shocked and disappointed all three men. These after all were the whistle-blowers, or at least that was how they all saw themselves if not each other. He explained that the government was going to seek a global civil settlement and emphasized that everything had to be settled or nothing would be. The structure was fragile and would not stand if even the smallest element were missing. Although the meeting was civil, it didn't take Hirst long to recognize that the mix was too volatile to yield favorable results. He decided that it would make more sense to use the standard mediator's technique of meeting separately with the parties to get a clear idea what each would take and then shuttling back and forth sweet-talking, cajoling, and jawboning until they had moved close enough together to seal the bargain.

During these initial individual sessions that afternoon, Campbell and his lawyer, David Rude, said that they wanted 50 percent of the total pot and that they would not budge from that position. It was harder to get a firm commitment from Corapi and Zerga. Corapi had become progressively more reticent and distant from the proceedings as time wore on and hardly spoke. He did interject at one point, however, that he was indifferent to what Campbell got. He said to Zerga that they needed to concentrate on what would satisfy them. Hirst was delighted to hear this because it was precisely the message he was trying to get across. When he asked them again how much it would take, Zerga, who had been mulling it over while doing most of the talking for their side, said $2.5 million each. Zerga did not intend to include in that amount anything he and Corapi might recover in the California insurance case, but he neglected to tell this to Hirst.

After the first day the negotiations continued by telephone. Among other things, Hirst was working to increase the size of the pot. The one way he saw to do this was to take advantage of a side letter to the Tenet settlement that provided for the government to be reimbursed if it identified unnecessary procedures that had not been taken account of in the $54 million settlement. Tenet was not at all happy about this, but the company was eager to accomplish the global settlement and eventually agreed to pay another $5.5 million, 15 percent of which would go to Corapi, Zerga, and Campbell. Hirst also persuaded Tenet to put up a million dollars to settle the California Insurance Code lawsuit, half of which would go the state and the other half to Corapi and Zerga.

During this same period, Hirst was also meeting with the lawyers for the doctors. By January, he too would be a defense attorney, working out of the Wells Fargo Building, where Malcolm Segal, who represented Realyvasquez, and Matthew Jacobs, who represented Moon, had their offices. Like Hirst, Segal and Jacobs had both been assistant United States attorneys in Sacramento. Chuck Stevens, Tenet's lawyer, had been the U.S. attorney in Sacramento and his office, too, was in the Wells Fargo Building. It was a small, tight little community and the lawyers tended to get along well with one another. Hirst, Segal, and Jacobs met regularly to discuss how to settle the state tort cases, negotiations that did not include the plaintiffs' lawyers, who were kept completely in the dark about their progress. They were also working out parameters for determining how much each doctor would have to pay the federal government to settle the federal case.

Hirst was adamant that the doctors' monetary settlement, like the one he negotiated with Tenet, should reflect the government's view that they were guilty of fraud. With this in mind, he insisted on triple damages and penalties for each case. The lawyers representing the doctors were resistant, but as in the Tenet negotiation it became clear that the federal government would settle for no less. Although the government had unmistakably signaled its preference for a civil settlement and had told Corapi, Zerga, and Campbell that there would be no criminal prosecution, it had not absolutely forsworn this option. And another possibility, absent a global settlement, was case-by-case civil prosecution of the doctors. Neither of these scenarios was particularly attractive to the prosecution, but they were even less appealing to the defense. Either option would add to the clients' already massive legal costs and there were no guarantees in either case that they would win. As a result, they accepted the formula, but with the understanding that they would not be obliged to admit to fraud. And, the same as Tenet, they would be able to characterize the settlement in their words.

The next big question that had to be resolved was the number of cases for which each doctor would be held responsible. This too was worked out in tough negotiations involving Hirst, Segal, Jacobs, and James Brosnahan, a well-known San Francisco criminal defense lawyer who also represented Moon and had been an assistant U.S. attorney in Phoenix and San Francisco, and Steve Enochian and Bruce Locke who represented Brusett. After some back-and-forth the parties agreed to use the total number of tort cases, 769, as a baseline and then they whittled it down, principally by eliminating all but the Medicare and Medicaid cases. They ended up with a number around 300.

These issues were hard enough to resolve, but there was another long-standing problem of a different kind altogether that slowed the talks and increased the anxiety for Hirst and everyone else—the intense dislike that Moon and Realyvasquez felt for each other. The two men had never gotten along and it made perfectly good sense that, to the extent that either of them actually believed he was innocent, he also thought the other, if not guilty as charged, was solely to blame for the trouble they were in. Realyvasquez even said on the record that he believed Moon "deserved the scrutiny he had received." In any event, because neither doctor wanted to appear more guilty a roadblock developed. Moon insisted that he would not pay a penny more than Realyvasquez and that he would not agree to pay anything until Realyvasquez had agreed to pay the same amount at the same time. Hirst tried to persuade each doctor that settling first would work to his advantage because it would leave the other doctor the sole target of the government's attention. But neither one took the bait. There was also a problem with Brusett. He had far less money and other assets than Moon and Realyvasquez, each of whom had many millions of dollars in cash, real estate, and other investments. In Moon's case, two weeks before the raid the FBI identified a brokerage account in his name with $17 million in it. And Realyvasquez's ranch alone was worth several million dollars.

Meanwhile, Hirst was taking care of his personal business and continuing to talk periodically by phone to Rude and Marks. The latter seemed especially eager for his clients to settle, but also seemed to have little influence over Zerga, who was driving the bus. Within about a week Hirst sent a draft agreement to the parties. It offered Campbell half of everything except the California insurance money, which was what he wanted, and Corapi and Zerga would get more than $2.7 million each, which included half of the million dollars Tenet put up to settle the insurance case. Campbell and Rude were pleased with the draft and accepted the terms. Zerga, who had left the meeting in Sacramento thinking that the talks had broken down, was surprised to receive it. But it gave him more than he had asked for and even though he got far less from the insurance case than he had hoped for, he finally decided it was time to put all this behind him. It had been three long years and enough was enough. He and Corapi looked at each other and Zerga said, "Let's do it and be done with it." He got no argument from the priest, who had been ready for a long time.

Around this time, Mike Skeen, whose frustration had turned into a slow-burning anger, decided he couldn't live with himself if he didn't make a last-ditch effort to get the criminal prosecution back on track. This would require an end run around the U.S. attorney's office. With the support of the FBI, he and Jerry Wilson, an agent with experience in healthcare fraud cases who had been working with him, flew to Washington and met with the top healthcare fraud staff at the Department of Justice. Skeen hoped that they would be able to convince the Justice Department officials that the obstacle presented by the anomalous professional opinion of one cardiologist who was a known opponent of government oversight of medicine could be overcome because he would not be a credible witness. The tone of the meeting was professional. Each side gave its position, with the Department of Justice officials representing the views of the U.S. attorney's office that the case had become essentially unwinnable.

Halfway through the hour-long meeting it was clear to Skeen that the government position was not going to change. Toward the end Skeen's and Wilson's goal had shifted and the participants in the meeting briefly discussed the elements they thought should be included in a civil settlement if one were reached. Everyone around the table agreed that one nonnegotiable condition should be that the doctors surrender their medical licenses for life. There was a consensus that in the absence of a criminal trial these doctors should never again touch another patient. Skeen and Wilson flew back to California disheartened, but with the consolation that at least they had put an end to the gross abuse of patients in Redding and the surrounding counties.

But Mike Skeen was not quite ready to give up on sending the doctors to prison. Having failed to persuade the Justice Department to reverse U.S. Attorney McGregor Scott's decision not to seek an indictment, he made a highly unusual approach to Shasta County District Attorney Jerry Benito to discuss the possibility of prosecuting the doctors on state charges. He felt comfortable doing so because he had discussed the possibility of going down this road more than once with his superiors and they had always been supportive. The two men met privately in Benito's office. Skeen told the DA that the FBI thought the cases should be prosecuted and that since the U.S. attorney was not going to do it the FBI would provide whatever resources he needed—money, full-time agents, whatever was necessary—to pursue state charges such as battery and elder abuse. Skeen was persuasive and Benito agreed to meet with members of the investigative team to discuss the matter. Skeen hoped that Laura Ferris, his main contact at the U.S. attorney's office, whose knowledge of the case was encyclopedic, would attend the meeting. The two of them had previously discussed the possibility of state charges if the federal criminal case fell through.

Skeen asked Ferris to find out two things: if the U.S. attorney's office would support the FBI's initiative and whether Scott would allow her to attend a meeting to brief Benito. She said she would get back to Skeen, which she did a couple of days later. The disappointing answer was that Drew Parenti, the special agent in charge of the Sacramento FBI office, would have to make a formal request to Scott, who seemed certain to reject it. Skeen put in the request to Parenti anyway and Parenti passed it on to Scott who turned it down as Skeen expected he would. Skeen was then told by Parenti to drop the effort because the FBI did not want to get into an open conflict with the U.S. attorney.

At the same time, the doctors, who were unaware of Skeen's effort to instigate a state case against them, were determined that any agreement they signed would insulate them from prosecution in the California courts, and they had made this crystal clear to the federal prosecutors. Shortly after the meeting between Skeen and Benito, Benito received a phone call from the U.S. attorney's office asking him to release the three doctors from all state claims. He said he could not do it because he was unfamiliar with the details of the case. Benito cannot remember who the person was who called him, but he received a follow-up call that he is sure was from Larry Brown, McGregor Scott's deputy. He told Brown the same thing he had told the first caller. He was unable to grant a release because he did not know the cases well enough to make a sound judgment. This did not satisfy Brown. He told Benito to expect a call from Judge Halpin, which seemed both odd and inappropriate to Benito, who could not imagine that Halpin, whom he knew well, would insert himself into a matter of this kind.

Nevertheless, Halpin did call soon thereafter. Benito was not available, but when he returned the call he immediately told the judge about the calls from the U.S. attorney's office and repeated the now familiar litany that he could not grant a release to the doctors because he did not know the details of the cases. After that, however, the story gets a bit murky. Benito remembered clearly that Halpin had tried to persuade him in the interests of achieving a settlement to go along with the request to grant a release. Halpin's recollection, on the other hand, was that Realyvasquez's lawyer, Malcolm Segal, had called only to ask him to get Benito to return the calls from the U.S. attorney's office and that was all he did. The trouble with Halpin's account was that Benito had already explained to Brown and someone else from the U.S. attorney's office why he could not release the doctors from state claims. It seemed fair to wonder why Segal would have asked Halpin to intercede with Benito to return these phone calls if Benito had already discussed the matter with both Brown and someone else in the U.S. attorney's office. Segal was not willing to comment at all.

Sometime in early November, despite the fact that neither the question of release from state claims nor settlement of the surgeons' tort cases had been fully resolved, the U.S. attorney scheduled a press conference to announce a final agreement. The release from state liability had appeared to be an absolute condition for settlement, but there didn't seem to be any way to get around Benito's refusal to grant it. However Scott and the defense lawyers very likely realized that without the FBI's help and with serious statute of limitations problems it would be difficult if not impossible for the state to prepare a case. In any event, the condition was dropped from the agreement.

Somehow, whether intentionally or by oversight, Scott had neglected to notify Mike Skeen and Jerry Wilson of the November 15 press conference. Skeen learned about it when he returned a call from Benito on Friday, November 11. The DA asked him whether he knew there was a press conference scheduled to announce the settlement. A very surprised Mike Skeen said he did not. Indeed he said he had no idea they were even close to a settlement. Benito said, well, they are, and proceeded to tell Skeen about the series of phone calls he had received from the U.S. attorney's office and from Judge Halpin. Benito sounded angry to Skeen, which the FBI agent attributed partly to the fact that Benito did not particularly like Scott, who had been his boss when Scott was the Shasta County DA.

Skeen immediately called Rosemarie Barnes, secretary to Mike Parenti, the FBI's special agent in charge in Sacramento. He said, "Look, obviously I'm not supposed to know this information because I didn't learn it through normal channels, but I just wanted to make sure that the SAC knows that supposedly there's going to be a press conference on Tuesday." Barnes took the message and a little while later called back to say that Parenti knew about it and that Nancy Nelson, the assistant special agent in charge, would be at the press conference. Skeen then checked with Wilson, who also had not been notified, suggesting that both agents had been left out intentionally, perhaps because of their dogged effort to overturn and then circumvent the U.S. attorney's decision not to prosecute Moon, Realyvasquez, and Brusett.

Over the weekend before the press conference Skeen was about as down as he'd ever been. He knew he had a good life. He was in love with and extremely happy with his wife, Roxanne. He loved her precocious daughter, Emily. They had a beautiful house on five acres with a pool and great views. His son and daughter-in-law, both of whom he loved and got along with well, lived in nearby Lake California. And he enjoyed his rambunctious Rottweiler, Gretchen. The pain in his shoulder from an old injury was getting a bit worse and probably needed surgery, but he had lived with that for a long time and it did not contribute to his gloom.

Only one thing was troubling him. The criminal justice system, in which he believed and to which he had dedicated twenty years of his life, had failed. He was totally convinced that the government had enough evidence to convict the doctors and that even if there was some chance of their getting off there was still a strong moral obligation to prosecute them because their offenses were so egregious and so well documented. Although he never explicitly said McGregor Scott was to blame for the failure, he regularly referred to Scott as "the decision maker."

Skeen also ruminated unhappily about the FBI's failure to put a wire on a doctor or a hospital employee during the period the affidavit was being drafted, which would have improved their chances of getting hard evidence of a conspiracy. He thought this kind of evidence could easily have made the difference between a decision to seek a criminal indictment and what seemed to him the totally unsatisfactory decision that was ultimately made to seek a civil settlement. But there was really no one to blame for this failure. There were two good reasons why no effort had been made to surreptitiously record conversations with hospital administrators. First, the FBI would have had to find someone who was well situated to do the job and was willing to wear the wire. And once they did so, they could not have expected that person to have all the necessary conversations within a few days because it would have been too difficult and too obvious. Second, the FBI had concluded that for each day of delay another five patients would undergo unnecessary procedures, which seemed like reason enough not to delay the execution of the search warrant.

What they did not count on, though, was that it would take three months to prepare and execute the search warrant instead of the few days it usually required. Had they realized it would take that long and found someone to wear a wire during that period, Skeen thought, things might have turned out very differently. In his better moments, however, he was proud of the FBI for pursuing the case vigorously right up until the end. And he got some satisfaction out of the fact that he had contributed to ending the unnecessary procedures.

The night before the scheduled announcement the agreement was still not completed. By morning there were still unresolved issues. Nevertheless, the parties thought they were close enough and agreed to go ahead with the announcement. The U.S. attorney's office issued a press release under the headline: "DOCTORS ACCUSED OF PERFORM-

ING UNNECESSARY HEART SURGERIES AT REDDING MEDICAL CENTER AGREE TO PAY MILLIONS TO SETTLE FRAUD ALLEGATIONS AND ACCEPT RESTRICTIONS ON THEIR MEDICAL PRACTICE." The first line beneath the headline read: "The Agreement Preserves the Right to Revoke the Doctors' Licenses and Exclude Them from the Medicare Program."

Agreements of this sort are frequently rich in terms of art and subtle escape clauses and this one was no exception. For example, while the agreement did preserve the right to revoke the doctors' licenses and exclude them from the Medicare program, it did neither. What it did explicitly do was preserve the right of the doctors to contest any such action should the government take it. This was especially irritating to Skeen because everyone at the Washington meeting he had attended had agreed unconditionally that there should be no settlement unless it included revocation of the doctors' medical licenses. But the agreement did ban Moon and Realyvasquez from performing "any further cardiac procedures or surgeries on any Medicare, Medi-Cal or TRICARE [U.S. military] patients." This provision severely limited their ability to profitably practice their specialties.

Moreover, the state medical board was now free to move against the doctors' licenses. In Moon's case the process was well underway. In October 2004, the board had filed a much more extensive accusation against Moon than the original one, filed in early June 2003, for, among other things, "gross negligence" in his diagnosis and treatment of Corapi. Dave Thornton, the board's director, said he expected that the end result of the process would be that Moon would either voluntarily give up his license or the state would revoke it.

Realyvasquez's case, however, had stalled at an early stage, largely because of Deputy Attorney General Stephen Boreman's position that the standard of care in northern California did not require surgeons to question diagnostic judgments of referring cardiologists, even if they disagreed with them. Boreman said after the settlement that the case against Realyvasquez remained open, but no accusation had been filed against him as it had against Moon.

Moon and Realyvasquez were each fined $1.4 million. While this was not a trivial sum and it might represent fair payment to the government for its losses, it was unlikely to change the lifestyle of either doctor. Kent Brusett, whose resources were much smaller, was fined $250,000, payable over ten years. Since Brusett was not barred from practicing his specialty, cardiac surgery, on Medicare, Medi-Cal, or TRICARE patients, the $25,000 annual bite out of his income seemed insignificant. The agreement also provided that the doctors, including Moreno-Cabral, who was named in the settlement but was not penalized, "deny liability and [the] settlement is not an admission of liability, nor an admission of law or facts by the settling parties." Within a few days of the announcement the surgeons also agreed to settle the tort cases for the limits of their insurance, with one exception. Kevin Miller, the surgeon who operated on Paul Alexandre and was practicing in Colorado, did not settle. Judge Halpin set a trial date in the Alexandre case for September 2006. The surgeons' insurance company paid $21 million to the plaintiffs in late February 2006.

Under the terms of the settlement, which still had some loose ends to be tied up, Campbell ended up with $4,457,938 and Corapi and Zerga each got $2,712,281. About half a million dollars went to the state of California.

On the day the settlement was announced Realyvasquez and his lawyer, Malcolm Segal, issued a press release of their own. It said that there never was a basis for criminal charges against Realyvasquez, adding:

> Having waged a three-year defense against the baseless criminal allegations, Dr. Realyvasquez has chosen to settle the civil dispute with Medicare and Medi-Cal by reimbursing Medicare for a portion of the fees received for patients he treated. He has also given his insurance companies full discretion to settle or continue to dispute the remaining state civil cases in Redding so that he can put an end to the biased and unfair attack on his surgical career.

The release went on to say that Realyvasquez had "simply given up on the legal system's ability to ensure complete justice will ever prevail. . . . I cannot continue to fight a system that is not interested in the truth." Ironically, Realyvasquez seemed to have been as disenchanted as Mike Skeen was with the systemic failures and the result they yielded.

Needless to say, not everyone saw the outcome in the same light as Realyvasquez and Segal. Doug Mudford, even though he and his colleagues had reaped millions of dollars in fees in the civil cases, was physically sickened by it. Two days later he sent me an email message that said, "It still has not quite sunk in that it took the U.S. attorney three years to determine the heart cases were too hard to prosecute; three years of all the clients (those still alive) waiting for news of indictments. When was it decided that because a fainthearted U.S. attorney decided not to bring criminal charges, all the doctors are exonerated for unnecessarily cracking chests open?" Mudford went on in a bitterly ironic vein about Realyvasquez and Moon. Realyvasquez's publicist, he wrote, "is damned good because RV's saga has taken on an heroic sheen. Soon we'll have a statue in his honor . . . no wait, Moon has already beat him to it. Redding will soon unveil the sculpture city hall accepted from Moon. It resembles a stack of coffins so it seems appropriate."

CW1 was equally angry, emotional, and even more cynical. She also sent me an email message. Hers said:

> I can't even begin to tell you how disappointed I am in the decision that was made not to criminally prosecute either Moon or RV. What's worse is that Pat Campbell got 4.5 million and he continued to refer patients to those two despite his claim that he was trying to stop it. I guess I was wrong in trying to do the right thing. What was I thinking? I should have gotten a lawyer and just filed a whistle-blower's claim and then I would have gotten the money and would have had the better life for it. The message for all of those families and all of us who tried to stop it was WHY BOTHER? The system is corrupt and you can't stop it. Even if you hurt, maim and destroy others you can continue to live a wonderful life, and never have to worry or to work again. . . . I'm sick and tired . . . and am currently rethinking what the hell I am going to do to heal myself from this whole ordeal. I think I am going to cash in all of my annuities, sell my house and travel around the world and try to get a sense of peacefulness.

As for Pat Campbell, he too sent me an email message in which he wrote that the doctors had "bought their way out of prison," which, he wrote, would "encourage more misbehavior elsewhere." But, he added, "I am not going to go public and add fuel to the fire. I achieved my main objective—Tenet and their accomplices are no longer abusing patients for profit (and ego in the case of Moon) in Redding. And the DOJ was forced to take out the knife they placed between my shoulder blades, an added bonus to be sure. After taxes and attorneys' [fees] I will end up with enough money to have a few more options and not worry about college expenses. I guess I should just be happy and thankful for those positives."

Joe Zerga said that he and John Corapi were satisfied with the settlement, or at least with the amount of money they received, and they were glad that it was over. Zerga thought the doctors should have gone to jail and he thought Campbell was a coward, not a true whistle-blower. But the sense of outrage he felt in the beginning seemed to have diminished. Corapi continued to deliver his sermons and homilies on the weekends and to hunt and fish during the week. He stopped returning email messages and telephone calls before this book was completed. Zerga said Corapi was too fed up with the whole business to talk about it with anyone anymore.

When it was all over and he was sitting on a rented chair behind a rented desk in his box-filled office in the Wells Fargo Building, Michael Hirst said he was persuaded that in these cases "unnecessary surgeries were done." He thought what Moon and Realyvasquez had done was about greed, and not just about greed, but also about "power and control." He said he was "highly skeptical about corporate involvement in healthcare," especially because he worried about "the profit motive tainting physicians' decision making."

Hirst's concern about excessive zeal for profits taking precedence over the best interests of patients was hardly idle. When doctors allow themselves to become beholden to corporations, as Moon and Realyvasquez did to Tenet in return for six-figure fees and perks such as easy access to hospital aircraft, management's bottom line becomes indistinguishable from their own. It is not surprising therefore that the less scrupulous among them get sloppy about their professional and legal obligations to patients while actively promoting their own and the company's financial interests.

In recent decades it has become a lot easier to do this and get away with it, particularly in subspecialties such as coronary medicine where rapid advances in technology have dramatically expanded treatment options. Overly aggressive practice, including using the newest and least tested forms of treatment, can generate high revenues while avoiding the scrutiny of peer review because other practitioners are not yet familiar with the devices. This almost certainly was what Moon was doing with IVUS. He made aberrant diagnoses that other local cardiologists could not easily challenge even though he claimed to be finding multiple examples of very rare conditions such as spontaneously dissecting arteries. Moon's use of IVUS also made it easier for Realyvasquez to perform bypass surgery on patients whose disease he could not personally verify.

Having made his last best effort to send Moon and Realyvasquez to prison, Mike Skeen began trying to put the last three years behind him, but he wasn't able to. As always, when he talked about it he spoke softly, but there was no mistaking his seriousness or sadness. "People have asked me," he said, "how am I taking it and am I moving on? I can't because I strongly believe what should have been the right thing to do [wasn't done]. I still believe that. To me personally it's an injustice and I feel very strongly that very heinous crimes have been committed, and people walked, and that always rankles me. I am a little concerned about Dr. Brusett. In my opinion, from the investigation, I'm confident that he knew what was going on and that he was a part of it, and he's a relatively young guy and I think that he will just continue to practice and I'm troubled by that. I think most people would agree that this has been ended, but it has not been resolved."

And as far as the relatively uninvolved citizens of Redding were concerned, the ones who were neither doctors nor patients, it was hard to say what they thought. Many of them seemed to have lost interest as the case dragged on. A headline in the *Record Searchlight* the day after the settlement was announced said, "RESIDENTS EXPRESS MIXED FEELINGS ABOUT SETTLEMENT." Although Skeen didn't claim to know what most people thought, his opinion was the same. "If you did a poll," he said, "you'd probably end up near the numbers you had at the beginning. Fifty percent thought that these poor doctors were persecuted and their careers were ruined and 50 percent scratched their heads and said, 'You know what, it probably was going on.'"

As for the doctors, they continued to maintain their innocence. They did not sign the settlement agreement reached in November 2005, most likely because it did not provide an ironclad guarantee that the state of California would not prosecute them. Their failure to sign the agreement meant their lawyers would still not let them talk to me, so I did the next best thing. Late in the afternoon of January 12, 2006, I paid a visit to Maja Sandberg, the vascular surgeon who worked with and was personally close to Fidel Realyvasquez at the office suite across from Redding Medical Center that they had shared. It was dimly lighted and empty except for two young women behind the reception desk, as it had been on each of my previous visits. Sandberg, who had known Realyvasquez for twenty years, had gone to pick up her daughter from school and was due back at the office shortly. I had been waiting only a short time when a man materialized from behind the desk, walked over to me, and with a faint but knowing smile asked, "Are you Mr. Klaidman?" Before I could answer, he said, "I'm Fidel Realyvasquez." It was the first time I had seen him, but I recognized him from pictures. I smiled too and said, "I know who you are. It's nice to meet you at last."

We stood talking for a few minutes, mostly about my first brief telephone conversation with him during the summer of 2003. At the time he said he was eager to talk to me, but his lawyers had forbidden him to do so. Then, dashing my minimal hopes, he added that he was still constrained from discussing the case. A moment later Sandberg walked in, at which point I realized she must have told him that I would be there. I had come partly to ask Sandberg if Frank Sebat's sworn statement accurately described Realyvasquez's concern about doing bypass operations based on Moon's diagnoses from intravascular ultrasound. I wasn't sure why Realyvasquez had decided to come. Was it just to see me in the flesh; or did he want me to see him so that I might judge him more sympathetically, or did he want at least in some small way to explain himself? Whatever his reasons for being there, though, I wanted to take maximum advantage of the meeting without scaring him off with questions that were too aggressive.

I told Realyvasquez what I had come to discuss with Sandberg and emphasized his involvement. I then offered to read a brief passage I had written about the intensive-care chief Frank Sebat's concerns that Moon was sending patients to Realyvasquez for bypass surgery based on incorrect diagnoses made with intravascular ultrasound. They both agreed to listen to the few paragraphs and comment on them. The three of us walked down a narrow corridor to Sandberg's office. She sat at her desk, backlit by the late afternoon sun filtering through the window behind her; I sat on a couch opposite her, and Realyvasquez leaned against a wall out of the sunlight. I read the account, which was based on Sebat's deposition as it appears in chapter 15. Realyvasquez listened, but was noncommittal about whether the events had occurred as described. Sandberg said she did not remember the conversation Sebat recounted, but when asked specifically whether she denied that it had taken place, she said that she could not do that.

I then asked Realyvasquez whether he had been comfortable performing bypass operations on patients whose angiograms did not show blockages that warranted surgery. He said he had been comfortable because he was confident that the intra-operative flow studies he had done with the most sophisticated and up-to-date measuring equipment had satisfied him that he was bypassing flow-limiting obstructions. He then provided a lengthy, highly technical explanation of why these tests convinced him that the native arteries he was bypassing were indeed sufficiently blocked to require bypass surgery. However, I found the physical principles of fluid dynamics Realyvasquez used to explain the flow studies confusing. Furthermore, the government's experts, the plaintiffs' experts, and the independent experts I consulted did not find Realyvasquez's earlier version of this explanation credible.

The sun had gone down, and Realyvasquez had been standing for about an hour. Judging from his increasingly defensive tone, I was beginning to think it was time to leave. I thanked him for talking to me and we walked out into the corridor together. Sandberg went off to do something and Realyvasquez and I had a moment alone. I asked him what he had been doing in recent months and what his plans were for the future. He said he had been spending time with his children and overseeing the house he was having built on the coast. Then I asked him whether he planned to continue practicing medicine when the settlement became final. His answer was delivered without hesitation and in a manner suggesting that his decision was irrevocable: "I'll never see another patient again."

Around the same time, I tried to reach Chae Moon through his lawyers, but they were unwilling to permit him to talk to me. Eventually one of his criminal lawyers, Matt Jacobs, said that if the settlement ever became final he would ask Moon if he would agree to an interview. As far as I know, Moon still plays golf regularly at the Riverview Country Club. And as of March 2006, each doctor had received permission from the Shasta County Planning Commission to subdivide his land and build houses for sale.

In May, the state medical board finally filed an accusation against Realyvasquez charging him with gross negligence in three cases, including Zona Martin's. The accusation asked that his license be either suspended or revoked, which, given the fact that he had said he has no plans to practice medicine again, seemed a rather toothless penalty. In each case the document specifically charged Realyvasquez with failing to independently evaluate whether the patient had needed surgery. Reason had prevailed, it seems: Deputy Attorney General Stephen Boreman's objection that in northern California a surgeon was free to mindlessly follow the referring cardiologist's treatment recommendation had finally been scrapped.

In June 2006, faced with a threat from the federal government of civil lawsuits, the doctors finally signed the settlement agreement. But it took almost two more weeks to make the deal final because John Corapi, who also had to sign, was bear hunting in the Canadian woods.

And before the month was out, Tenet got what it had wanted from the beginning—a global settlement of all claims against the company by the United States government. The price was more than $900 million dollars, but the payout was scheduled over four years and based on "the company's ability to pay." By far the largest amount, $725 million plus interest, went to settle all claims involving outlier payments. The rest of the money was reimbursement for various forms of overcharging, and penalties for improper financial relationships such as paying kickback to physicians to refer Medicare patients to Tenet hospitals. Tenet CEO Trevor Fetter said his company "was humbled because of what happened" and he admitted that it had "made mistakes in its conduct before 2003." Fetter said reforms were underway. And once again, as it had done after the psychiatric-hospital scandal of the late 1980s and early 1990s, the company entered into a corporate integrity agreement with the federal government. What does all this mean? Is the settlement, once again, just a cost of doing business? Or will there be a real change in corporate culture? Will the company survive? Given Tenet's recent history, perhaps it's best to wait and see what its future will be.

Not being able to interview Moon at all and having had so little time with Realyvasquez made the reporting for this book more difficult. But it was not a crippling handicap. It did not keep me from forming what I believe to be a well-considered opinion based on three years of interviewing and research about how the outcome in Redding should be understood.

The overriding question was why after more than three years of investigation during which an impressive body of evidence against them was developed neither Moon nor Realyvasquez was prosecuted or convicted of a crime. Was justice done or miscarried as a result of the federal government's decision not to bring them to trial? Should one or both of them have gone to prison? Was justice done for Shirley Wooten, who suffered and died as a result of her unnecessary surgery, for her husband, Bob, and her sons, Shannon and Kevin, who lost a wife and mother prematurely? What about Zona Martin, who can barely move and who can't talk as a result of her surgery, and her daughter, Donna, and grandson, Donald, whose lives have been entirely given over to caring for her? And Paul Alexandre, who is in constant pain and can't work, or fish for salmon—his greatest source of pleasure? And his wife, Janeen, who must care for him and support him?

The documentary evidence to which I was given access, which included medical records and sworn depositions of expert witnesses for the plaintiffs and the defense, persuaded me that many of the procedures at issue in these cases were unnecessary. The harder question, of course, is whether the offenses I believe were committed by these doctors constituted malpractice or criminal fraud. I feel strongly that a jury should have decided this question. I do not believe the fact that a single government expert witness had disagreed with many others should have derailed a prosecution case built on a trove of powerful evidence.

Besides, who knows what else might have come to light at trial? For example, Matt Jacobs, one of Moon's team of criminal lawyers, shared with assistant U.S. attorney Laura Ferris in confidence the astounding fact that the experts they had hired for Moon's defense had classified roughly half the angiograms and intravascular ultrasounds Moon had performed as unwarranted. This means that based on the judgments of the defense experts Realyvasquez operated on a substantial percentage of those patients unnecessarily. Regrettably, but unsurprisingly, Jacobs provided this information to the assistant U.S. attorney only after criminal prosecution of Moon and Realyvasquez had been ruled out and the settlement had been announced.

AUTHOR'S NOTE

It is hardly original to observe that medicine in America, not unlike most other countries in the world, but for different reasons, is a mess. In the United States more than 40 million people have no medical insurance and therefore more often than not lack access to adequate healthcare. Millions of others with minimal insurance are better off, but not by much. The fortunate majority of Americans who are well insured complain that the care they get often is rushed and impersonal, resulting in, among other things, an epidemic of errors, some of which are fatal. And doctors are unhappy. They feel they are unloved, unrespected, and no longer in charge of their professional lives. Indeed for many doctors medical practice has become more a business than a profession, more a job than a calling, which can't be good for the quality of care they deliver. There is widespread agreement that a major restructuring of the medical system is necessary. But the country's polarized population and political system seem incapable of getting the job done.

These are among the problems that have interested me for the last twenty years. In two earlier books, I examined the role of news media in interpreting medicine for the public and the interaction of industry, academic medicine, and medical practice in developing new forms of treatment for coronary disease. If anything, since the first of these books was published in 1991, things have gotten worse. My interest in the subject hasn't flagged, but I admit to having been frustrated by the small number of readers these books reached. However, other than writing still another book, I didn't have any idea what to do about it. Eventually, though, it occurred to me that if I could find a story—a true and compelling narrative—I might be able to write a book that would attract a larger and broader audience and therefore possibly do a bit more good.

Finding the story took longer than expected and the story itself was not the one I'd been looking for, but I knew it had the makings of a book. My wife, Kitty, and I were living in Berkeley, California, for a year to spend time near our daughter, Elyse, her husband, Elyakim, and our two grandsons, Liam and Itai. Because Kitty, who is a painter, wanted to keep up with local cultural and other events, we had subscribed to the *San Francisco Chronicle*. On Thursday, October 31, 2002, I picked up the *Chronicle* from our doorstep and immediately noticed a front-page story that seemed astonishing to me. Forty federal agents had raided a hospital and two doctors' offices in a small city named Redding in far northern California. The FBI was investigating allegations that cardiologists and cardiac surgeons at the hospital, Redding Medical Center, had performed perhaps hundreds of unnecessary procedures, including coronary bypass and valve surgeries.

My interest was in systemic flaws in American medicine, not criminal fraud. But the more I thought about it the more obvious it seemed to me that vulnerability to fraud was a major systemic flaw in American medicine. I was also aware, of course, that the launching of an investigation, even one involving forty federal agents and a raid on a hospital to haul away records for fear that they might be destroyed, proved nothing. My previous book, *Saving the Heart*, had dealt with cardiac medicine and I knew that two well-qualified clinicians could evaluate the same patient's disease and reach very different conclusions about how it should be treated or even if it needed to be treated. Suppose the cardiologists and cardiac surgeons in Redding were guilty of no more than being aggressive practitioners who believed they were practicing good, up-to-date medicine and their local colleagues were simply bumpkins who were behind the curve? Well, it didn't take me too long to recognize there was a book in that, too. This story was not just about medicine, it was also about justice, irrespective of whether the victims were patients or doctors.

After some further thought and several months of preliminary research, I traveled to Redding to try to get a better sense of what had happened, what effect it was having on the community, and who the key players were. Most of all, though, I needed to know what it would take to get the access I would need to write the book. Two quick trips during the summer of 2003 convinced me that access would be difficult. To get it I would have to live in Redding for as long as it took, which turned out to be eight months. Afterwards I traveled to Redding as needed from our home in Bethesda, Maryland.

On the whole, people were generous with their time and helpful. It was more difficult to get supporters of the doctors to talk to me than, for example, patients who believed they had been subjected to unnecessary surgery. And the doctors who were subjects of the investigation, with one notable exception—my brief conversation with Fidel Realyvasquez—were unwilling to talk to me at all. I was, however, able to talk to many other doctors, nurses, technicians, and former patients who knew them well. I also had access to sworn depositions, voluminous medical records, and a great many other documents, all of which made it possible to reconstruct the history of what happened with a high level of confidence.

To make the book as readable as possible, I have sometimes reconstructed conversations and used quotation marks. I did this when one or more parties to the conversation had a clear and consistent memory of it and when no other participant credibly denied that the conversation had taken place essentially as I had recorded it. I also used quotation marks when the conversation was part of a sworn statement such as a deposition or FBI affidavit. When one party to a conversation said he or she did not remember what was said, I made a personal judgment based on my assessment of the credibility of the parties.

I believe the story, as I tell it here, reflects to the best of my ability, honestly and fairly, what the information I was able to gather indicates. I am, however, neither judge nor jury. I neither convict nor sentence. I have done my best to enlighten.

STEPHEN KLAIDMAN
ALTEA, SPAIN

NOTES

1. This account of the taking of Jeramy Harrell by private security police is based largely on Joe Sharkey's account in his book *Bedlam* (New York: St. Martin's Press, 1994), pp. 23–45.

2. W. Afield, "The Profits of Misery," report of a hearing of the Select Committee on Children, Youth and Families, U.S. House of Representatives, 1992.

3. Quote from Harvey Friedman, deposition, in *Dorothy A. et al. v. National Medical Enterprises, Inc. et al.*, Plaintiffs Consolidated Response to the Defense Motions for Separate Trials, p. 7.

4. *Dorothy A. et al.*, p. 9.

5. In the civil suit referred to as *Dorothy A. et al. v. National Medical Enterprises, Inc. et al.*, eighty psychiatrists were named as defendants. This suit involved eleven hospitals in Texas. PIA at one time operated eighty-two hospitals in thirty states. NME Litigation Report, October 1996.

6. NME Litigation Report.

7. *Dorothy A. et al.*, p. 18.

8. Joe Sharkey, *Bedlam* (New York: St. Martin's Press, 1994), p. 227.

9. The following account is based on "Prisoners of the System," *Houston Chronicle*, December 6, 1992, and "Few Doctors Lost Licenses over Scandal," *Houston Chronicle*, March 24, 1997, and all quotes are from these two articles.

10. Elizabeth Cohen, "Rage reduction therapy: Help or abuse?" Cable News Network, October 24, 1996.

11. Plaintiff's Twelfth Amended Original Petition, *Dorothy A., et al.*

12. Joaquin Miller, *Unwritten History: Life Amongst the Modocs* (Hartford, CT: American Publishing Co., 1874), p. 17.

13. Bill Wallace, "Cardiologists Dogged by Past Lawsuits," *San Francisco Chronicle*, November 30, 2002, p. 19.

14. *The Dartmouth Atlas of Health Care 1999*, John Wennberg, principal investigator and series editor, p. 156.

15. Mary Roach's deposition in Moon's federal suit against Mercy Hospital in the Charles Kenneth Brown case, pp. 32–33.

16. Maline Hazle, "Documents Reveal Source of Complaints," *Record Searchlight*, November 15, 2002, p. 1.

17. Institute for Health and Socio-Economic Policy, "Tenet Health Care Corporation, Drugs and Hospital Charges: Impact on Health Care Costs in California and Nationwide," February 4, 2003. This study was sponsored by the California Nurses Association.

18. Institute for Health and Socio-Economic Policy, "Comment on the Tenet Health Care Report," February 5, 2003, sponsored by the California Nurses Association.

19. Denny Walsh, "Doctor Didn't Blow Whistle, Court Is Told," *Sacramento Bee*, September 26, 2003, p. B1.

ACKNOWLEDGMENTS

Writing a book is always a lonely enterprise, but few if any books have been written without help. That is certainly true of this one, which has benefited from the contributions of many people. I want to thank them all, some individually and by name and others, especially those in Redding who served as valuable sources of information, collectively and anonymously. My thanks to Mark Levin and Daniel Okrent who were responsible for helping me find my agent, Chuck Verrill. Chuck's enthusiasm for the book and his professional skill resulted in my current happy and productive relationship with Scribner. Thanks, Chuck. At Scribner I have had the good fortune to have as my editor Colin Harrison. Scribner is of course the publishing house where the great Maxwell Perkins worked and Colin is a worthy successor to Perkins in an age where real editing has become increasingly rare. *Coronary* is a far better book than it would have been without his thoughtful, insightful, and detailed suggestions, virtually all of which I took. I also want to thank Karen Thompson for all the intelligent and good-natured support she gave to Colin and to me.

Although I have written extensively in the past about coronary disease, I am not a cardiologist, or even a physician, and therefore I relied on a number of cardiologists and cardiac surgeons for expert advice. My thanks therefore to Nelson Schiller, Mitch Sklar, Paul Corso, Stu Seides, and Tom Fogarty, each of whom helped me evaluate claims made by various physicians, nurses, technicians, and lawyers who were directly involved in the Redding cases.

I also want to give special thanks to our dear friend Penny Steiner, who opened her home to my wife, Kitty, and me numerous times on our trips to Redding after we gave up our apartment there.

For anyone I have forgotten, and I'm sure there are some, my apologies and my thanks.

INDEX

ABOUT THE AUTHOR

STEPHEN KLAIDMAN is a former editor and reporter for the *New York Times*, the *Washington Post* and the *International Herald Tribune*. He was a senior research fellow at the Kennedy Institute of Ethics and a senior research associate at the Institute for Health Policy Analysis, Georgetown University. He is the author of *Saving the Heart: The Battle to Conquer Coronary Disease*, *Health in the Headlines*, and *The Virtuous Journalist* (with Tom Beauchamp).